COVENTRY LIBRARIES

Please return this book on or before
the last date stamped below.

PS130553 DISK 4

COUNDON

1 3 JUN 2008

09. SEP 08.

23/9   B.U.

17. OCT 08

01. NOV 08

10^ JAN YJ

17 APR 2009

12. MAY 09.

09. JUL 09.

30. JUL 09.

06. AUG 09.

08. JAN 10.

ST. CATHERINES LODGE

11 FEB 2010

COP. LODGE
27 MAY 2010

3 NOV 2012

29/11 BI

-3 JAN 2013

2014
- 6

PW CLOSE

12 JUN 2014

ST. CATHERINES LODGE

- 4 AUG 2016

1 3 MAR 2018

SOV. H&E

1 1 JUL 2019

To renew this book take it to any of
the City Libraries before
the date due for return

Coventry City Council

Sisters in Arms

SISTERS IN ARMS

British Army Nurses Tell Their Story

———

Nicola Tyrer

Weidenfeld & Nicolson
LONDON

First published in Great Britain in 2008
by Weidenfeld & Nicolson

1 3 5 7 9 10 8 6 4 2

© Nicola Tyrer 2008

A CIP catalogue record for this book
is available from the British Library.

ISBN 978 0 297 84658 1

Typeset at The Spartan Press Ltd,
Lymington, Hants

Printed in Great Britain by
Mackays of Chatham plc, Chatham, Kent

Weidenfeld & Nicolson

The Orion Publishing Group Ltd
Orion House
5 Upper Saint Martin's Lane
London, WC2H 9EA

An Hachette Livre UK Company

www.orionbooks.co.uk

To Keith

'The most important people in the Army are the Nursing Sisters and the Padres – the Sisters because they tell the men they matter to us – and the Padres because they tell the men they matter to God.'

Field Marshal Montgomery

Contents

List of Illustrations ix

Acknowledgements xi

Preface xiv

Introduction 1

Part I: Home and Abroad

1 'Not when they have work to do' 9
2 The Making of a QA 15
3 A Baptism of Fire 27

Part II: Far East

4 'Do English women never cry?' 41
5 Into Captivity 59
6 Friday the Thirteenth 71
7 Shipwrecked 80
8 The Disappeared 93

Part III: At Sea

9 Sailing the Seven Seas 111
10 The Cruel Sea 121

Part IV: North Africa and the Mediterranean

11 Flowers in the Desert 137
12 Under Siege in Malta 151
13 Operation Torch 160
14 Life of Comradeship 169
15 Swept off their Feet 179

Part V: Europe

16 'The QAs are here'   191
17 'Come and see what we are part of'   206
18 Operating in the Orchards   214
19 The Liberation of Europe   228

Part VI: India and Burma

20 A Tiger for the Nurses   239
21 Contrasts in the Raj   248
22 'Hard-working and patriotic women'   257
23 Bringing Home the Prisoners   267

24 Last Act   277

Source Notes   285
Select Bibliography   294
Index   295

List of Illustrations

Section One

Irene Anderson in uniform (Irene Leighton)

Meta Manson (Meta Kelly)

Mary O'Rourke (Mary English)

Dorothea Chisholm (Dorothea Davies)

Brenda McBryde (John Fuller)

QA tending a patient in No. 8 General Hospital, Nantes, France, April 1940 (Imperial War Museum)

QAs tending patients in No. 83 Dublin Hospital in Boulogne-sur-Mer (Imperial War Museum)

Margot Turner and Daphne van Wart (The Trustees of the Army Medical Services Museum)

British prisoners of war in Singapore, 1942 (Hulton/Getty)

Allied forces surrender party, 15 February 1942 (Hulton/Getty)

QAs aboard destroyer after being rescued when their troopship was torpedoed near North Africa, February 1943 (Photos by Margaret Bourke-White/Time & Life Pictures/Getty)

Molly Budge in her tent (Molly Jennings)

QAs queuing for water in the desert (Molly Jennings)

QAs washing their veils in the desert (Molly Jennings)

Field Marshal Montgomery visiting No. 2 General Hospital, Tripoli, 1943 (Molly Jennings)

Section Two

Sunbathing in Denmark, April 1945 (Molly Jennings)

Tea dance in the compound of No. 2 General Hospital, Tripoli, 1943 (Molly Jennings)

Wedding of Jane Hitchcock, Egypt, 9 May 1942 (Molly Jennings)

Wedding of Sarah McNeece and Harry Savile, Dacca, 30 April 1945 (Sarah Savile)

QA tends a patient in a field hospital, Italy, 1941 (The Trustees of Army Medical Services Museum)

QAs in Normandy (Imperial War Museum)

QAs transporting a casualty, Bayeux, 20 June 1944 (Imperial War Museum)

Contaminated huts being burned at Bergen-Belsen, 1945 (Molly Jennings)

Two QAs nursing a Russian Jewish victim of Bergen-Belsen, 1945 (Popperfoto)

A QA nurses a liberated POW from the Changi jail, Singapore, September 1945 (Popperfoto)

Photos of Irene Anderson's wartime experiences in India (Irene Leighton)

Dame Katherine Jones (The Trustees of the Army Medical Services Museum)

Acknowledgements

Many people helped me in this enterprise, but it would not have got off the ground without the help of the QAs themselves. I owe the following nurses, and their families, a great debt of gratitude for their generosity in granting me their time, their willingness to trust me with their unique and precious photographs, books and mementoes, and their patience with what must at times have seemed my tedious rechecking of facts: Daphne Ingram; Mary English; Mary Davies; Meta Kelly; Irene Leighton; Audrey Hayward; Sarah Saville and especially Molly Jennings, who was not in the best of health when I first interviewed her, and who sadly died on the eve of publication. I am indebted to them all for the vividness of their recall and for making their time available to me.

The former QAs' relatives have been equally helpful: Suzanne Woodruffe faithfully relayed my supplementary questions to her mother Molly Jennings and generously copied her extensive photograhic record of her war service; Maxine Porch stepped in when deafness made phone conversations with her mother Sarah Saville tricky; John Fuller kindly allowed me to quote from his late mother Brenda McBryde's books and to include a photograph of her; and Kathryn Ingham generously allowed me to reproduce material from the a website she has created to celebrate her mother Freda Laycock's remarkable war service.

A great deal of the information in this book came from archive material and for this my thanks are owed to the staff who manage the collections of unpublished material that prove so rich a source to anyone writing about the Second World War: Captain Pete Starling, Director of the Army Services Museum at Keogh Barracks, Mytchett, Surrey, and his former colleague Hannah Bentley, at that time Assistant

Curator, are experts in their field and have been unfailingly prompt and helpful in dealing with my various queries; Rod Suddaby, Keeper of the Department of Documents at the Imperial War Museum, lent me books from his personal library and helped flesh out several of the sea disasters in which QAs lost their lives; and Stephen Walton, archivist of the department of books store at the Imperial War Museum, Duxford, who was of great assistance in locating the testimony to the Tokio War Crimes Tribunal of QAs and British medical staff describing atrocities committed by the Japanese in Hong Kong and in the aftermath of the fall of Singapore.

When it comes to knowledge of the QARANC regiment two people stand head and shoulders above the others: one is Major Judy Evans, the Regimental Secretary – without Judy there might well have been no book, as it was she who introduced me to those QAs who had had a particularly interesting war service, sending me fresh names as new people contacted her; the other is Colonel Eric Gruber von Arni, lately Colonel QARANC, a leading authority on the history of military nursing. My calls on Eric's extensive knowledge of the subject have been legion, and his wisdom has contributed much to this book.

Many books have proved invaluable sources of information. For much of the factual background to the war I have to thank Ivor Matanle's scholarly yet compulsively readable *World War II*. I am grateful to the following for permission to quote previously published material: Charles G. Roland and Wilfrid Laurier University Press for permission to draw on *Long Night's Journey into Day, Prisoners of War in Hong Kong and Japan, 1941-1945*; Barbara Angell for allowing me to quote from her book *Wilma a Woman's war the exceptional life of Wilma Oram Young*; Eric Taylor for permission to reproduce from *Front Line Nurse* the hilarious anecdote in which King Farouk of Egypt met his match at the hands of a British army nurse; and Clare Hardy, author of *SS Ceramic: The Untold Story*, who introduced me to Eric Munday, the only survivor from the SS *Ceramic* when it sank off the Azores with the loss of a considerable number of QAs' lives. It is through Clare that I had the opportunity to hear his almost unbelievable story from his own lips.

In the case of unpublished archive material and books that were published many years ago I have made every effort to trace the copyright holders and ask their permission to quote from their accounts, but with the passage of time in some cases the trail has sadly gone cold. Where inquiries have borne fruit relatives have been generous in granting permission for me to quote from their sources. I was particularly delighted to receive permission from the following: Gillian Haley, niece of Maud Buckingham who was Matron at Imtarfa Hospital in Malta during the year-long siege; Anthony Perkins, who kindly allowed me to reproduce sections of his late wife's dramatic diary of her time in France with the British Expeditionary Force in 1940 and her knife-edge escape as the Germans invaded. Sister Helen Luker's diary was one of the first I read while researching this book and the meticulousness of her accounts, and the way she decorated her diaries with bus tickets, theatre tickets and pressed flowers moved me deeply.

I would like also to thank my editor Bea Hemming whose enthusiasm for the book has been so encouraging and whose clear-sighted suggestions have invariably been the right ones. Lastly my thanks go to my husband who has generously given me so much help at every stage. He believed in the project from the moment it hatched, nudged it on when I felt stuck, and helped with all the practical side – researching, editing and proof-reading.

Preface

The underlying purpose of this book is to convey my deep and growing admiration for the war generation, a group of remarkable men and women who are now, inevitably, disappearing and will soon be gone. This admiration for the qualities they epitomise – guts, modesty, restraint, altruism – was first kindled in a book I wrote ten years ago about the Land Army. The land girls were dogged and good-humoured in the face of hard work, foul weather and unsympathetic bosses. Working at the front line the Queen Alexandra nurses faced far greater peril, but reacted to it with the same self-deprecation and steely self-control.

Like many baby boomers born soon after the war I missed out on the opportunity of hearing my own parents' war stories first hand. I would give anything to turn the clock back and talk to them about those extraordinary years that changed everybody's lives. They died before I was old enough – or wise enough – to take any interest in their war service. My father was in the Air Force in the Far East and my mother worked for the American Red Cross. She had been offered the incredibly glamorous opportunity of transferring with them to Berlin – an avenue she was prevented from pursuing by discovering she was pregnant with me.

My lack of interest wasn't just because I was young and living in the present and they were old. In the sixties and seventies the fashionable stance among the young was to be opposed to war. Dapper old men in mirror-polished shoes and blazers who talked about their war service were ridiculed as militaristic old fools. Anti-war fervour reached such a pitch at my university that there was an unchallenged campaign to prevent money raised in Rag Week from being paid to its historic benefactor, the Earl Haig Fund – on the grounds that Remembrance Day glorified war. A boycott of poppy-wearing was encouraged among the young and hip. Even then that troubled me. I lived in Richmond in Surrey and regularly saw the wheelchair-bound amputees who lived in the Star and Garter home for wounded ex-servicemen and whose care was funded by the income from poppies. We grew up in a climate which judged the dropping of atomic bombs on Hiroshima and Nagasaki as an act of unparalleled wickedness. Only now are people of my age starting to address the alternative – the deaths of thousands more Allied troops at the hands of the Japanese.

I realise now that in being glibly – and often ignorantly – anti-war, we did the men and women who fought those wars a terrible injustice. As we grow older and they fade away many of us feel an intense regret that we did not hear their stories from their own lips. When people denounce the bombing of Japan I think of Oscar, the husband of a close friend of my mother's. Tall and so thin his watch strap hung loose on the tightest hole, he remained on an invalid's diet all his life. He was very withdrawn. My mother said he used to be very witty before the war, but had been a prisoner of the Japanese. The name Changi, however, meant nothing to me. I know others have similar regrets. Kathryn Ingram, whose mother Freda was a Queen Alexandra nurse, knew that she had nursed the living skeletons in the filth and disease of a German concentration camp. What she did not discover until after her death was that her exemplary behaviour so impressed a fellow officer in the Royal Army Medical Corps at the camp that he accorded it special mention in his official report. Kathryn's pride, as she has since discovered the extent of the task facing nurses like her mother, is immeasurable.

The war generation, unremarkable though they may look now with their stout sticks and thinning hair, led extraordinary lives. In writing this book I came upon story after story which made the hair on my neck prickle or made me gulp with emotion. There were the three men who survived the sinking of the mighty *Hood*, the navy's most prestigious battleship, which went down with the loss of 1,415 lives. One of the high points of my research was meeting a man who was the only survivor of the torpedoing of SS *Ceramic*, a troopship which went down off West Africa with 655 lives. He celebrated his 21st birthday aboard the U-boat which had killed all his shipmates and all twenty-six of the Queen

Alexandra nurses aboard, some of whom he had danced with days before. As for courage it would be hard to beat the two QAs who ignored the Captain's order to abandon the torpedoed troopship *Strathallan*, hit off the coast of Algeria. Facing what appeared certain death they opted go down into the bowels of the sinking ship and tend the horrific burns of the engine-room staff.

I admire them, not just for what they did, but for the people they are. Courteous, self-reliant and unassuming they embody qualities which are becoming rarer in modern society. In the decades since the Second World War we have become more materialistic, more self-centred and more prone to complain. Post-war psychologists have branded the famous British stiff upper lip, the cornerstone of so many stories in this book, undesirable emotional repression. Contemporary literature and drama focus on selfishness and cruelty on the grounds that these are the qualities that really drive the human spirit. But among people whose parents were the war generation, and among the younger public too, one detects a hunger for the uplifting qualities of bravery and self-sacrifice. One senses it in the huge groundswell of public admiration, spread by the internet, for the have-a-go heroes who have emerged from the curse of suicide bomb attacks; men like John Smeaton, the baggage-handler at Glasgow airport who tackled the driver of the blazing jeep and Angus Campbell, the off-duty fire-fighter who tackled a would-be suicide bomber on the London Tube. In an era when the police urge members of the public not to have a go, but to think of their own safety, and where they themselves wait in lay-bys rather than attend a house where people are at risk of being murdered, selfless acts of courage lift our spirits.

Among the thinning ranks of the war generation there are still plenty of unsung heroes. We have much to learn from them.

Introduction

The founding of the Queen Alexandra Imperial Military Nursing Service on 27 March 1902 enshrined a belief not traditionally subscribed to in the army that where it comes to nursing sick and injured soldiers a woman's gentle touch can work miracles.

This was something of a departure from received wisdom for the fighting forces. Women had always been involved with nursing sick civilians, and much of the makeshift nursing of a fighting army was carried out by the wives of the soldiers. But the calling had a reputation for drunkenness, promiscuity and the associated spread of venereal disease. Many commanders believed women created more problems than they solved. The idea of women being regularly used as nurses in the army was not established by the end of the eighteenth century. Wellington's army fought the Peninsular War without any nurses.

Historically, battle casualties were operated on by surgeons and nursed, if they were nursed at all, by male orderlies with only the most basic grasp of care and hygiene or by the wholly untrained wives of soldiers following the army. No educated women were to be found at the bedside of the injured because it was not thought decent for a lady to nurse men. Whether the unfortunate victims survived or died from their injuries was mostly down to luck.

It took a public scandal to force the army to address the expendable way it treated its wounded. A journalist working for *The Times* newspaper during the Crimean War exposed the disgusting condition of the wards at the Barrack Hospital in Scutari, Turkey, where the wounded lay on floors covered with excrement with no dressers or nurses to care for them and without even bandages. This moved Florence Nightingale, an exceedingly well-connected woman who had already taken steps to acquire a nursing training for herself in Germany, to go to the Crimea with a party of thirty-eight nurses. More than a hundred years after her death the affectionate nickname bestowed on her by grateful soldiers – the Lady with the Lamp – is synonymous with caring and gentleness; but this formidable woman changed a culture. It is to her intellect, energy and vision that the QAIMNS owes its existence.

Florence Nightingale's great aim in life was to transform nursing into a respected profession with a formal, standardised training. On her return from the Crimea a fund was raised to commemorate her pioneering work there. She used the money to set up the first training school for nurses at St Thomas's Hospital in London. The initial intake numbered fifteen. The Nightingale School of Nursing was the crucible; from here nurses wishing to make a career out of army nursing emerged to staff the military hospitals that sprang up across Britain and the Empire in the second half of the nineteenth century. The first of these was the Royal Victoria Hospital at Netley. Demolished in the 1960s, it was once a grandiose domed building overlooking Southampton Water in Hampshire, with three floors of corridors of a quarter of a mile each. It was staffed by graduates of St Thomas's.

By now the army had accepted that it needed its own trained nurses at home and overseas. But it lacked funds. A charitable organisation came to its aid. In 1880 the National Society for Aid to the Sick and Wounded in War (the forerunner of the British Red Cross Society) offered an annual grant of £1,100 for 'training a certain number of nurses at Netley and subsequently maintaining them at the other Military Hospitals, whose services may afterwards be available in case of War'. The posts were advertised in the two newspapers read by the educated classes, *The Times* and the *Daily Telegraph*, where it was stated that 'preference will be given to widows and daughters of officers of H.M. Services'. The posts would entail one month's trial followed by a year on probation. A period of two years in a military hospital would follow. By the following year the ladies had been chosen and the Army Nursing Service was born. Now Netley became the hub from which trained nurses fanned out to other military hospitals, not just in Britain, but in Ireland and the Mediterranean bases on Malta and Gibraltar.

Only women from the 'right' background were considered and applicants were regularly rejected because of what was deemed 'unsatisfactory social status'. What might seem to us mere snobbery was justified by Mrs Jane Deeble, the first Superintendent of Netley, and the widow of a doctor, in terms of imposing discipline. To her, a military nurse had to be 'a class of woman entirely superior to that of the wardmaster and the sergeants, because she must be a terror to the wrongdoer. When a Sister comes in it must be "Oh, here is Sister"; she should be the shadow of the medical officer, and she should be superior to all the female relations of the patients if she is to have proper influence.'

In 1897, with trouble already brewing in South Africa, Queen Victoria's third daughter Princess Christian started the Army Nursing Reserve. When two years later the Boer War broke out, a hundred nurses from the Reserve went over to nurse the huge numbers of casualties, many of whom were victims of disease. They were joined by a contingent of nurses from the London Hospital. Their dispatch had been organised by Princess Christian's sister-in-law Alexandra, Princess of Wales, wife of Queen Victoria's eldest son the future King Edward VII, an enlightened woman who had already shown a keen interest in the advancement of nurses.

Conditions in South Africa were taxing in the extreme. Wearing floor-skimming Victorian dresses over the customary whalebone stays, the nurses lived in tents like the men and worked round the clock in temperatures of up to 103°F. If female nurses still needed to prove themselves to the military medical establishment, this is where the breakthrough came. Sir Frederick Treves, a highly respected army surgeon, who was commanding a field hospital, was deeply impressed by the four nurses who worked with him:

> They seemed oblivious to fatigue, to hunger or to any need for sleep. Considering that the heat was intense, that the thirst which attended it was distressing and incessant, that water was scarce, and that the work in hand was heavy and trying, it was wonderful that they came out of it so little the worse in the end. Their ministrations to the wounded were invaluable and beyond all praise. They did a service during those distressful days which none but nurses could have rendered, and they set to all . . . an example of unselfishness, self-sacrifice and indefatigable devotion to duty.

They brought to many of the wounded and the dying that comfort which men are little able to evolve, or are uncouth in bestowing, and which belongs especially to the tender, undefined and undeniable ministrations of women.[1]

Sir Frederick's percipient observation of the cheering effect of a female presence on injured men played its part in the decision of the commanders of the Second World War to place nurses nearer the front line than they had ever been before.

Acceptance that women made superior nurses to orderlies was finally made explicit in a Royal Commission set up to assess the care of the wounded during the South Africa campaign. Noting that the soldiers 'seem to prefer to be attended by them to being attended to by orderlies' it stated that nurses '. . . would appear to be far better than orderlies, and their general employment in fixed hospitals ought to be now generally recognised by the authorities, and be provided for in future wars'. The only area of nursing from which women were to be excluded was venereal disease.

Before the Boer War ended it was decided to reorganise the army nursing and medical services. In the heyday of the Raj there were thirty-nine nurses, nine nursing Sisters and four Superintendents working in India under the banner of the Indian Nursing Service, many of them relatives of officers based there. January 1901 had seen the coronation of a new king and queen and it was decided to amalgamate the British and Indian army nursing services and ask the new queen to be its president. Queen Alexandra's Imperial Military Nursing Service had arrived.

The new corps needed a badge, which the Queen designed herself. A Danish princess, she chose an emblem deriving from her country's medieval past. The white cross is from the ancient Order of Dannebrog, and the QA motto, *Sub Cruce Candida* (Under the White Cross), is also the motto of the Order.

By the end of the first decade of the new century members of the fledgling force were working in Africa, Canada, Gibraltar, Jamaica, India and Hong Kong. In 1909 two Sisters from the QAIMNS were dispatched from Malta to Sicily, where an earthquake had killed and injured hundreds. The Sisters lived in tents near the Officers' Mess tent.[2]

Five years later the QAIMNS was plunged into the brutal era of modern warfare as nurses found themselves caught up in the mobilisation of the largest army Britain had ever put into the field. For women still nursing in the quaint Victorian uniform of floor-length dresses and bonnets tied with bows, the scale of the casualties came as a shock. The Great War ushered in an era of deadly new weaponry – bombs, landmines, torpedoes, tanks, flame throwers, machine guns – and with it the era of mass killing. For the first time nurses had to contend with poison gas, trench foot, trench fever, frostbite and the damaged nerves of shell-shock victims. This was the first war fought across the globe and the army nurses set up their hospitals wherever there were soldiers fighting, sharing the same hostile climate and primitive conditions as the men. They nursed the legions of casualties at the battles of Mons and Passchendaele in Flanders. In Salonika they cared for the host of men injured in the disaster of Gallipoli. Emancipated as few women before them, they worked in Egypt, Mesopotamia (now Iraq), East Africa and even ice-bound Russia. In August 1914 the corps had numbered only three hundred, but by the end of the war 10,404 nurses had served in the force.

It was not yet army policy to have nurses at the front line, but now, for the first time, war came to the unarmed. Hospitals were bombed from the air by the new aeroplanes, hospital ships were torpedoed by U-boats which infested the eastern Mediterranean. Nearly two hundred QAs died on active service during the war. In keeping with the creed of self-discipline instilled into them during their training they acquitted themselves with honour. Sixty-five military medals were awarded to military nurses during the war, one to a young nurse who continued to nurse an injured soldier while fifteen bombs fell within 80 yards of the tent they were housed in.

The war to end all wars turned out to have been nothing of the sort. Twenty-one years later a new peril engulfed the world. This time the army would tear up the rule book about the proper place for 'ladies' in warfare. This time QAs would serve at the front.

It would prove their finest hour.

I

HOME AND ABROAD

1

'Not when they have work to do'

They were ordinary girls from ordinary backgrounds, yet few groups of women in history have had more extraordinary adventures – or faced more ordeals – than members of Queen Alexandra's Imperial Military Nursing Service (fondly known as the QAs) during the Second World War. Two hundred and thirty-six paid with their lives. Theirs is a story of guts, self-sacrifice, inspirational leadership and dogged good humour in the face of suffering, privation and death.

Army commanders had noticed how, in those sad wards of the Great War, the spirits of mutilated victims had revived at the sight and touch of a nurse. When war was declared in September 1939, therefore, nurses were positioned as close to the front line as possible. It was a radical decision, matched nowhere in the Axis war machine: German, Italian and Japanese casualties were all cared for by men on the battlefield. Its implication for the nurses was incalculable. This was to be a war that showed no respect for the 'fair sex'.

For much of the war, waged from the air or from under the sea as much as on land, there *was* no front line – the enemy attacked indiscriminately. Between 1939 and 1945, wherever there were Allied troops risking their lives, there were QAs. A thousand newly enlisted QAs went over with the British Expeditionary Force in 1939. Trapped in the lightning advance of the Germans as they invaded Holland and Belgium, they rescued thousands of wounded British troops by loading them on to hospital trains – trains that might later be blown up or bombed. At the docks they helped carry the injured on to waiting hospital ships under wave after wave of attacks by the Luftwaffe.

Their darkest hour came when the Japanese invaded Hong Kong and Singapore. During a horrific massacre on Christmas Day, which included their senior doctor and dozens of patients, QAs were raped and murdered. Many QAs were taken prisoner and died as a result of starvation and illness. Those who survived devotedly nursed the sick, and it is from this ordeal that some of the most inspirational examples of courage and leadership spring. In all, thirty-one QAs died at the hands of the Japanese.

Wherever the troops went the nurses went with them. Over a hundred fell victim to the unseen but deadly enemy – the U-boats that hunted convoys crossing the Atlantic, the Mediterranean and the Indian Ocean. Ships were blown out of the water without warning, survivors having no choice but to jump into the burning oil spreading over the surface of the sea or to drift for days on life rafts.

When the Allies invaded North Africa the QAs were there too, sharing the rigours of desert life with the men of the First and Eighth Armies. Conscious of their appearance, the young women dreamed of baths rather than the unsatisfactory canvas washstand stripwash dictated by water rationing. Somehow, even in these harsh conditions they imported a woman's touch, decorating the wards with desert flowers, setting their hair and fighting doggedly to look after their complexions when sand invaded the pores of their skin.

With Rommel defeated in North Africa the QAs followed the troops to Sicily and Italy. Several lost their lives when the Germans bombed hospital ships, and their bravery during the terrible battle at Anzio, which raged for days and caused terrible casualties, won the admiration of the doctors who worked with them. In addition, they took part in the greatest adventure of all – the opening of the second front and the Normandy landings. From camps along the south coast, while waiting for their orders, they looked up and saw the skies studded with the thousands of planes and gliders carrying the first wave of troops. Thousands of QAs sailed to France, disembarked from assorted ships and landing craft on to the legendary Mulberry harbour, and witnessed at first hand the greatest seaborne invasion in history.

The war forced them to develop emotional strengths that few suspected they possessed. Day after day they faced terrible sights but, as professionals, they could not afford the luxury of tears. No training could have prepared them for the hideous injuries that war inflicts. Some had never seen a man die before. Overnight they had to learn to put on brave faces when men the same age as themselves were brought in groaning in agony – in some cases with both legs amputated, in others with head-to-toe burns, blinded, with mangled chests or with jaws blown away.

It was QAs who took care of the group of men whose sufferings, by general consensus, exceeded those of all other Second World War victims – the prisoners of the Japanese and the survivors of the Nazi concentration camps. QAs worked on the hospital ships that took the POWs liberated from the Japanese to British military hospitals to nurse them gently back to health. The sight of servicemen who had been driven mad by their sufferings having to be straitjacketed as they were brought up for fresh air on the deck was, for one QA, the worst experience of the war.

The first women to go into Belsen and several other Nazi concentration camps were QA nurses. It was they who shaved and bathed the stinking diseased victims and tried to restore human dignity to those reduced to the level of animals by their brutal captors. The suffering they found there, and the inhumanity of those who had inflicted it, would haunt them.

But the story of the QAs is not only about suffering and death. Nor were the nurses merely pious heroines virtuously doing their duty. These were flesh-and-blood women. They slept in curlers, which led to much embarrassment when there was a raid in the night and they couldn't get their tin hats on. When they were off duty they hummed the latest dance tunes, sighed after Spitfire pilots, bounced around in the backs of army lorries on their way to dances in the desert or shared moonlight swims and beach picnics with fellow officers. Non-medical observers were always impressed at the way the QAs were able to switch with apparent ease from the most harrowing work into carefree leisure mode.

In those days there were seldom days off, or even half-days, and when they came off duty the girls would tumble into bed to get a couple of hours sleep before going on again. Like all young people they were irreverent, and secretly mocked their superiors. Plenty about army ritual struck them as absurd. The failure of the hidebound army tailors, used to making uniforms for men, to take female curves into account when the corps abandoned its grey dresses and white veil caps for khaki battledress made them groan in despair. These were girls who wore dainty, lace-trimmed underwear made of crêpe de Chine or silk, and the army's doomed efforts at concocting regulation underwear provoked particular hilarity. 'Good news this morning: some replacement uniform and underclothes arrived from England including ghastly khaki knickers. These pants are hilarious, huge and elasticated at the waist and legs, but we could hardly have expected army-supplies to have equipped us with glamorous cami-knickers.'[1]

Some aspects of Army protocol appeared ludicrous to them. The view of one QA on procedure in the event of shipwreck was probably widespread. 'Standing on the boat deck watching the docks recede we were amused to hear a talk on the use of iron rations being given to a group of men by an NCO. After impressing on the men that iron rations were only to be used on the order of an officer he continued: "If you are torpedoed and you are in the water for more than 24 hours you may open your iron rations without waiting for an officer's orders."'[2]

Above all the QAs were women of character. They were the stiff-upper-lip generation. Their upbringing and training had dinned into them that service to others was far more important than personal fulfilment, and that to complain was unacceptable. Self-discipline was paramount and they put up with hardships unimaginable to their children and grandchildren. When things got really bad, in the best British tradition, they turned the nightmare into a joke. The troops also cracked jokes in the darkest hours and the QAs loved them for it. A nurse whose ship was torpedoed describes how they were about to board the Royal Navy rescue ship after twelve hours in lifeboats filled with the dead and injured. Suddenly a soldier appeared on a small raft, paddling with his hands. Seeing the sailors he put up his hand and shouted, 'Hey! Taxi!' 'We thought he should receive a medal just for his marvellous attitude.'[3]

There was deep affection and camaraderie between the troops and the QAs. The soldiers liked the Sisters for their pluck, and for their willingness to muck in whatever the conditions. The Sisters, for their part, had boundless admiration for the British Tommy's unwillingness to complain in the face of pain, which was in marked contrast to the wounded POWs. The soldiers showed their respect for the Sisters in a variety of ways. American troops took pleasure in teasing and embarrassing nurses and whereas the Australians were renowned for having hopelessly untidy lockers, the British patients' lockers were always immaculate for the daily 10 a.m. inspection. Being a tiny handful of women among a sea of men presented certain problems. For the early years of the war the uniform was skirts and dresses, so climbing up on to the back of a three-ton army lorry presented a decency problem. In these situations the men turned away.

Bravery was a huge issue for people who fought in the Second World War. People worried whether, when the time came, and the shells started whining and buildings began collapsing, they would be able to behave with dignity, be an example to others, do the right thing. The inspirational QAs' story shows just how brave many of them turned out to be: there are the young nurses who, when their ship was torpedoed, refused to take to the lifeboats because they couldn't bring themselves to abandon their helpless patients in the ship's hospital; there are Sisters who declined to take their place on life rafts after being shipwrecked in the seas off Singapore and who, ignoring their own wounds, opted to stay in the water, leaving the safer space to children and civilians.

Time and again it was Matron who came into her own as leader. The army Matron, no less than her civilian counterpart, was seen by many young nurses as a battleaxe – the female counterpart of the regimental sergeant major – wedded to the army, a stickler for discipline and often a bully. But in danger, that discipline turned Matron into a rock to whom others looked for strength and comfort. Amid the terror of the Japanese attack on Singapore, when the Sisters' home suffered a direct hit, Matron thought nothing of her own safety as she tore into the shattered building to check on her girls. Later, still under fire yet showing no fear, she shepherded them all to the blazing docks and the getaway ships. One of her young nurses confided in a letter home that although the situation was very worrying, as long as she had Matron around she wasn't afraid. In the terrifying siege of Malta, in which for months the hospital itself came under fire on a daily basis, Matron's upbeat letters were full of motherly concern for her nurses and for the privations of the civilian population, with no mention of her own feelings.

On occasion, the guts of some of these women put even seasoned fighting men to shame. The distinguished Allied commander, Lieutenant General Sir Brian Horrocks, was at Arnhem in Holland when the Germans cut off the road to their rear. While visiting his men in a

Casualty Clearing Station in a converted school in Nijmegen, he was talking to the Head Sister when he heard the sound of a large enemy shell approaching:

> After a time in war, one gets to know instinctively whether or not an approaching shell is likely to land nearby. This one, I could tell, was going to be very, very close indeed. I would dearly have liked to take cover under one of the beds, but as the Sister seemed quite unmoved, I felt I had to grin and bear it. Then came a resounding crash, and all the windows were blown in. The Sister never even blinked. She finished what she was saying, then looked round and said, 'What a bore – we shall have to get all that repaired.' She did not know the meaning of the word fear, but had the gentlest of touches when it came to tending a wounded soldier.[4]

On occasion the nurses even won the grudging admiration of the enemy. In one detention camp in Hong Kong, where the food was typically inadequate and medical supplies withheld, the Japanese officer in charge was so impressed with the selfless dignified way in which the Matron and Sisters devoted themselves to the sick and needy, despite being weak themselves, that he saluted them when they left his camp.

But it was at a hospital in Hong Kong in the aftermath of the raping and killing that marked the Japanese victory that a QA Matron uttered a phrase which encapsulated everything the corps stood for. A Japanese soldier had been brought into the hospital in the fighting and had died of his wounds. Knowing the Japanese custom, the Matron had taken the Japanese flag the soldier carried in his pocket and laid it over his body. When a horde of Japanese soldiers burst into her hospital the Matron was tied up at gunpoint and treated roughly and insolently, this at a time when mass atrocities were taking place all over the island. She repeatedly demanded to be freed, contrasting the humane way she had cared for the Japanese patient with the way the Japanese were treating her. Finally a Japanese officer asked to be taken to identify his dead compatriot and when he saw him, he was moved and wept. The Matron, standing beside him, maintained her dignity, even though she had no idea what her fate would be. Astonished at her self-control he asked her, 'Do English women never cry?' To which she replied, 'Not when they have work to do.'

2

The Making of a QA

Queen Alexandra's Imperial Military Nursing Service was an elite corps. Since 1926 its members had been entitled to equivalent rank with officers and, in 1943, after robust campaigning by the Matron-in-Chief, they were granted wartime commissions with full military rank. Yet whether or not there was a war on, the army planned to keep the corps exclusive. To be accepted a recruit had to 'fit in'. That meant being not merely a fully qualified nurse with up to four years training behind her, but also a girl from a respectable middle-class – ideally professional – family. She had to be British, preferably English, have had a good education, speak well and know how to behave.

Pre-war Britain was a highly class-conscious society in which hospitals occupied a clearly delineated hierarchy, catering for different types of patient. At the top came the university hospitals, followed by the general hospitals, with the municipal hospitals seen very much as poor relations. As one English QA, the daughter of an accountant, delicately put it, 'The municipal hospitals tended to attract a lot of girls from Scotland and Wales.' It was nurses from the general hospitals who were favoured by the QAIMNS. Interviews, which could take up to an hour, were conducted by a matron who, while stressing the discomforts of active service, probed into the recruit's background, asking questions about her schooling, her family, their occupations and her hobbies. A girl was likely to be asked if she played tennis.

In the heyday of Empire, Britain had a huge standing army overseas and in peacetime the purpose of QAIMNS was to provide nursing staff for the military hospitals in those countries where Britain maintained a garrison. Before the outbreak of war the total strength of QAIMNS worldwide was 624. These Sisters, who often came from army backgrounds themselves, were Regulars, permanently employed in military hospitals. With the outbreak of the Second World War they were joined by members of the Territorial Army Nursing Service (TANS), together with thousands of newly qualified civilian nurses, bringing the size of the corps to over ten thousand. A palpable rivalry existed between them, with the Regulars regarding the Reserves as interlopers.

When Hitler gained power in 1933 and launched Germany into wholesale rearmament, Matrons were encouraged to apply substantial pressure on those nurses approaching the end of their training to join the Reserves. As soon as war was declared the Reserves and TANS were merged into the QAIMNS. Administered by matrons answering to the army's Matron-in-Chief – a distillation of the most formidably organised women in the country – it is hardly surprising that the system worked like clockwork. By 1936 most trained nurses who wished to enlist had received instructions telling them which unit they were to join in the event of general mobilisation. Within a few days of war being declared a group of one thousand QAs sailed for France with the British Expeditionary Force.

Most nurses needed little persuasion to sign on. They were young, intensely patriotic and hungry for adventure. So eager were they to take part in active service that those who began their training in 1939 fretted that the war would be over before they had had the chance of joining up. Although the navy and the air force had their own considerably smaller nursing services, the army seemed the obvious choice. The uniform, a strikingly attractive combination of grey dress and scarlet-trimmed cape, undoubtedly played a part. Nurses poured into the corps in such numbers that at one stage civilian hospitals suffered a staffing crisis and recruitment had to be halted.

The reaction of Molly Budge was typical of those who were already qualified when war was declared. She was working as a midwife in Lambeth, south London, delivering babies in tenement houses where poverty meant that mothers gave birth in rooms shared with their older children. 'As war was declared I went to Millbank Military Hospital, which was just across the river, and signed on for overseas service. My father had been in the artillery, in charge of horse-drawn guns, in the First World War and he was very dismayed at my eagerness to go to war. But I didn't want to stay in a hospital in England. I wanted to go where the action was."[1]

Once a nurse had been accepted as a QA she was sent to a mobilising unit. There she would be given inoculations for typhus, typhoid and smallpox before being toughened up and moulded into the army's idea of a nurse. These units were military hospitals, some purpose-built, others based in requisitioned hotels, schools and elegant country houses. Throughout the war the units maintained a steady throughput of new recruits, as civilian nurses completed their training and joined up, some QAs returning from active service to the unit in which they had started years earlier. The purpose of these units was twofold: to train the recruits, physically and professionally, for what lay ahead; and to create a mobile hospital unit that would remain together, in different locations, for the duration of the war. The unit comprised doctors, pharmacy and laboratory technicians and army privates trained in first aid who were known as orderlies. Women who had joined up at the same time from the same civilian hospital often found themselves allocated to different units and did not meet again until much later in the war, if at all.

Many new QAs were unimpressed by the leisurely pace and complicated bureaucratic rituals of peacetime army nursing. Audrey Hayward was posted to a military hospital in Shaftesbury, Dorset. She arrived in December 1940 and remained there for five months, finally sailing to West Africa on 17 May 1941.

It was a bit of a culture shock after civilian nursing. The patients seemed all quite fit and young compared with what I'd been used to. They were mostly road accident victims. When they were up they wore hospital uniform – blue serge trousers and jacket with a white shirt and red tie. There was a tremendous emphasis on ritual and order. The patients had lockers beside their beds and everything had to be arranged in a particular way. The top shelf contained a huckaback towel folded in three and with the folds to the front. Then you put their razor and below that their hospital uniform folded so that from the front it ran blue white blue with the red tie threaded through the whole thing. It struck us civilian sisters as absurd. The soldiers kept their rank when they were ill, too, and the Sergeant was the boss of the ward.[2]

Many, like Audrey, found the rigidity of the army hierarchy – which made the civilian Matron look flexible by comparison – hard to accept.

A patient complained of chest pain one day and noticing that his notes said he had a chest infection I mentioned to an older nurse that I would tell Sister.

'Why would you do that?' she barked.

'I thought it would help,' I stammered.

'When you join the Army you don't think, you obey,' she snapped.

On another occasion I went and asked for a kaolin poultice and was told in no uncertain terms that I was not expected to use my own initiative. Rank was paramount and everyone had their role. When it was time for a cup of tea there was even a tea orderly to pour it. I suppose it was very important that we became initiated, but after civilian nursing it did seem very ritualistic. We had to master endless forms – all of which had numbers. If you wanted to request an X-ray you had to fill out a numbered form, even medical history notes had numbers. The whole thing was like stepping back to a different age, where everyone was cocooned, instead of getting on with things. There were a lot of ambulant patients and they were kept in for far longer in military hospitals than they would have been in the world of civilian nursing.

Audrey's conviction that she had gone back in time was strengthened by the elaborate and old-fashioned uniform list with which she was presented in Shaftesbury. The uniform had to be bought at Harrods and was so expensive that the government grant to equip her only covered half the cost – the QA's parents were expected to make up the difference. Every item was made to measure and used only the finest cloth.

We had to have four or five ward dresses, a walking out suit and hat. We had a grey mess dress, which was made of the finest wool, pintucked down to the waist with a white collar, long sleeves and cuffs which buttoned. On duty we wore a cap, or veil, made of starched lawn which hung down our backs in a point. Then there was a grey elbow-length cape with red trim. This was the QA's trademark and was said to have been designed by Queen Alexandra herself so that the licentious soldiers should not be able to see the nurses' figures. If this was true it was nonsense as some of those capes were fairly fitted. On top of this we had a heavy wool greatcoat, also grey with a half belt at the back. We also had to have a tropical kit. This consisted of white overalls with pearl buttons you put in with shanks, and epaulettes where you put your pips – two for a lieutenant, three for a captain. Then we had to have white stockings, white shoes and a white felt hat with appropriate ribbon. Just to complete the feeling that you had strayed into an earlier century the whole thing had to be topped off by a white parasol with a red lining! We scoured the shops of Lowestoft for a red-lined parasol. In the end we managed to find a green-lined one which I decided would have to do. Needless to say it was never used.

At the same time as rationing started to bite and material grew scarce, the realities of modern warfare began to make themselves felt – the white veils proving a nightmare for nurses working in tents in the desert – and the ladylike uniform was gradually replaced by the more practical khaki. By the time QAs were sailing across the Channel after the D-Day landings, parasols and pintucks had given way to full battle-dress, including boots and gaiters.

The newly enlisted QA might be a novice as far as the army was concerned but she was no stranger either to hard work or to unquestion-ing obedience. The pre-war nurses' training was exceedingly harsh by the standards of today and the culture of humiliation it fostered would be unacceptable now. Matron and her senior Sisters dominated and bullied not just the junior nurses, but the patients too. The nurses lived in nurses' homes attached to the hospital, where the Home Sister, in boarding-school-headmistress mode, turned the lights out at 10.30 p.m. Windows were fixed so they could not open wide enough to admit a late homecomer. Men were barred from the premises. Most of the time a nurse did not address a superior unless spoken to. In 1939 many nurses worked sixty-seven hours a week on day duty and seventy-two on nights. Their two hours' off-duty time between 2 p.m. and 4 p.m. was spent attending lectures. Nurses were not allowed to sit down when on duty and many had problems with swollen feet. The amount of food they were given was inadequate for young people leading such physical lives and most of them remember feeling permanently hungry while they were training. In the early months they were treated little better than skivvies. Every morning they had to pull the beds out from the walls before throwing the previous day's tea leaves on the floor to gather the dust, which was then swept up. Some even had to count the cutlery every day.

Victorian hospitals loved brass. All the beds had decorative brass knobs and the lockers had brass rails round the top and brass knobs. All this had to be polished daily by the nurses. The beds then had to be completely stripped and remade, some Ward Sisters insisting that the turndown on a bed had to be exactly nine inches – and woe betide the nurse who got it wrong.

Many girls couldn't take it and left before their training was completed. Those who stuck it out found that they had toughened up quite a bit since they first left home. If you could cope with the Matron of a civilian hospital you could cope with the army.

Some QAs actually found army life more congenial. This is how one new recruit put it:

> Right from the start, I had formed an impression of the QAIMNS that was an entirely good one. For one thing there was very little talk of discipline, but an unspoken presumption that one was a mature and professionally-trained person attached to a distinguished army nursing service . . . In my training days I had been constantly belittled, never praised . . . My bruised spirit recovered in the warmth of an encouraging and accepting milieu. So that I developed a greater confidence in myself and a new assurance in my work.[3]

One of the busiest mobilisation centres throughout the war was the Peebles Hydro. In peacetime this imposing Gothic pile set in glorious countryside some 25 miles south of Edinburgh had been the Peebles Hydropathic, a five-star spa hotel catering for the well off. In wartime, however, its bedrooms were so chilly that the girls gathered wood to build fires in the stone fireplaces, its elegant tennis courts were covered in khaki tents, and the grounds echoed, not to the sound of guests languidly playing croquet, but to the despairing bellows of the Sergeant Major charged with getting the nurses fit.

The QAs who came here were struck, as Audrey Hayward had been, by the endless forms that had to be filled out in a military hospital and there was much giggling over the army's obsession with the locker layout – they were even given a photo to memorise. But if the locker arranging struck the new recruits as overly fussy, the rest of their training was very much to the point. They were put through their paces physically. They were made to hike up and down the steep Scottish hills in battledress and tin hats with full packs on their backs, expected to vault five-bar gates and taught self-defence. Crucially, they learned how the army dealt with casualties in the field, a meticulously disciplined system that had been honed down over the years, which all QAs would come to admire.

Whitby-born Brenda McBryde (later Fuller) became part of the 75th British General Hospital on her arrival at Peebles:

> We learned how to keep medical records in the field, how to purify water, the lay-out of a general hospital under canvas, how the field kitchen worked . . . We became familiar with the progress of a wounded man from the time he was picked up by stretcher-bearers and hurried to his Regimental Aid Post (RAP) then taken by ambulance to the Field Dressing Station (FDS) or Casualty Clearing Station (CCS) for urgent surgery, then down the line to the base hospitals . . . Here he would receive treatment before being evacuated by sea or air to the United Kingdom or sent back for service with his company.[4]

The doctors who lectured at Peebles pulled no punches when describing the kind of injuries the battlefield inflicted. The officer in charge of surgery told them: 'If the man has been shot through the popliteal vein and his foot is cold and gangrenous, don't waste time, cut it off.'

The dental officer's lectures, written with hard-boiled medical officers in mind, made his inexperienced young audience flinch. 'Fractured jaw . . . Treat for shock. Pick out any loose teeth and bits of bone then put a stitch through the tongue and tie it to a button on his jacket before you send him down the line on a stretcher.'[5]

The Peebles regime not only taught the new recruits the ins and outs of caring for the injured, but also to become rank-conscious, to feel and behave like the army officers they were. This meant that young sociable girls surrounded by handsome soldiers ever eager to catch their eye had to accept the army rules forbidding fraternising with Other Ranks. While at Peebles they mixed only with officers. When they went into Glasgow or Edinburgh even on social business they always wore uniform and were always accompanied by officers. Getting used to saluting was a problem for young girls fresh from civvy street, as Gwladys Aikens discovered during her stay in Peebles: 'I was stopped in the street in Edinburgh by a senior officer. He had passed by and saluted; I had stood there thinking how very handsome and official he looked. He had come back to me and said rather abruptly, "When another officer or other rank salutes you, Sister, you don't just stand there and blush, you return the salute immediately." '[6]

Some QAs had already experienced battlefield conditions before joining the Army, having trained in cities that had been badly bombed during the Blitz. After London, Liverpool was probably the most bombed city in Britain and its inhabitants suffered appallingly. The massive port at which the convoys carrying troops and supplies ceaselessly embarked was mercilessly pounded for three years by the Luftwaffe, killing four thousand of the town's citizens and destroying ten thousand homes.

Dorothea Chisholm was training at Liverpool Royal Infirmary when war broke out and was on duty during the air raids:

> The injuries inflicted on civilians by the Blitz on Liverpool were some of the worst things I saw during my entire service. The hospital was hit directly three or four times and our Night Sister was killed in one of the raids. She was a generation older than me and had done night duty for thirty-five years. If a bomb explodes too near you it sucks all the air out of the lungs and all the dust and grime sets up an infection and you die of pneumonia, which is what happened to her. In those days we didn't have routine access to antibiotics . . .
>
> We used to tell the patients, who were terrified, to put their heads under the pillow so they wouldn't hear the noise so much. One night when I was on night duty they brought in a young girl

who had been sitting on a settee when a bomb fell on her house. She was very badly injured – the springs had gone through her abdomen. Normally we moved the beds out into the corridor when there was a raid because there weren't any windows there so we thought they'd be safer. Because of her injuries this poor girl had been slung up on a type of support system known as a Balkan Beam and couldn't be moved. She was absolutely terrified so I stayed with her. We put our heads under the pillow and hugged until it was over.[7]

The exploding bombs and the noise of the ack-ack guns right next to the hospital were deafening and terrified the patients. The air filled with dust and broken glass. After a raid the corridors would be lined with stretchers containing the injured.

Every morning there would be row upon row of people waiting to have their dressings changed. There were terrible burns from the fires – it was particularly upsetting to see kiddies who had been burnt – and people who had hips and chests crushed by falling masonry. There were dockers whose bodies had been smashed by being blown into the dry docks and merchant seamen in agony from crushed limbs . . . One night someone brought in a lost child and no one knew where his parents were. The doctors were shouting out, 'Does anyone know who this child belongs to?' Somewhere else there was a husband and wife who had come in badly injured. They were filthy dirty because their house had fallen in on top of them and they were being got ready to go to theatre . . . Suddenly the distracted woman called out, 'Oh thank God! There he is!' Mother and child were reunited.

Self-discipline was what Matron expected and the young nurses did their best to maintain the tradition. One girl Dorothea knew had been told to give the patients cups of tea. She went through the ward collecting all the empty cups on a big tin tray. As she walked back with them there was a huge bang and a window frame fell in right beside her. 'She didn't flinch. She just kept walking down the corridor. It wasn't till she got to the kitchen and put the tray down that she fainted.'

Not yet twenty, Dorothea found self-control very hard. 'I was so upset by what these people were going through I had to run into the sluice room to hide my tears. What you were seeing and what your own nerves were being subjected to in the air raids built up and suddenly you'd find yourself crying at the oddest moments. Once when I was at Liverpool I got free tickets to the Liverpool Empire to see Margot Fonteyn and Robert Helpmann dance together in the ballet. It was magnificent and I loved it – but I cried through most of the performance.'

Dorothea was not the only one to experience the brutal incursions of war on her own doorstep. While Brenda McBryde was at Peebles awaiting mobilisation she received her own abrupt initiation. She and another QA agreed to take a six-week course in plastic surgery at a burns unit at Bangor, where most patients were badly disfigured Battle of Britain pilots. It was an experience that tested the young nurses' ability to suppress their own emotions in the face of pain to its limit.

> The scarred hands of one RAF pilot were contracted back towards the wrist to a position where they were virtually functionless. His face was young and handsome but his raw, red hands were like bunches of boiled prawns . . .
>
> The next patient was sitting with a bundle of cane on his lap and the beginnings of a basket. He was one of the success stories, we were told, but to . . . me he looked like a major disaster. Three years ago, he had leapt from his burning, spiralling plane, a little knot of flame at the end of a parachute. His limbs were mobile now but his face was still in the process of being rebuilt. The new eyelids were still puffy, still showing the stitchmarks, and the large round graft on one cheek was the pale skin from his left buttock that had not yet taken on colour from the face's blood supply. Twin tunnels in a stub of bone was all he had left of a nose.[8]

The surgeon described the operations the man had had to undergo to stop his mouth from twisting over to one side. 'What we did,' he explained, 'was to strip a length of fascia from his leg muscle and insert one end here, stitching it to the corner of his mouth. Then we made another incision here by the cheekbone on the same side of the face, inserted long sinus forceps to the corner of the mouth to pick up the free end of the fascia strip, pulled it through and secured it. Now he can smile.'[9] Trying to look as if she was taking a professional interest,

Brenda wondered silently what the poor young man would ever find to smile about. But she acquired a deep reverence for the infinitely patient hands of the plastic surgeons and their pioneering technique of skin grafting that offered hope to these ravaged bodies. 'There were men with burnt elbows stitched inside the raised skin of the abdomen, immobilised there till the graft should "take". New lower jaws were fashioned from ribs. Uppers of burnt feet were stitched to the underside of calves. Men with extensive body burns were lowered into warm saline baths and encouraged by physiotherapists to keep muscles flexible with the gentlest movements possible under the water.'[10]

A crucial task that had to be undertaken before any of the units could embark for overseas service was packing up the equipment a mobile military hospital would need in the field. The laborious job took days.

> Bales of straw, sacking, cans of paint, wooden crates and tins of smelly brown grease were all stacked in the Great Hall. Each piece of hospital equipment was to be wrapped, labelled and crated in category so that the whole could be reassembled with the minimum of delay 'over there', wherever that might be. Each surgical instrument had to be greased to prevent rust, wrapped in oiled paper, sewn in sacking and packed in crates which were then stencilled with an identifying number. Our fingers grew sore from sewing the coarse sacking and the stink of lubricating grease pervaded our hair, skin and clothes. After a few days the Great Hall began to look like some medieval workshop with figures hammering, painting, sewing.[11]

The final task that had to be accomplished before the newly fledged QAs were ready to embark on active service was the purchasing of kit that would provide them with warmth and shelter on any kind of terrain. The list comprised a tin trunk, a camp bed, a bedroll, a canvas wash bowl and tripod, a collapsible canvas bath, a canvas bucket and a 'Beatrice' paraffin stove.

As the end of their mobilisation period approached the tension mounted. Speculation was rife as to when they would be leaving – and for where – and the townspeople of Peebles, seeing them striding about in uniform, would regularly ask them when they were leaving for overseas. But 'Walls have ears' was the watchword and they were under strict orders not to discuss their movements with anyone. Not that they knew themselves. When the long-awaited news was announced it was in a locked room with a guard posted outside.

As the end of their stay at Peebles approached, one unit decided to show its appreciation of the kindness of the locals by organising a concert.

> The army assembled a decent-sounding band consisting of a sergeant, a few doctors and nurses, and a couple of other officers. A couple of the other QAs, one of the sergeants and I composed a song about the people of Peebles . . . We named our creation Peebles Air and rehearsed diligently.
>
> With all of us working on different skits, songs and dances we knew we would have a worthwhile production. We had chosen a date and time, put up a few posters and made tickets to hand out at the door. It must have come as quite a shock to the people of Peebles when, a few days before the scheduled . . . concert, the whole general hospital vanished without a trace.[12]

3

A Baptism of Fire

Everyone found the 'phoney war' of 1939 tedious, including the nurses who had been mobilised in a rush and sent to France. Helen Luker, a nurse with ten years' experience at St Thomas's Hospital in London, was among the first to arrive in France in the autumn of 1939. Germany's assault on Western Europe was expected at any moment. On 3 September, following Germany's rejection of the British ultimatum and her invasion of Poland, war was declared. The British Expeditionary Force, numbering half a million men, went at once to the aid of her French allies and by mid October were in position defending a stretch of the Franco-Belgian border.

The QAs followed in a matter of days, the first six arriving in Cherbourg on 10 September. By the turn of the year there were more than a thousand in France and Belgium. Helen Luker was posted to a 1,200-bed military hospital in La Baule, a small resort near the Loire estuary on France's Atlantic coast. Then suddenly the drama stopped, and the weeks of the phoney war grew into months.

Eager for action, Sister Luker found life in La Baule tedious in the extreme. She had not even been issued with QA kit and was still wearing her old St Thomas's uniform. Glumly she wrote that she was 'doing the work of a probationer, under a rather elderly sister who had seen service in the last war'.[1] It is a tribute to the organisational skills of the Matron-in-Chief, however, that Sister Luker had been prepared for what would happen in the event of war, for not just months but years.

'In 1936 we received our instructions in the event of General Mobilisation, the units we were to join, our travelling warrants to those units from anywhere in Britain . . . So I carried my papers everywhere with me; during the Munich crisis in 1938, I was on a walking tour of Scotland, and whether in a shepherd's cottage in Glen Dessary or a tiny whitewashed house at Aviemore, I listened to the 9 o'clock news on the wireless!'

When war was declared, as instructed, Sister Luker got herself to the country's largest military hospital, Netley in Hampshire. There, despite the careful forward planning, chaos reigned. She was subjected to a crude form of physical training – being made to walk at least six miles a day – suffered a raft of painful injections, was made to fill in endless forms and was required, somehow, still to find time to assemble uniform and kit.

Those six months marking time at La Baule dragged by. No one knew what Germany would do. The celebrated Maginot Line, a super-solid rampart of fortifications along the length of the Franco-German border built to keep the Germans out of France, was deemed impregnable. Few anticipated that Hitler might ignore neutrality and invade France through Holland and Belgium, the frontiers of which were not protected.

Suddenly, with only thirty-six hours' notice, Helen Luker was told that she was moving. Her posting, dated 15 April 1940, instructed her to proceed to No. 12 Casualty Clearing Station, a tented unit in the French mining town of Bethune, near Lille, not far from the Belgian frontier. Less than a month later the phoney war would be over and Helen Luker would be caught up in the extraordinary rescue operation that has come to be known as the miracle of Dunkirk.

On 10 May 1940 the Germans unleashed the full might of the Luftwaffe on towns and airfields in Holland, Belgium and northern France, killing thousands and making tens of thousands homeless. Sister Luker kept a diary of this first engagement of the war which gives a vivid insight into what it felt like to be caught up in it.

Her entry for 10 May reads: 'We are woken at 4 a.m. by terrific air raid. There are four light enemy planes and three heavy bombers. Much anti aircraft firing and incredible trace bombs. I watch from the garden . . . We have black coffee and rum at 5.30 a.m. Evacuation of all possible patients – the CCS is nearly cleared. Continual air raid warnings all day . . .'

Extraordinarily, even as the net was closing, life in the as yet hardly used casualty station continued its agreeable course. The staff listened to the radio and heard that Neville Chamberlain had resigned and Churchill had taken over.

Every time there was an air-raid warning everyone had to don tin hats and gas masks, but despite the deteriorating situation a semblance of normal life continued. 'I am off at 5 p.m. Bicycle into Bethune for shopping. Asked by Maj Longridge to join the party which is dining out. In the end 8 of us go out for dinner at the Pas de Calais – quite a good dinner, champagne and everyone in good spirits . . .'

By now the town was starting to fill with fleeing civilians. Helen Luker's diary entry for 17 May reads: '. . . hundreds of Belgian refugees – a most ghastly sight. Some on foot, some on bicycles, and others in cars and with as many belongings as they can carry.'

On 18 May the staff have 'a terrific tea party in a tent – all rather depressed with news but trying to keep the flag flying!' Optimistically they decide that the news on the wireless is a 'little better'.

On 19 May the good life ended abruptly. Convoys of wounded started to arrive – the first battle casualties that Helen Luker had seen.

'We began working soon after 3 and after that we continued continuously for the rest of the day. We each had two sets of trestles and the stretchers were brought straight in from the pre-operative room and out to the tents afterwards. Lt Jule was operating, Major Butler anaesthetising, Straklen was the orderly . . . Lees the orderly in the sterilising room kept things going there. Some cases were simply frightful – whole areas blown away. Others were peppered with small shot . . . some sights made me feel quite sick.'

Suddenly, the order came to get out. They were to dismantle the hospital, pack their patients into ambulances and make a run for the coast, in the hope that a ship would pick them up.

May 20

The night is very cold. We work on. As soon as we nearly finish one convoy another comes in. We have another break at 3.30 a.m. – beef sandwiches and more 'hot sweet tea'. We all feel completely exhausted and 'gone at the knees'. Our last case was a most *terrible* gangrenous back. Have breakfast at the mess at 8.30 a.m. Return to theatre and am told we are to pack up. Do some clearing then back to rooms and pack my own luggage. After lunch we clean theatres completely most terrific and very sad business . . . We take a last farewell of 12 CCS leave at 5.30 p.m. . . . the roads are simply *jammed* with refugees and we crawl along. The sight is an absolute nightmare, mostly women and children on farm waggons drawn by horses – thousands on bicycles, walking. We try to eat some food by the roadside at about 10 p.m. but feel too grim for words.

Helen Luker clearly had no idea how close the Germans were. While she listened to the BBC they had been advancing at speeds never previously witnessed by tank columns. The Dutch had capitulated on 14 May and by the 17th the Germans were in Brussels. Panzer corps surged up the Somme and by the evening of 21 May took the town of Abbeville. As the corps that had taken Abbeville turned north, another Panzer corps pushed west from Brussels. Gradually the BEF – with its medical support staff – was being forced back to the sea by a ring of German steel.

The staff of No. 12 CCS were headed for Abbeville, and from there to Boulogne, but by the evening of the 21st the Germans were already there. The medics ran into a German road blockade, but though one of the ambulance drivers capitulated, the one Luker was in drove on and managed to get through. Her diary entry for 21 May reads:

> At about 1 a.m. we are warned by an officer not to proceed via Abbeville . . . and he orders another route . . . [via] minor roads to Montreuil . . .
>
> I see much evidence of trouble – dead and wounded civilians . . . three French soldiers, wire across the road. Driver of second ambulance thinks group of . . . soldiers tanks and guns are French – surrenders. We drive on leaving all kit luggage and bicycle. Eventually reach Montreuil . . . meet some officers escaping from No. 13 CCS. Reach Nos. 14 and 18 GH [General Hospitals] a few miles north and report to CO. *Terrific* air raid . . . We lie in trenches for half an hour . . . Put into ambulances at 2.30 p.m. Roads fearfully congested. Onto hospital train at Amiens. Reached Boulogne at 5 p.m. Disembarked [*sic*] on George V.* *Fearful* air raid as we left . . . no bombs on us. Saw two ships mined. We lie on deck . . . during raids . . .

---

* A celebrated Royal Navy battleship which made many return trips to rescue stranded troops at Dunkirk and went on to have a distinguished war. Her chief claim to fame was that she was one of the two battleships responsible for sinking the *Bismarck*, reputedly the most modern battleship on the seas at that time, and the pride of the German navy.

Sister Luker got safely back to Britain, but with Luftwaffe planes swooping over the Channel and strafing the rescue ships, it was touch and go. The retreat was a catastrophe on a colossal scale. Tens of thousands of men were trapped on the channel beaches of Boulogne, Calais and Dunkirk. Meanwhile the roads were crammed with thousands of panic-stricken civilians – Belgian, Dutch and French, fleeing headlong from the advancing Germans.

The miracle of Dunkirk came about through a totally unhoped for stroke of luck. For reasons which are still debated even today, on 24 May Hitler ordered his tanks to halt at a small town on the coast just before Dunkirk. It was just the break the British commanders needed. By the time Hitler had given the order to advance again the British had surrounded the town with artillery, which prevented the Panzers from getting on to the beach. The evacuation had begun. Between 26 May and 4 June a total of 861 ships, from naval destroyers to pleasure boats, evacuated 338,226 British troops, as well as many French and Belgians.

QAs were involved at every stage of the operation, plying to and fro across the Channel to bring home the wounded, and manning hospital trains in Britain to ferry them on to proper medical care. Because of the nature of the emergency the vessels were not always hospital ships, but vessels of all types, hastily adapted to perform operations on very sick men.

One QA who had qualified at the London Hospital in 1923 kept a vivid record of the back-to-back trips she made under heavy bombardment from land and air, between 20 and 31 May – those last days before France fell. Initially the trip was Boulogne–Dover, but after 24 May they had to go to Dunkirk. Sometimes the bombardment was so intense they could not get into port and were ordered away by the navy. Several crew members and orderlies had to be taken off because of stress.

> May 20th.
> We sailed at 3 a.m. arriving at Boulogne at 11.30 a.m. We spent an hour in the town itself, which was terribly changed. Headquarters had been badly bombed, and there were a number of fires. The town and all the roads were thronged with Belgian and French refugees. We were constantly stopped by them, and asked the way to ships for England . . . We waited all day for our patients to arrive. There was a bad raid that night, causing a number of fires.[2]

When they returned to the port they found the ship under siege from refugees, but the QAs insisted that casualties take priority. At 5 p.m. . . . we took on very badly wounded casualties. One of them had to have his leg amputated immediately. We did two other major operations on board, all of which were successful, and the patients did well.'

By 24 May it was no longer possible to get into Boulogne – the following day the Germans overran the town and took five thousand British and French troops prisoner. On altering course for Dunkirk they found a scene of utter devastation:

Two ships had been sunk in the harbour, one of which, having gone down quite straight, was still flying the White Ensign. We could not get up to the Quai Felix Faure, as there were ships there. A hospital ship was on the quay, but no one answered our hails. At this point there was an attack by dive-bombers, and a salvo of bombs fell on either side of the ship. Pieces of bomb casing and debris fell on the deck. We sailed away, as there was a risk of our being hit and blocking the harbour. We could see huge fires all along the coast on our way back to Dover, where we arrived at 11.30 a.m.

By lunchtime they were underway again, this time accompanied by the hospital ship HMHC (His Majesty's Hospital Carrier) *St Andrew* and an aerial escort. This time they took on 230 stretcher cases. In these tense conditions they had to wait for the tide before sailing for home, and despite having all lights on and the red cross of the hospital ship plainly visible were fired on and bombed.

May 25th.
Arrived Newhaven 4.30 a.m., disembarked casualties, and sailed again for Dover.
May 26th.
We sailed at 10.45 and were again shelled from the coast, this time north of Calais. We altered course to mid-channel and returned to Dover.
May 27th.
Sailed again by 11 o' clock for Dunkirk. At 3 p.m. we were attacked by enemy aircraft, and two bombs fell close to the ship. We arrived

at Dunkirk harbour at 6.15 p.m. We arrived back at Dover at
midnight.

May 29th.

We were attacked at 5.30 by several enemy aircraft, including dive-
bombers; the attack was severe and lasted an hour. The decks were
machine-gunned at close range. The vibrations of explosions caused
damage to the ship's engines, instruments and fittings, and much
glass was broken. The ship was alone when the attack began, and
two destroyers came up and engaged the aircraft with gunfire. We
arrived at Dunkirk at 6.15 p.m. and were again ordered to leave by
the Naval Patrol.

May 30th.

We put off six RAMC personnel and members of the crew, suffering from shock at Dover.

May 31st.

We sailed at 5.30 a.m. and arrived at Dunkirk at 8.50 a.m. The quay
was much broken and on fire in places; the patients were embarked
with no gangway, just lifted over the ship's side. The Naval Officer
in charge on shore was so calm that one literally did not realise the
aerial battle that was going on all the time . . .

Not all the rescued troops were able to leave France via the Channel
ports. Many units retreated south-westwards towards Le Mans and
were picked up by ships from ports in Brittany and Normandy such as St
Nazaire, Brest and Cherbourg.

Mary Evans, a QA who spent two years aboard the hospital ship
HMS *Somersetshire*,* made a series of trips bringing wounded troops
stranded in France home from St Nazaire. In a BBC radio broadcast a
month after the end of the war Sister Evans described the desperate
conditions that prevailed as the overladen ships struggled to accommodate the huge numbers. *Somersetshire* was built to transport 560 patients.
'When there are over that number, we sling canvas cots and put
mattresses on the decks . . . On our third trip back from St Nazaire in
the summer of 1940 we were carrying over a thousand. We were

* Two years later *Somersetshire* would once again come to the rescue of gallant men – this time
taking off the wounded trapped in the siege of Tobruk and earning the nickname The Old
Tobruk Warrior.

attacked by aerial torpedo that night while we were crossing the Channel . . . we just put out our lights and ran for it.'[3]

At the very beginning of her service Sister Evans had received startling evidence of the affection naval men have for their ship – and the efforts they will go to to save her:

> Within the very first week of being at sea, we picked up the crew of a torpedoed oil tanker. They came on board at one o'clock in the morning, covered with oil and badly bruised. We fed them and washed them, and meanwhile our ship circled the blazing tanker, in the hope of picking up more survivors. And I'll never forget this – when six of the crew had recovered just a little, they went back to their tanker with the captain, in the dark and through the burning oil, with the submarines still circling all round. They boarded their ship and brought her safely to harbour.

While the ships were plying back and forth between France and England, a minutely organised schedule of hospital trains, fully staffed by QAs, waited in Britain to do their bit – speeding the wounded to rest and recuperation in British military hospitals.

Sister Edwards, who had been posted to Ambulance Train 58 in November 1939, described the operation as they waited for the men coming back from Dunkirk and St Nazaire:

> First we stood by at Southampton for four days – sixteen trains altogether. Then we were given orders to move . . . We went at it solidly for ten days, evacuating the men from the coast as they came in. We made three journeys to Dover – I found it particularly impressive to watch all the different ships bringing the men across – everything from hospital ships to rowing boats. I know a great deal has been said about those little ships – but it really did give you a lump in your throat to see them.
>
> . . . Two boys were brought onto the train both of them walking cases, they were suffering from tiredness and shock more than anything else. One of them said . . . 'Blimey we've got to Heaven' – and then as two nursing sisters came towards him 'and look, here come the angels.' Then one of the sisters spoke to him, and he looked quite bewildered and then he said, 'Wot's more, the angels speak English.'[4]

Not all QAs were lucky enough to get home by the end of May. The staff at No. 4 General Hospital at La Baule on the Atlantic coast were among the last to get out of France – days before the surrender on 22 June. In mid June they were still nursing under the charge of Miss C. L. Robinson, an elderly Matron close to retirement. The nurses had all their belongings packed in readiness for a quick getaway. Miss Robinson was clearly relieved when the Commanding Officer told her on 15 June that they were getting out the next day. Not a moment too soon as it turned out:

> The Home Sister and I went round and quietly paid all our bills in the shops as we did not want to alarm the French people by our departure. My Assistant Matron . . . stayed with me to help get away as much of the luggage as possible. At 5 o'clock, when about half of it had been loaded on a lorry, the CO said: 'If you do not get off yourselves now you will miss the train': so Miss Hall and I started for the station, carrying as much as possible. It was a very hot June day and the perspiration rolled off our faces as we hurried along . . . We got there to find the ambulance train on the point of moving out, and managed to scramble into the last carriage . . .[5]

The train was laden with badly wounded stretcher cases. As soon as it began moving, planes appeared overhead and started machine-gunning the carriages. 'One or two of the shell-shock patients . . . who had had experience of being attacked on other trains, jumped off to take cover . . . We slowly continued our journey and these attacks happened several times, but the train was not hit although a part of the line behind us was blown up, and had to be repaired before the second ambulance train could follow on.'

The train reached St Nazaire at 7 p.m. on 16 June and unloaded all the passengers, only for them to be ordered back on board as a massive air raid began. The casualties were eventually unloaded but then had to be embarked on the hospital ship, a laborious business which required great courage and dedication. 'It took a long time to load up the hospital ship, as we had a great many stretcher cases, and they had to be carried over between the bursts of firing. Eventually we had them all on board without casualties . . .'

Matron Robinson was very worried about the rest of her QAs who were due to follow on in the second ambulance train. She later learned that in the general pandemonium they had missed the train, but had managed to get to a ship by another route.

Once aboard Miss Robinson felt safe at last, but the feeling was short-lived:

> We put out from St Nazaire about 1 a.m. on the 17th and about 1 a.m. on the 18th an enemy plane dropped two bombs by us. Neither hit us, one falling in front, and the other on our port side, but after this, all lights were put out on the ship, which had, of course, been previously fully lit up [to show it was a hospital ship], and the captain sailed in a circle to elude further enemy planes. When morning came we were pleased to see RAF planes round us as we felt we were now quite safe. We reached Southampton about 8 p.m. on the 18th.[6]

Dame Katharine Jones wrote with some pride that she had sent a thousand QAs to France with the BEF in 1939 and had brought a thousand back. The troops were less fortunate. The Dunkirk rescue was an uplifting example of a beleaguered nation snatching a sort of victory from the jaws of defeat, but it was costly in terms of lives. By the end thirty thousand soldiers were killed, wounded or missing. The loss of equipment was equally costly. Arms, vehicles and equipment of all kinds were abandoned in the scramble to get away. Of No. 11 General Hospital, which had been based at Le Havre, all that was salvaged was one typewriter. Everything else was destroyed.[7]

The rout of the BEF and the evacuation from Dunkirk had been a grim introduction to war for QAs who only a month earlier had been longing for some real casualty nursing. Now, for the first time in history, nurses had found themselves on the front line. After it was over the captain of a hospital ship wrote to the Matron-in-Chief:

> As Captain of this ship I should like to give expression to my admiration and deep regard for the Nursing Sisters aboard. We recently made two trips to Dunkirk and two to Cherbourg, in each case being the last Hospital Carrier to enter and leave the ports. Our second trip to Dunkirk was under extremely severe conditions, bombs and shells dropping all about us and men being wounded

and killed alongside our ship on the pier . . . During all this our Sisters were really splendid. Never a sign of excitement or panic of any kind . . . I feel quite sure that their magnificent behaviour was an important factor in steadying the members of the RAMC personnel with whom they worked.[8]

It was a testimony that was to be echoed many times before the war was over.

II

FAR EAST

4

'Do English women never cry?'

To a newly qualified young nurse leaving home for the first time, a posting to Hong Kong must have seemed like a passport to paradise. As the luxury liner *Empress of Australia* slipped out of Liverpool one warm July night in 1940, protected from the danger of U-boats by its comforting convoy of Royal Navy fighting ships, the mood of the fifty-five QA nurses destined for Singapore and Hong Kong must have been one of eager anticipation. They were leaving a battered homeland where cities had been devastated by months of bombing by the Luftwaffe, food rationing, clothing coupons and the depressing, all-pervasive blackout. Ahead lay a leisured journey to the sun in first-class accommodation, punctuated by the almost forgotten luxury of three-course meals and, most important of all, freedom – freedom to flirt or fall in love with the hundreds of young officers travelling with them. At journey's end lay the exotic East – where they would don the white tropical uniforms (so flattering both to their complexions and their figures), nurse sick soldiers and, their day's work done, sip gin fizzes and Singapore slings on airy verandahs.

As the carefree girls took their last look at a vanishing Britain little did they dream how dramatically the lives of some were about to change – or how soon some of them would lose that precious freedom. They could not know that an enemy with no respect for nurses, doctors, prisoners of war or wounded men was planning an assault on their paradise islands, an attack so savage its culprits would one day be arraigned as war criminals.

But that was still months in the future and the mood as they sailed was upbeat. Daphne van Wart (later Ingram), a petite, vivacious brunette of 26, was one of the QAs who left Britain for Hong Kong that day.

Before leaving she had visited her aunt on her two-day embarkation leave and had told her merrily, 'Don't worry about me. I'm going to such a safe place.' According to Daphne, the dangers of pleasure, not the privations of war, were uppermost in the minds of the authorities at that time. 'We were travelling with the Matron-in-Chief, Far East, Miss Jones. On the train on the way up to Liverpool she gave us a pep talk on how to behave with the officers and the need to avoid affairs with married men.' Daphne, a sharp-brained, if physically frail woman, now in her nineties, says they didn't take too much notice.

'There was a lot of socialising on the ship. I had a boyfriend, a gunner, and he was married. He was honest about it. Matron was fairly strict but the liner was huge and there were fifty-five of us. She couldn't be everywhere.'

Little did the nurses suspect, as they giggled at Matron Jones's spinsterly preoccupations, that five months later Violet Maud Evelyn Jones would be dead, a victim of the Japanese bombing of Singapore.*

Life on board was exciting, but an abrupt reminder that the rest of the world was at war came when the *Empress* was diverted to rescue two hundred women and children who had been torpedoed just off Cape Town.

At Hong Kong five QAs disembarked, leaving the other fifty to sail on for Singapore.

As the five Sisters settled in, in that September of 1940, they found a colony where readiness for war had given way to a dedicated pursuit of the good life. Before embarking, Daphne had been based at the Shorncliffe Military Hospital, near Folkestone in Kent, where treating the high number of casualties among the troops in the retreat from Dunkirk had been exhausting, round-the-clock work. She was surprised at the generous amount of off-duty time in Hong Kong – 'far more than in England'. Dedication to this life of pleasure had taken its toll on the health of the troops. At the outbreak of war there were reputedly ten thousand prostitutes on Hong Kong island – one of the soldiers' favourite dance halls being dubbed the 'gonorrhoea racetrack'. The Second Battalion of the Royal Scots had been abroad for seven years

---

* Matron Jones was killed on 13 February 1942 when the Japanese bombed the ship on which she and other nurses were fleeing following the fall of Singapore.

and was, says Daphne, 'riddled with VD and malaria and unfit to fight'.

The colony of Hong Kong was composed of the island itself, with its capital Victoria overlooking the magnificent harbour and, across a narrow strait, a piece of the mainland bordering China, the peninsula of Kowloon and various islands. This constituted the New Territories. Hong Kong's only airport, Kai Tak, was on the eastern edge of Kowloon.

Few of the inhabitants in that carefree year of 1940–41 seem to have been deeply concerned about either Japanese expansionism or the vulnerability of the colony in the event of attack. They were too busy having a good time. 'I had a wonderful year,' Daphne recalls. 'It was very social, as it often was overseas. Male officers far outnumbered us girls and there were endless parties. I went sailing. I played squash and tennis. I went dancing . . . nobody thought there was going to be a war.' None the less, for anyone who wanted to notice, there were signs of a gathering storm. Everyone knew that the island's mainly Chinese population of 1,750,000 had been swollen by hundreds of refugees fleeing Japanese brutality. For a decade the Japanese had been carrying out raids in China and Manchuria and the massacre of three hundred thousand unarmed men and women in Nanking in 1937 had shocked the world. But the Europeans took the view that this was a private fight between two age-old oriental enemies and that it would never target them.

The island was a sitting duck. In peacetime Hong Kong was an important naval base, the headquarters of the Royal Navy's China Station, a key staging post of the British Empire. In 1941 however, both the RAF, still recovering from the ravages of the Battle of Britain, and the navy were stretched to the limit defending the homeland and maintaining Britain's fragile lifeline across the Atlantic. Churchill and his War Cabinet could spare no more equipment.

All the navy could muster was three destroyers, four gunboats, a fleet of eight motor torpedo boats and a handful of smaller vessels. By a grim twist of fate two of those destroyers sailed for Singapore the very night the Japanese landed on Hong Kong island. The RAF arsenal consisted of three obsolete Wildebeest torpedo bombers and two Walrus amphibians.

The management of human defences was not much better. In September 1941, just three months before hostilities began, a new General and a new Governor arrived, along with two Canadian battalions, totally unfamiliar with the island's terrain. The men entrusted with the defence of the island were made up of two British regiments, the Middlesex and the Royal Scots (the same soldiers whom Daphne van Wart described as unfit to fight), two Indian regiments, a regiment of artillery and two Canadian battalions. This added up to a total garrison of a little over twelve thousand.

Such was the determined optimism of the authorities that, a week before the Japanese invaded, an intelligence officer was imprisoned for spreading alarm and despondency because he told HQ that the Japanese were about to invade the colony.[1]

Events moved rapidly. On 7 December the Japanese attacked Pearl Harbor, devastating the US Pacific fleet. On the same day they turned their aggression on British interests and bombed Singapore. On 8 December the 38th Infantry Division of the Japanese Army launched a ferocious attack on Hong Kong, totally destroying the airport at Kowloon and with it every hope of rescue from the air. On 10 December, off the coast of Malaya the Japanese sank two of the Royal Navy's most prestigious battleships, HMS *Repulse* and HMS *Prince of Wales*, with the loss of 840 lives.

By 12 December the Japanese flag flew over Kowloon Hospital. Three days later all the medical staff – nurses, doctors and volunteers – were prisoners. The speed with which the drama of war engulfed the lives of these colonials was poignantly captured by one nursing volunteer:

> One's heart is torn by the thought of the partings that took place on that Monday morning – from husbands, lovers, children, needy ones, from homes and animals, even from jewels and books . . . The Indian girl came, the Japanese woman with the English name and the just-grown-up son, the large Turkish lady . . . the Portuguese and many Eurasians, and the handful of Europeans like myself; I am English. Gradually they all turned up. A wife and mistress came together, having said goodbye to their man.[2]

From Kowloon and from the air the Japanese continued to pound the island of Hong Kong across narrow Lye Mun passage. Casualties

44

among the British, Indian and volunteer troops were heavy as the deadly accuracy of the Japanese shelling and bombing forced them from their fixed positions.

Bowen Road Military Hospital was the colony's biggest medical centre for the military sick. Built in 1907 in the same style of super-confident imperial invulnerability as Netley and staffed by twelve QAs, it commanded a slope overlooking Victoria Harbour and was directly in the firing line. It was indeed a change from its privileged early days, when sedan chairs were chartered to take patients from the lower levels up the hill for fresh air each morning. As the Japanese troops pounded the massive, four-storey edifice, from the mainland, they could watch the nurses through their binoculars scrambling to reach their air-raid shelters. In their white uniforms and veils, once deemed so glamorous, they were dangerously obvious.

Daphne van Wart, who was based at Bowen Road when the war began, says, 'I soon changed into a pair of navy slacks and a shirt which I never took off for the remainder of the war.'

As the top floors of the hospital collapsed, operations were moved to an emergency operating theatre in the basement and the CO, Colonel Shackleton, issued an emergency memo: 'Owing to danger from snipers, personnel will not proceed above the ground floor of this hospital.'

With the kitchens out of action, staff also faced a frightening water shortage. The island's reservoir had been bombed in the first days of the attack and water had been rationed to a pint a day per person for drinking and washing.

The inevitable happened ten days after the initial air attack. On 18 December the Japanese invaded. They landed at night on the north-east corner of the island. In Kowloon the behaviour of the Japanese towards medical personnel and civilians had been humane and civilised. Here, with a conquering army running apparently out of control, it was to be shockingly different.

Early on the morning of the next day the Japanese stormed into the island's medical store at the Salesian Mission in the Shau Kei Wan district on the eastern side of the island. In defiance of international convention all the male medical personnel were marched away from the mission and bayoneted or shot. Some Japanese tried to behead the prisoners with their swords. The women were released unharmed, though they were forced to witness the massacre of their male colleagues.

Despite everything the medical response to the emergency was highly organised. All sizeable buildings – schools, convents, hotels, even the local racetrack – were turned into emergency hospitals to care for the mounting casualties, each staffed by one or two doctors, two or three QAs and a small group of locally recruited VADs (members of the Voluntary Aid Detachment) and orderlies. Bowen Road Hospital increased its peacetime capacity of 168 beds to four hundred. Medical supplies were taken and stored in the cellar of St Albert's Convent, a Spanish institution, where four hundred could be tended. A further four hundred could be nursed at St Stephen's College, a Chinese boys' school in the extreme south of the island, while the Hong Kong Hotel was adapted to take two hundred patients.

The day after the Japanese landed (19 December) the local radio station went off the air, but news of the massacre at the medical store at Shau Kei Wan soon became known. It was also well known that Japan had not signed the Geneva Convention guaranteeing humane treatment for prisoners of war and the sick.

As the battle continued, there was no time for the medical staff to get into the cellars during bombardments as a ceaseless stream of stretcher-bearers brought in fresh casualties. All the hospitals were overwhelmed and stretchers were left wherever space could be found while fresh beds were made up.

Daphne van Wart had been transferred from Bowen Road to St Albert's Convent after the fighting started. The Matron at St Albert's was Kathleen Thomson, a very popular no-nonsense New Zealander who had been based in Shanghai. The Home Sister, whose job was to produce hot meals for the exhausted nurses when they came off their gruelling shifts, was Brenda Morgan, a lively, likeable Lancastrian.

Physical conditions at St Albert's were appalling. Patients had been injured by flying glass and so the wards were shuttered, plunging the interior into permanent gloom. For a while Daphne and the two other QAs who worked with her did their rounds with a hurricane lamp, feeling like Florence Nightingale. But then it was decided that even this light made them too conspicuous from the air and so the medical staff worked on by the light of pocket torches.

'It was very frightening,' says Daphne. 'You could hear the shells getting nearer and nearer. The Japanese were trying to knock out a mobile gun at the bottom of our road.'

From now on, still desperately thirsty, the nurses were included in the daily tot of rum issued to the troops – 'It made a great difference to our morale,' says Daphne.

The Sisters' Mess was an old house in the grounds of the convent. At lunchtime on 18 December the gunfire seemed closer than ever. Daphne ordered the off-duty night staff to take shelter in the cellar. Brenda Morgan was out in the grounds with Kathleen Thomson trying to persuade a terrified dog the nurses had been given to come in for safety. Suddenly there was a colossal blast and the nurses' quarters received a direct hit. The blast killed Brenda and seriously wounded Kathleen. It could have caused even more bloodshed, but Brenda had been late serving lunch that day. 'I was only spared because I was on night duty. If lunch had been on time all the day staff, which numbered many of the forty VADs, would have been in the nurses' home and there would have been a bloodbath,' said Daphne.

The tragedy in effect claimed two young lives. Brenda Morgan had just become engaged to a young officer. As Daphne recalls, 'He was so upset when he heard that he stood up in silhouette and deliberately made himself a target. He was killed immediately. When his remains were found after the war he was identified by his fiancée's hospital badge which she had given him as a keepsake.'

While Kathleen Thomson was sent to another hospital to recover from her injuries, Mary Currie (later Davies) was sent to St Albert's to take over as acting Matron – she had been Theatre Sister at Bowen Road. Mary, a tall Scots woman with a brisk manner, was destined to become one of the heroines of the battle for Hong Kong and the focus of one of its few uplifting incidents. Her stubborn refusal to be intimidated by the bullying of an enemy already infamous for their cruelty would win her the admiration not just of her staff, but even of the Japanese themselves.

Mary Currie was one of those women who seemed able instinctively to hit on the right course of action in a crisis. All the emergency hospitals were relying heavily on volunteer nurses who had joined the local Voluntary Aid Detachment when war broke out. Some of these young women were single, others were colonial housewives who had the briefest of medical training when they volunteered to do their bit. VADs were looked down on in some professional nursing circles, but the QAs who worked with them when Hong Kong was fighting for its life had nothing but admiration for the effort they put in in those last terrifying days. Fearing the worst, Mary Currie decided that where a mother and daughter were both VADs they should work side by side. 'I felt, in my heart of hearts, that we would all be captured. I knew that we few Sisters would not be able to cope with everyone and, when the time came, it would be better for mothers and daughters to help each other.'[3]

Mary kept a diary, written as the events were actually happening, of the days and hours leading up to the capture of her hospital. It is part of a nurse's training to make reports and keep records, but it is still astonishing – and a tribute to the character of this indomitable woman – that in such conditions, she made time to describe the inevitable.

Dec 19th.
3 a.m. called by Night Sister to interview CO.

Japanese had landed on the island. State of emergency declared. Enemy reported to be close to St Albert's Convent. Called staff. Gave orders for all to wear tin hats and Red Cross armbands.

Bombing and shelling intense from 6 a.m.

All patients evacuated from rooms to corridors.

Casualties brought in off field throughout day. No road communication to Bowen Road Hospital. Queen Mary Hospital offered to take 100 severe casualties. Assisted in theatre throughout day. Both theatres working continuously.

No. 1 theatre hit by shell during operation . . . evacuated theatres to first floor.

Lighting difficulties very great, only able to operate in daylight.

Field Ambulance moves into hospital.

Dec 20th.
Persistent shelling and bombing round and on hospital all day . . .

Operating continued in both theatres from 9 a.m. to 6 p.m.

Many casualties admitted from Field. Some serious cases evacuated to Queen Mary Hospital.

<u>Dec 21st.</u>
Told by CO capture of hospital imminent.

Telephone communication shut.

Water supply cut. Drinking water supplied by Field Ambulance.

No rations received after 18th Dec. Rations for patients and staff cut by 50%.

Field Ambulance left hospital at 7 p.m. to escape capture.

<u>Dec 22nd.</u>
No communication from outside. Trench mortars falling on building. Windows shattered and parts of walls knocked down by shell fire. Wounded Japanese officer brought in amongst casualties.

Fighting takes place in hospital grounds. All staff slept in clothes.

As day broke on the 23rd the Japanese were so close that one of the many snipers firing into the hospital wounded a patient in the face. At 11 o'clock it was all over. The Japanese burst into the hospital. An RAMC sergeant who bravely rushed out with his hands up shouting 'hospital' was seized and tied up. The rest of the medical staff – Mary Currie, two nurses from the Hong Kong Volunteer Defence Corps, an RAMC officer and two orderlies were tied together with their hands behind their backs and taken out into the grounds. There their tin hats were removed and they were made to sit on the ground in front of a machine gun under the eye of Japanese soldiers with fixed bayonets. They were left there until 4 p.m. while the Japanese searched the building, insisting they did not believe it was a hospital.

For the whole of that day the fate of the captives hung in the balance and they feared the worst. But, in an incident previously briefly mentioned, something had happened before the Japanese overran the hospital that was to ensure that on this occasion, medical staff were treated with humanity.

On 22 December one of the casualties brought in was a Japanese officer. He had a very serious buttock wound and two hours before the Japanese stormed the hospital, he died. As staff were dressing the body for burial they found the Japanese flag in his pack. Mary Currie remembered a story from her childhood about the burial of a Japanese warrior and the way his comrades wrapped the body in the Rising Sun.

She instructed her staff to do the same. The officer was laid out, his body wrapped in the flag, his rank insignia and medals were pinned to his chest and he was taken to the mortuary to await burial.[4]

Mary and her staff lay helpless on the ground while the Japanese swarmed through the hospital grounds searching for concealed Allied troops. A Japanese soldier cuffed her viciously with his rifle butt as he tripped over her long legs. Instead of being cowed she was furious, accusing the enemy of failing to honour the Geneva Convention, a failing made all the more shameful, she pointed out, as the British had shown respect for their sick. The soldier did not understand Mary's tirade, but a Japanese officer who spoke English and claimed to have studied at Oxford overheard the conversation.

'After a good deal of questioning he released me to show him the body of the Japanese officer. After inspecting the body he ordered the soldiers to remove it . . . and made me stand at its head,' said Mary. Eyewitnesses noted what an odd pair they made, emerging from the mortuary, Mary towering at least six inches over the diminutive Japanese.

At about 4 o'clock the staff, still tied together, were marched into a room on the ground floor of the hospital. Mary was sent in last and a machine gun was placed ominously in front of them. But she was not done yet. As soon as the English-speaking officer returned she asked that the staff be untied and allowed to care for the patients.

'He answered that I would take him round the wounded men. We did a complete tour of the hospital and he told the patients that Hong Kong would belong to the Japanese in two days but they respected International Law and would not hurt wounded men.'

Later the officer told Mary that his Commanding Officer wanted to see her. When she came face to face with him he thanked her, through an interpreter, for looking after the dead officer. He said the dead man had been a close friend and he wept as he spoke. 'You have been very good to this man. You may ask a favour in return.'[5] Mary again asked to be released to look after the patients, but this was declined. Her second request was that the interpreter remain in the hospital and accompany her until his troops were withdrawn. This thoughtful request was granted – and the nurses at St Albert's had Mary Currie's quick thinking to thank for being spared the ordeal others were at that very moment undergoing.

At the end of the interview the interpreter told Mary Currie that the women of her staff had behaved with great bravery and calm: 'Do English women never cry?' he asked. To which Mary gave her immortal reply: 'Not when they have work to do.'

The Japanese nodded. 'That is very praiseworthy. We Japanese admire fortitude.' He bowed again and walked away.[6]

The Japanese were not the only people to have found Mary Currie's bulldog resolve inspirational. After the war a group of nurses from the Hong Kong Volunteer Defence Corps who were with her at St Albert's that Christmas wrote to the Secretary of State for War and the Matron-in-Chief, urging that Mary Currie's courage be recognised. That letter, signed in fading ink by thirty-six names, survives in a file at the Army Medical Services Museum, and more than sixty years later still makes moving reading:

> Casualties were numerous, filling the wards; the hospital and environs were constantly under shell-fire, and in the days preceding the actual capture of the hospital the surroundings were infested with snipers who made anything moving their target. Throughout these dangerous and arduous days Miss Currie was untiring in her care of patients and staff alike, and her courage and devotion to duty were an inspiration to us all. Following the capture of the hospital by the Japanese forces on 23rd December 1941 all were called upon to endure the most terrifying experiences and, in our opinion, the coolness, leadership and bravery of Miss Currie contributed in great part to the high standard of morale maintained throughout.[7]*

Two days after the hospital fell it was Christmas Day. But in place of the festive turkey at St Albert's there was hunger. The Japanese had bayoneted the food tins while they were searching the hospital for pockets of resistance. And instead of herald angels, the sky was thronged with vultures marking the bodies of the wounded and the dying. To the deep distress of the staff the Japanese would not allow

* Mary Currie was awarded the Royal Red Cross, 1st Class, in April 1946.

them to go out into the surrounding hills to retrieve casualties. 'I am sure we could have saved more lives if they had,' says Daphne van Wart.

For a while the staff at St Albert's were allowed to continue nursing. They had to bow to Japanese officers or they were liable to be beaten up, but on the whole the Japanese interfered relatively little. As the patients recovered the nurses equipped them with new clothes and two army blankets and sent them to the men's POW camp at Kowloon.

Elsewhere on the island the Japanese were behaving with considerably less restraint.

On 12 December the buildings of Happy Valley racecourse, home of the Hong Kong Jockey Club, were hurriedly transformed into a two-hundred-bed emergency hospital. On the night of Christmas Day 1941 a horde of dirty and dishevelled Japanese soldiers, apparently unsupervised by any officer, arrived in the hospital. An eyewitness describes how the soldiers surrounded them and looked at them with 'toothy grins. A more repulsive mob one could not imagine.'[8] For most of Christmas Day the Japanese attention was confined to leering. Then one of the staff told Matron that the Japanese had taken away some of the Chinese girls, who were members of the St John's Ambulance. The girls, young teenagers of 15 or so, were later found weeping and distraught. They had been raped.

In a state of deep disquiet the nurses retired to their quarters for the night. Not long afterwards the beam of a strong torch lit up the darkness.

> There stood a group of Japanese soldiers. The one who held the torch . . . flashed around, showing us all huddled beneath our blankets. They advanced. 'Get up all,' one commanded. They scrutinised each one in turn, almost blinding us as they shone the torch in our faces one by one. It was a terrible ordeal, as we did not know what was to happen, and when they selected about four, we feared the worst. As they selected each one the spokesman said 'Go Jap. No come kill all.' . . . They went away, taking the girls with them . . . I could not say how long it was before we heard running light footsteps, and one of the girls rushed in sobbing. Very soon the others followed, and almost before we could get them quieted, the torch reappeared . . . they looked under the table and found

those who had taken refuge there. They made the same threat, 'No come kill all.'

The ordeal continued throughout the night. A total of six European and six Chinese nursing assistants were raped. They were all wearing uniform. Some returned not just dishevelled and traumatised but badly injured from their ordeal. One girl managed to escape and fled to Bowen Road to report the outrage to the senior medical officer. He asked the Japanese for the immediate evacuation of the nurses. At about noon on Boxing Day at the Jockey Club a Japanese soldier began to drag a woman away in broad daylight, but released her hurriedly when an officer appeared. Following this, the nurses were taken to Queen Mary Hospital on the western side of the island.

The identity of the nurses who were raped at the Happy Valley racetrack has never been disclosed, nor has the service to which they belonged. Some of them were almost certainly European VADs from the Hong Kong Volunteer Defence Corps. And due to the emergency they were staffed by one or two officers from the RAMC and two or three QAs. It is highly likely, therefore, that QAs were among the victims.

The Europeans were stunned by the rapes. A letter written to the Matron-in-Chief by Miss Jones, Principal Matron, Far East, at the height of the battle for Hong Kong reveals the naïve faith of the British in the ability of the uniform to protect the women.

From Alexandra Military Hospital, Singapore, Miss Jones wrote: 'We are all very distressed about our people in Hong Kong . . . I feel they will get fair treatment if only because of their training. Unless the Japanese have made great headway within the last eight years, they will appreciate anyone with medical or nursing skills, and they have so far spared anyone wearing the Red Cross.'[9]

Meanwhile, in another hospital on Hong Kong even more horrifying events were taking place. Once again nurses were among the victims. In this instance we do know who they were because after the war they denounced the perpetrators at the International War Tribunal. Women – their own or foreign – counted for little in Japanese culture, where women were seen as inferior beings, or as comforts. Throughout the war the Japanese refused to recognise the officer status of QA nurses, ordering them to do menial tasks in preference to male orderlies, and later, as POWs, denying them the pay which they were entitled to as officers.

St Stephen's College was an imposing two-storey edifice built on a grand scale round three sides of a square. Its twin gabled ends looked out over a pleasant grass-covered hillside which sloped down to the neck of land that connects the main body of Hong Kong island to the Stanley peninsula on its south-east corner. Built as a boys' school in the heyday of Empire and hurriedly converted into a four-hundred-bed military hospital just before the outbreak of war, its very stones seemed to symbolise the lofty confidence of the colonial era. On Christmas morning 1941 there were about 160 patients in the hospital. The medical staff was headed by Lieutenant Colonel George Black, a 65-year-old civilian with the HKVDC, and Captain P. N. Whitney (RAMC). The British nursing staff consisted of two members of the Territorial Auxiliary Nursing Service, Amelia Gordon, known to everyone as Molly, Elizabeth Fidoe and five VADs: Miss Andrews-Levinge, Mrs A. Buxton, Mrs E. M. Begg, Mrs W. J. L. Smith and Mrs Simmons. In addition there were five Chinese nurses.

Christmas must have been the last thing on anyone's mind that most unfestive of Christmas Eves as the enemy closed in. By now it was not so much if as when.

Molly Gordon described 24 December as a 'dreadful day – we were shelled, machine-gunned and dive-bombed throughout'. It was only four days since the Japanese had landed on the north-east corner of the island and they had advanced with deadly speed and purpose, inflicting heavy casualties and forcing the Allied troops ever further back. Molly Gordon noted, as she made her way back to the hospital from her living quarters on 23 December, that 'the whole route was trenched and occupied by troops with machine guns'. Now the hospital *was* the front line.

At about 6 a.m. on Christmas Day a group of drunken Japanese soldiers burst into the hospital, with 'a terrific howl' (Amelia Gordon) and embarked on an orgy of cruelty. Dr Black and Captain Whitney, their Red Cross armbands clearly evident, went out to meet the invaders and were dragged away. Molly Gordon, an unmarried career nurse in her middle years, was made to remove her steel helmet and cracked over the head with it while the soldiers ripped off her Red Cross armband and stole her watch. Meanwhile, to the horror of the terrified onlookers, another group of Japanese soldiers rushed down the main hall and began bayoneting and shooting patients in their beds. 'Any patients who were too slow in getting up out of bed, or who could not move owing to wounds were bayoneted or shot. Some of the HKVDC tried to escape and others put up a bit of a struggle but they were mostly bayoneted or shot. The St John Ambulance Brigade men were all put in one room and systematically butchered, only one remaining alive to tell us what happened.'[10]

Molly Gordon reckoned that between fifty and sixty patients were killed.

Later that day, in an ominous development, the men who had survived the massacre were separated from the nurses. Eighty-six male patients and staff were herded into a room 9 feet by 12 feet. There was no room for the wounded to lie down, nothing to eat or drink – thirst was a major problem and only when people began fainting did the Japanese distribute the most meagre rations – and no sanitary facilities. The men began by using their boots as receptacles but were eventually reduced to relieving themselves on the floor. The stench was appalling. They were expected to kneel whenever a Japanese entered the room, but this was impossible because of the lack of space. Anyone within reach of a Japanese was lashed with a rifle or a leather strap.

At intervals during the day the door burst open and a group of Japanese dragged a soldier or patient at random out into the corridor. This happened up to four times and each time the man's screams, followed by shots, could be heard by everyone in the room. The terrified state of the men in that room was such that many tried to jump out of the window.

For the early part of the day the nurses had been corralled with the men, which must have offered them some comfort, but after some hours the Japanese took the women away and so began their appalling ordeal. At the Tokyo War Crimes Trial after the war Molly Gordon bravely described what they endured that night:

> After two hours (about 9 a.m.) we were marched in single file upstairs – dead bodies and blood covered the stairs – and at the top of the landing several Japs hit us as we passed. We were then put into different classrooms, I going into a small room with four VADs Mrs Smith, Mrs Begg (wife of Sergeant Major Stewart Begg), Buxton and Simmons where there were five Chinese women (wives of

British soldiers). We remained here all day . . . A particularly bad lot of Japanese (five in all) came in at 4.30 p.m. and removed Mrs Smith, Begg and Buxton – these three we never saw again.[11]

The Chinese girls told the British nurses that the Japanese had taken out the three VADs to kill them, adding that they would return for them shortly. The plan was to kill everyone in the hospital if Hong Kong did not surrender that evening.

After a while the Japanese moved the nurses again, this time ordering them to dress the wounds of Japanese casualties. The room contained five decomposing bodies of Red Cross staff killed in the massacre, which had been partly covered by mattresses, and the smell was overpowering. Molly and Elizabeth Fidoe were ordered to sit on the bodies of their colleagues.

A little later two soldiers removed Mrs Fidoe and two removed me. I was taken to another room, where there were two dead bodies, and made to take off all my clothes whilst they removed theirs. Before touching me they apparently became afraid someone was coming and made me put on my clothes again and I was returned to the room where Mrs Simmons and Mrs Andrews-Levinge still were. Mrs Fidoe rejoined us almost immediately in a weeping state and told us she had been raped. We were all hurried back into the original room with the mattresses . . . We were left in peace a short time only – three soldiers came in and took me to a small adjacent bathroom, knocked me down and all raped me, one after the other, and then let me return. Mrs Fidoe was then taken and underwent a similar experience. Both Mrs Fidoe and I were taken out a second time and raped as before. We were all now very desperate and discovering there was a Yale lock on the door we pulled it to, locking ourselves in.[12]

The formal language of a deposition leaves little room for emotion and Molly Gordon tells her harrowing story almost dispassionately. But Mrs Andrews-Levinge, who was mercifully not selected by the Japanese, described the devastating effect of the repeated gang rapes on the women. (Fellow prisoners recalled that many months later Molly Gordon had not recovered from her ordeal. She never worked again.)

Very shortly four Japanese soldiers came and took away one of the Chinese women, who returned weeping after an interval of ten minutes or so. Another Chinese woman was taken shortly afterwards. I believe both these women were raped . . .

Mrs Simmons was first made to strip and later was taken away and brought back after ten minutes; and on her return Miss Gordon was removed. All returned weeping . . .

Several parties of two or three Japanese soldiers kept arriving and Miss Gordon and Mrs Fidoe were taken away alternately and both raped twice. Miss Gordon, after the second occasion, was in a very collapsed condition and at her wits' end and Mrs Fidoe volunteered to take her place next time should it be necessary.[13]

Eventually that interminable Christmas night came to an end. The nurses locked themselves in and were thus spared further suffering. A grey dawn exposed the evidence of just what the Japanese had done. James Barnett, a Canadian Padre, made a tour of the hospital with Elizabeth Fidoe. They found the bodies of Lieutenant Colonel Black and Captain Whitney lying in separate rooms. Both bodies had been stabbed and slashed with swords or bayonets. They found what was left of the bodies of the young men who had been taken out of the room and tortured before being shot. Their ears, tongues, noses and eyes had been cut away from their faces.[14] They found the bodies of about seventy patients who had been bayoneted in bed and twenty-five members of staff.

No one had seen the three VAD nurses who had been taken away by the Japanese soldiers early on Christmas Day – Mrs Smith, Mrs Begg and Mrs Buxton. Mrs Begg's husband, a Sergeant-Major who was at the hospital when it was overrun, was beside himself with worry and kept asking for news of his wife, who was known as 'Jimmie'. At 9 a.m. a Japanese officer told them that the three nurses were dead. Elizabeth Fidoe and James Barnett were taken to a clump of bushes in the grounds of the hospital. There, huddled together and covered by a blanket, were the bodies of the three nurses – all three had been horribly mutilated during or after the rapes – one witness said they had been 'cut to pieces'.[15] Mrs Begg had been attacked with a sword and her head was almost severed from her body.

At 12.45 a.m. on 26 December, no longer able to resist an enemy with total command of the air and seas, the colony surrendered.

With the surrender some sort of order was re-established. Officers appeared and began to impose discipline on their rampaging troops. At 8 o'clock on Boxing Day morning at St Stephen's two Japanese officers ordered the nurses out of their hideaway and took them downstairs. There they were given a tin of bully beef and some milk – the first food they had had since Christmas Eve. Then, in accordance with the Japanese belief that menial work should be carried out by women, Elizabeth Fidoe, Molly Gordon, Mrs Andrews-Levinge and Mrs Simmons were ordered to clean up the corridors, which were stained with blood and strewn with feathers from the destruction of scores of pillows. After that they were to attend to the wounded. With both doctors murdered, the nurses did what they could. The Japanese refused them permission to bury their dead. Instead the orderlies were told to pile the bodies up and set fire to them with kerosene. About a hundred and eighty bodies were burned that day.

For the four shattered nurses, three of whom had been raped repeatedly the previous day, only one thing mattered – to escape. Early in the afternoon rescue appeared in the form of a volunteer British officer, Captain Stoker, who, apparently unaware of the events of the previous night, arrived at the hospital from nearby Stanley Fort with a patient. Molly Gordon beseeched him to smuggle the four of them out. As good as his word, at 6 p.m. he returned in an ambulance and took them to Stanley Fort. For now, at least, their ordeal was over.

By 27 December the Japanese had left the building altogether and the water situation for the men left behind at St Stephen's was desperate. By disconnecting the hot-water cisterns they managed to get enough water to last for two days. Enough food was salvaged from the wrecked stores to give everyone meagre rations. On the evening of 29 December a Japanese officer ordered a lorry to take the remaining staff and wounded up to Stanley Fort. Most of the St Stephen's Hospital RAMC personnel were left there. The rest were marched back to North Point Camp. For all of them it was the start of the long road into captivity.

The colony, described by the Matron-in-Chief before the war as a 'very favoured station', had become a prison. Nobody would emerge from it for more than three and a half years.

5

Into Captivity

After the surrender of Hong Kong life at the different hospitals returned almost to normal – for a while. Daphne van Wart says doctors and nurses were allowed to tend their patients with relatively little interference from the Japanese. They were, however, expected to bow to any passing Japanese, however lowly his rank. If they didn't they were beaten.

Overcrowding became a huge problem when the Japanese decided to commandeer the Naval Hospital at Wanchai for their own wounded, and sent British patients to St Albert's. A tented hospital for the Indian wounded had already been set up in the grounds of the old convent and food soon began to run scarce. Water supplies had been re-established but there was no fresh food. There was only stale bread, so the patients' breakfast consisted of fried bread. The main meal was tinned stew and tinned vegetables. When the tins ran out the staff had to rely on the Japanese. Sacks of rice were supplied sporadically but no indication was given of how long each sack was expected to last.[1]

As the patients recovered the nurses were instructed to supply them with new clothes and two army blankets. They were then taken to Sham Shui Po, the men's POW camp on the mainland at Kowloon.

The relative freedom seemed too good to last. And it was. The Japanese decided to take over St Albert's for their own use and in February they told the nurses they had just one hour to pack up the hospital. They were to take whatever they could, plus a bedding roll. The naval Sisters who had been working at St Albert's were the lucky ones. They went to Bowen Road Hospital, which, by an extraordinary twist of fate, was destined to continue functioning with relative freedom throughout the war. The QAs, headed by Matron Kathleen Thomson, now recovered from her shrapnel wounds, were to go to a camp at Kowloon on the mainland. They were to be free citizens no longer. For the next three and three-quarter years they would be the first women in British nursing history to become prisoners of war.

The destination of the QAs was a French hospital called St Theresa's, run by nuns. Since the Japanese had told them that the nuns would be taking all supplies and equipment with them when they left, the staff at St Albert's took everything they could – against the clock. Mattresses, blankets, linen and medical supplies were hastily got together and loaded on to trucks, the whole hospital being cleared just as the hour expired.

Kathleen Thomson and her nurses were taken to Kowloon by coal barge and herded into a wire pen with other POWs. It was the monsoon season and they were left for hours without shelter in the wind and rain. A group of Japanese nurses came to jeer at them through the wire as they waited, and by the time transport arrived to take them to the convent night had fallen.[2]

They arrived at their new quarters in the middle of the night to find an unfurnished building in the convent grounds. The mattresses they had brought with them were unusable, having been unloaded and left lying in the rain. No food was provided so their sole subsistence was some cocoa supplied by one of the nurses, which they mixed with water. That night they slept in damp blankets on bare boards.

At 3 a.m. they were woken and Miss Thomson was ordered to report to the hospital at once, where, guarded by Japanese soldiers, she found a Major and a Sergeant Major from the RAMC. As they were marched into the office they were confronted by the Japanese Director of Medical Services for the area, Major Shunkiti Saito, who told them that, as a result of the generosity of the Japanese people, the hospital was being handed over for the exclusive use of prisoners of war. Miss Thomson was told to return at 6 a.m., when she would be allowed one hour to take over existing patients from the French Matron.

For months previously the patients had been deprived of proper food and vital drugs. As Daphne Ingram remembers, 'We were appalled at the state of the patients, emaciated and desperately ill and suffering from starvation. The nuns had done their best but had few drugs, and insufficient food for them. That morning there was enough rice for breakfast but nothing further until a sack of rice was brought in about 5 p.m.'

Many of the patients had dysentery and desperately needed building up. The nurses tried to make ground rice by mincing and crushing grains of rice. But they had no salt or sugar for flavouring and the patients could not be persuaded to eat the resulting paste. To the distress of the nurses, who knew they could have saved them with better food, many died.

The Japanese eventually gave them flour to make bread but stole twelve loaves out of the POWs' ration for themselves. Then a note was found in a loaf – supposedly written from a relative in another camp – and the bread ration stopped.[3]

At St Theresa's the Japanese bizarrely insisted that the dead be buried with full military honours, with the nursing staff forming a guard of honour, despite the fact that the deaths were the direct result of lack of food and drugs. The Japanese invariably contributed a wreath to the funeral, a gesture viewed by the outraged British as grotesquely cynical. After a time the nurses were permitted to keep a few hens – a lifesaver, as eggs were beneficial to their gastric patients.

The New Zealand-born Matron Kathleen Thomson was an impressive woman – brave, resourceful, and with an off-beat sense of humour which she drew on to keep up morale. The welfare of the patients was paramount for her. One of her biggest challenges was preventing the orderlies, who hated kow-towing to the Japanese, from exploding in mutiny. Her instinct to use humour to resolve problems led to an incident which, sixty years later, still seems both hilarious and moving.

The men were given orders to clean up the garden of the next-door house because the Japanese were giving a party for their girlfriends. The NCOs were furious and were determined to refuse such humiliation but Miss Thomson entreated them to submit. If they did not, she pointed out, the rations would be cut still further and the patients would suffer.

'Make a joke of it,' she appealed. 'Show them that they can't get you down.'

Next day Matron went to the top verandah of the hospital to see how the working party was progressing. Round the corner of the house came the tubby little sergeant – dressed in an ankle-length dress of mauve chiffon with a wide-brimmed hat to match, over his shoulder he carried a rake and he was singing in his pleasant Welsh voice. Behind him came Private Bache in a bathing suit and a large hat with a wreath of pink roses, wheeling a wheelbarrow and behind him a procession of RAMC orderlies in similar garb. [In the cellars of the empty house they had found trunks full of clothes belonging to the owners.] Last of all came the Japanese guards looking on in astonishment at the mad British.[4]

Sick POWs were regularly brought to the hospital in busloads from the men's camp at Sham Shui Po on the outskirts of Kowloon city. The death toll was high, with some dying on the journey and many soon after they arrived. One day a prisoner was unloaded whose laboured breathing spelt only one thing: the much-feared, highly contagious diphtheria. In those days diphtheria, a bacterial infection which causes the throat to swell up, leaving the sufferer fighting for breath, was very common and could be lethal. In prison-camp conditions – with no drugs to treat it and only the most primitive disinfecting facilities – the staff at St Theresa's were looking at a catastrophe. Fearful of becoming caught up in an epidemic themselves even the Japanese kept their distance. There was, of course, none of the normal protective clothing for staff, so the nurses took down the hems of their white uniforms and made themselves masks.

The epidemic was made all the more harrowing by the fact that the Japanese had a plentiful supply of the anti-toxin needed to treat the disease. Many packets of it could be seen piled up in a house within the monastery complex which the Japanese kept locked. Kathleen Thomson went doggedly every day to Major Saito to ask for access to the drug, but every day she was told there was none. Finally, ground down by Matron Thomson's daily visits, Major Saito grudgingly flung a meagre out-of-date supply of the precious anti-toxin over the fence. It contained enough for eight patients and a hundred had the disease. 'The Japanese were brutes. They didn't bring the men in to St Theresa's from the camp until they were already black in the face. And then Kathleen Thomson and the doctors had the appalling task of choosing who was to live and who to die. Many died.'[5]

Without the necessary drugs the only way doctors could make men who were gasping for breath more comfortable was by performing tracheotomies, opening a passage into the windpipe. In these terrible, primitive conditions these operations were performed without anaesthetic – and in secrecy. 'A doctor who was brought in from the officers' camp hid instruments for the operations in his socks. Matron removed them surreptitiously while he was scrubbing up while another doctor kept the Japs occupied outside.'

It was a very bleak time. Starvation was by now starting to wreak its effects on the nurses.

As Kathleen Thomson remembers: 'Food became more scarce, until sometimes there was no food at all in the hospital. Sometimes a sack of rice would be brought in late in the afternoon, and sometimes it would not. On those occasions we had a glass of hot water and went to bed.'

The health of the nurses deteriorated rapidly. One VAD died and several others became too weak to continue on duty. A plan Kathleen Thomson had hatched, whereby each nurse would memorise the names of a certain number of the next of kin of the dead (so that they could be contacted after the war) had to be shelved because lack of food was affecting their memories.

In the face of a mounting death toll which she could do little to stem Matron Thomson became increasingly concerned about the relatives of those who had died. One of the worst torments for POWs was feeling cut off from the world. They got no news of home, and their loved ones didn't know if they were alive or dead. The Japanese, keen to leave no evidence of their atrocities, forbade prisoners to keep any written records.

When prisoners died Matron Thomson faithfully recorded the names and addresses of their next of kin on the thinnest paper she could find and hid them in a talcum-powder tin. The tin had a spray of lilac painted on it and though the talc was long used up she said she kept it through her imprisonment 'to remind me of happier times'. Now she found a proper use for it. She replaced the talc with French chalk from the operating theatre. When the nurses were transferred to another camp she hid it in her suitcase and was proud that her database escaped detection, even though her luggage was searched. At the end of the war she wrote to the relatives of all those who had died in her care.

'I . . . met with a wonderful response. Relatives had received no news other than the War Office telegram stating that their dear ones had died in a POW camp and they were so grateful to know the details of their last days and particularly to know that they had had a Christian burial with a service conducted by an Army padre.'

One blisteringly hot day in August at the height of the diphtheria epidemic the Japanese announced that they were closing St Theresa's. The doctors and orderlies were to go to the men's camp at Sham Shui Po, while the nurses were to return to Hong Kong island where they would be interned in Stanley Internment Camp on the southern side of the island. It was a move that could have been handled humanely – very sick men were involved – but once again Major Saito* and his men showed a callous disregard for the helpless in his care.

With the utmost care, RAMC orderlies carried the diphtheria cases down from the top floor of the convent and laid their stretchers gently on the floor of the trucks waiting in the shade, hoping in this way to dispense with unnecessary handling – but the Japanese guard ordered the trucks to be unloaded again. All patients were to be assembled in the centre of the compound. Here, with no shelter from the blazing sun, desperately ill men lay on their stretchers for several hours until the drivers were ready to move off.[6]

Then it was the nurses' turn to climb into the lorries that were to take them back to Hong Kong island. Their gloom at having been forced to abandon such desperately ill patients turned to astonishment when, as they drove out of the convent gates, the infamous Major Saito saluted them. Matron Thomson thought it was because, even while he was mistreating them, this singularly heartless man had come to admire the nurses' dignity and courage. 'At first the Japanese treated us with the same contempt they had for their own women, but when they saw how we stood up to hardship and the dedication with which the nurses cared for their patients, they began to show a grudging admiration. Major Saito, with his parting salute, acknowledged this.'[7]

Conditions at Stanley were less harsh than they had been at St

---

* In 1946 Saito was condemned to death as a war criminal in Hong Kong, a sentence eventually commuted to fifteen years imprisonment.

Theresa's. Daphne van Wart believes this was because the camp contained children and the Japanese liked children. It may also have been because they were civilians and therefore not guilty of the 'cowardice' of surrender. Stanley was a mixed-nationality camp consisting of British, Americans, Norwegians, Dutch, some Chinese married to English men and a few Canadians. (In 1943 all the Americans and Canadians were repatriated.) It was a great relief to be able to write and receive letters, after having been out of touch with home for so long. Each prisoner was allowed a postcard of twenty-five words. Letters from home were two years old when they arrived.

The camp comprised the whole of the peninsula and added up to several acres. Provided they always remembered to bow to any passing Japanese, internees were free to wander about. Daphne van Wart says now: 'Luck played such an important part in what happened to people in the war. I could so easily have gone to Singapore where I probably wouldn't have survived. Stanley was reckoned to have been the second-best POW camp in the whole of the Far East, after Shanghai.' None the less Daphne says that for every prisoner the anguish was the same. 'We had no idea how long it would be before we were set free. The Japanese guards used to taunt us, telling us the war would last ten years.'

The other factor which made Stanley less harsh than some of the other camps was that, because it was mixed, they had men to do the heavy work. 'They had to cut grass to create fuel to cook the rice we lived on.'

The camp at Stanley included St Stephen's College, where the Christmas Day massacre had occurred. The nurses were housed in the college and slept three to a cubicle – on the floor for the first few weeks. Even though they were prisoners, they still had a Matron. The formidable Miss Dyson, a career QA with a reputation as something of a martinet, had been Matron at Bowen Road and was in overall charge of the QAs at Stanley, who addressed her as 'Ma'. She shared a cubicle with a naval nursing Matron.

The Hong Kong-based nurses had effectively disappeared off the face of the earth. No one at home knew of their fate following the fall of the island at Christmas 1941. Keenly aware of the anguish families at home must be suffering, Matron Dyson wrote to the Japanese authorities asking them to inform the International Red Cross of their whereabouts.

Under the heading 'British Civilian Internment Camp, Stanley, Hong Kong' and dated 4 November 1942, *By courtesy of the Japanese Authorities*, Miss Dyson wrote:

> Since our arrival in Stanley on August 10th it is thought that the British Government have no information regarding our transfer to a Civilian Internment Camp and owing to the recent incidents it is much feared that our relatives will be exceedingly anxious as to our safety and welfare presuming that we are still stationed in Hong Kong.
>
> I respectfully request that in order to alleviate what must be great mental distress that a cable may be sent to the Matron-in-Chief, the War Office, London, stating that all eighteen Members of the Army, Navy and Canadian Nursing Services are safe and well in Stanley Camp.[8]

Miss Dyson maintained an optimistic manner throughout her years in Stanley, convincing herself at every stage that the war could not last much longer. Eight months after the letter to the Japanese authorities, on 26 July 1943, she wrote a determinedly cheerful letter to her mother in which only oblique references to weight loss and diminishing energy levels suggest what they are undergoing.

> Dearest Mother . . . Glad to tell you that all members of the unit are fit and fairly well, but in excellent spirits, facing this life with cheerful courage, making full use of this enforced holiday by language courses, lectures, commercial and art classes, camp fatigues, all types of housework from laundry to kitchen, walking, the more robust swim, but games definitely too strenuous nowadays. We send greetings to you and all friends, assure you that we are ready for anything, full of hope, only waiting for the day . . . Weight now nine and a half stones, some fairy! . . . God Bless Darling, not much longer now, fondest love, Billy . . .

It is poignant to think that Matron Dyson and her fellow prisoners still had more than two years to serve.

Another camp resident was Molly Gordon. After her ordeal at St Stephen's College she had been smuggled out to Bowen Road Hospital, where she had remained until August, nursing wounded British troops and serious illness cases brought to them by the Japanese from various POW camps on Hong Kong. Molly was still so distressed as a result of what she had undergone that a decision had been taken by 'Ma' not to house her in the college, the scene of such traumatic memories. Instead she was billeted in the married quarters of the camp.

'I used to go and visit her,' Daphne says. 'She was a lot older then me, rather like an older maiden aunt. She was still in a dreadful state. We never spoke of what had happened. We just shared a cup of tea and chatted. She retired up to her native Scotland and I used to travel up to Edinburgh to see her.'

As time went on Molly did take part in the daily life of the camp. In the beginning, however, the QAs didn't do any nursing – part of a principled stand by the ever rank-conscious 'Ma', who declared, somewhat naïvely, 'My girls were not going to work in a civilian camp – my girls are going to be repatriated.' As time went on and lack of food undermined the prisoners' strength, Ma's defiant stance had to be modified. A rule was introduced, because of the starvation rations, that no one could work for more than six hours a day – 'We worked to give the Government Sisters a rest.'

Basic food rations were sparse in the extreme, with practically no protein.

> We had two meals a day, at 10 a.m. and 5 p.m. which consisted of 2 or 4 ounces of boiled rice and a watery vegetable stew . . . Occasionally we had a few cubes of meat or fish and very occasionally a fried pasty. We also got 2 or 3 rations of boiled water with which to make tea. We had no milk and very little sugar – one ounce per 10 days. The Japs provided grindstones and we used to grind rice and make a kind of pancake to eat which we cooked ourselves on an open fire. We also ground peanuts which we obtained later on from the canteen.[9]

The poor diet caused a range of problems, including diarrhoea, beriberi and muscle cramps due to lack of salt. Nurses were able to give sick patients injections of vitamin B, and to guarantee supplies of vitamin C they made an infusion from pine needles. As their body weight dropped the women stopped menstruating and didn't begin again until months after the end of the war. At one stage the Japanese allowed the prisoners to bathe in the sea, enabling them to harvest much-needed salt.

Some fared better than others in Stanley. People who had Chinese friends or relatives still at liberty in Hong Kong could receive weekly food parcels. A couple of the VADs were orthodox Jews and didn't eat the rations, relying on food sent in by Chinese friends. Nurses received no pay, since the Japanese refused to recognise their military status, but male POWs were paid and eventually they were able to send money in to their wives or girlfriends. A month before Hong Kong fell Daphne had been a bridesmaid at the wedding of a fellow prisoner in Stanley, whose husband was in the officers' camp and used to send money in for his wife and Daphne. 'I was a kept woman while I was in Stanley,' she smiled.

The Japanese made great play of allowing Red Cross parcels into the camp and in three years the whole camp received three Red Cross parcels. They contained bully beef, which was welcome, and sanitary towels, which, because of the effects of malnutrition, were useless.

Everyone's priority was to keep fit and well and prisoners with access to money were in a better position to do this. The Japanese ran a canteen in the camp, as well as a weekly public auction, and prisoners were able to buy extras. Soya beans, peanuts, occasionally lard and duck eggs, were all available.

'Married women sold wedding rings, gold watches and even fountain pen nibs to the Korean guards.' The Japanese exploited the situation. In a letter to a friend written from the camp Molly Gordon complained, 'The prices charged were exorbitant. In July this year I cashed a cheque for fifty dollars (Hong Kong) – and I received yen 2000 and for that amount I purchased 1 lb brown slab sugar, half a pound of peanuts and half a pound of lard.'[10]

Patients who became ill, however, had to trust to luck to get them better. In the same letter in which she complains of extortion in the canteen Molly Gordon pinpoints the contradictory attitude of the Japanese towards the sick. She says that apart from a small supply of Javgel septicide powder and Acriflavine, there were effectively no drugs. Yet their captors insisted that a history sheet be kept on each patient.

Molly's comments show that her wry sense of humour had not deserted her – 'And so often under the heading "Treatment ordered" was written by our MOS "good advice".'[11]

Apart from the diet, day-to-day life in Stanley was relatively pleasant, at least compared to other camps. Molly Gordon talks of spending her time cleaning and tidying, running clinics and playing bridge and mahjong. They were even allowed a daily Japanese newspaper, which was translated by Reuters journalists who spoke Japanese. The newspaper was so expensive that twenty prisoners contributed to buy one copy which was passed round, a privilege that was stopped when Germany surrendered. The internees were also allowed to hold Sunday services.

Their resourcefulness, both in terms of physical survival and dogged insistence on feeding the human spirit, is impressive. There was considerable free association between men and women in the camp and one couple even got married. According to Daphne Ingram they had managed to make some rice wine and gave it to the happy couple as a substitute for champagne.

They grew their own crops in plots using urine as a fertiliser. These included a form of runner bean, pumpkins, sweet potatoes and tomatoes grown from seeds from tinned tomatoes in the Red Cross food parcels. They were even allowed to educate and entertain themselves.

As Daphne Ingram recalls, 'We had books to read, they were brought in from the Hong Kong libraries early on in internment. There were lectures, concerts and plays to attend as there was a fair amount of talent in the camp. We were also fortunate in having two professional pianists and sometimes the Japanese formed part of the audience.'

At one stage the Japanese agreed to an open-air concert and took photographs which were circulated to the Red Cross in order to show them how well the prisoners were being treated.

'As cameras clicked children in the front row made a V sign and the guards were caught laughing at them. No pictures distributed. No repeat performance.' The war intruded only once, when an American bombing raid accidentally killed fourteen prisoners. It was, however, a sign that the tide of war had begun to turn.

As the years passed scarcities worsened. There was no electricity. In the fourth year water became very scarce and the prisoners were only allowed one pint of water each day for washing. As there was only one tap per block there was always a mad scramble to shower and wash clothes. But the resourcefulness of the internees never let up. They got round the lack of electricity by telling stories in the dark. They made thread for sewing by drawing threads out of bed sheets. When there was no soap the men made a substance called lye from wood ash and used it to wash clothes. When shoes wore out they made wooden clogs as in summer the tarmac was too hot for bare feet.

It was this resourcefulness that was to keep them going until the great day of liberation, still so far in the future.

6

Friday the Thirteenth

Singapore, with her massive guns pointing warningly out to sea and her heavyweight Royal Navy presence, was regarded by the British as an impregnable fortress. And as news of the fall of Hong Kong stunned the Allies, the fifty QAs who had sailed out of Liverpool in July 1940 must have been grateful that their destination was Singapore.

Their relief was short-lived. Six weeks after Hong Kong fell the Japanese war machine exposed Singapore's famous guns as impotent – they could not be turned around and the Japanese attacked from the land. In Hong Kong a handful of QAs had witnessed unspeakable horrors at the hands of an enemy with no mercy for the defeated. Now for the dozens more Sisters fleeing the blazing and encircled colony of Singapore in the second week of February 1941 the nightmare was only beginning. For the first time in the history of war they found themselves in the front line – dodging bombs and shellfire to rescue the wounded and becoming caught in crossfire between their own troops and the enemy.

The first bombs fell on Singapore on 7 December 1941, the same day that the Japanese attacked Pearl Harbor. Simultaneously they landed men and supplies at two points in Thailand close to the Malayan border. General Tomoyuki Yamashita had been given a hundred days to conquer Malaya and carry off Singapore, the jewel in its crown. That would have given him until mid March. In the event it was a month more than he needed.

Initially many QAs regarded the danger as an opportunity for adventure.

Dorothy Garvin, a curly-headed Scots QA, was in a hospital in Singapore, waiting to go Christmas shopping, when she and a friend were told by Matron to take the ambulance train up-country and bring casualties back down to the safety of Singapore. She described her reaction in a letter to her mother.

> Of course we were thrilled at the chance to go. We simply loved the work, it was just grand. We used to go away up country as far as we dare and pick up the casualties from the casualty clearing station. It was so exciting creeping up in the moonlight and we always got such a warm reception. You would hear the patients saying to each other 'There are Sisters on board.' We had a grand team and were as happy as larks and as black as tinkers . . . Joan and I were frightfully spoilt especially as we were often the only white women in the district or even native state. There was great excitement too when we met the two other ambulance trams with our pals on board.[1]

There was a problem moving the trains when the native drivers, frightened of the approaching Japanese, ran away. The Medical Officers had a go at driving the train until the army sent volunteers and Dorothy found herself having lessons in engine driving.

> We used to park in sidings, and sometimes between journeys I made oatcakes which we ate hot on the bank . . . When we were up all night with casualties and were bringing down Scotties the Scots Pte and I used to make real porridge which was greatly appreciated after no food. Some nights were frantically busy with terrible haemorrhages but we never lost anyone.
>
> I got terribly bitten by the mosquitoes and got between 200 and 300 bites, but just did not want to come off the train.

Dorothy returned to Singapore in mid February to find her hospital under siege and she herself caught up in the war in earnest:

> We went to bed to gunfire and the red glow of artillery fire. We had a curfew and even a torch light was fired on. Some nights I used to be so frightened to walk over to the Mess after duty . . . On the evening of the 11th the Matron said orders were for the Sisters to leave but she was staying and asked for volunteers for a skeleton staff. Quite a number left. After that it was pretty grim, the planes

were over the whole time and the oil dumps beside us were blazing. I could hear the enemy rifle fire two miles up the road, they were past us in lots of places. They got to the water supply. The Mess was bombed and we could not live there . . . I was helping a Bannockburn dentist . . . (now a prisoner) take out a tooth when there was a great bang and the MO shoved me under the bed as the roof came in 5 yards over our heads.

On the evening of 11 February came Matron's announcement that the Sisters were to be evacuated and request for volunteers to go. It came as a shock as nurses are trained never to abandon their patients. Several left, but learning that Matron was staying Dorothy decided to remain as well. It was to prove a fateful decision for them both.

That night the 30 of us who had remained slept on the NAAFI floor on mattresses. We slept like tops in spite of the incessant bombing . . . The next day the order came that all the Sisters were to be evacuated immediately. There was no gainsaying it tho' it broke our hearts to leave everyone . . . We were out on an Ambulance and whisked through . . . The guns round us had been [for] giving in several days earlier, but they just wouldn't when they heard there were still sisters in the hospital.

Meanwhile in the reopened Gordon Barracks at Changi on the island's east coast medical officers found themselves trapped between the British and the Japanese, a situation made more alarming by a news blackout caused by a lack of newspapers and broken radios. In fact, they had been without news for twelve days.

Catherine Maudsley, a Sister in the Territorial Army Nursing Service (TANS) had arrived in Malaya two days before war broke out and had become caught up in the headlong retreat down the peninsula to the 'fortress'. 'The 17th Combined General Hospital and the RE Barracks, Changi, and ourselves were two miles apart. In less than a week of reopening, we were again doing 16 to 18 hours per day . . . both hospitals were between the two front lines, the Japanese on the island of Ubin, about three quarters to a mile away and our own 16 inch guns behind us. With the repeated and almost continuous air raids the number of casualties increased and our beds rose from 500 to almost 1000 in one week.'

Barely ten days later they were retreating again as the unremitting Japanese air raids pounded the island. As one hospital was bombed out another tried to absorb its patients and homeless staff before being forced to evacuate in its turn.

> On Feb 7th the 17th CGH were bombed and blasted out of their hospital; the next day, Feb 8th, we received most of their patients and some of their staff for temporary quarters; also on the 8th the MO [Medical Officers] quarters of No. 1 MGH [Malayan General Hospital] were hit, rendering some of the MOs homeless, and they had to sleep on any empty beds we had in the wards. On the 9th we moved from our quarters over to the hospital for safety; the Mess was within mortar range of the Japanese, also the Japanese were aiming at our heavy batteries behind the Mess . . . On the 9th . . . the hospital and Mess were heavily bombed; the Mess was da-maged. Over in the Hospital, the barrack square had craters in the four corners and centre . . . The casualties rolled in that night from the surrounding camps; the day staff . . . came off-duty between 11.30 and 12 p.m. only to be called again at 1 a.m. to pack up the ward equipment and reclassify the patients prior to our evacuating in the morning.[2]

The strain of those last days, the fear of being killed or taken prisoner, was appalling. But the nurses' general restraint makes the rare appearance of emotion in their accounts, whether an admission of their own fear or their admiration of the bravery and leadership of others, deeply moving.

Evelyn Cowens had responded to an appeal for more trained nurses by joining the Emergency Military Nursing Service, a branch of the QAs. She was a member of the 1st Malayan General Hospital, then functioning in part of the large civilian hospital in Johore Bahru. At the end of Janury 1942 the enemy had drawn so close it was decided there was no hope of holding the Malayan mainland. The Matron of this hospital was Miss West, a woman whose bravery clearly inspired her frightened young charges.

In spite of large red crosses on all the buildings . . . the Japanese dive-bombed and machine-gunned us frequently . . . I can see Miss West now, after one of our worst air raids [during which one VAD was killed – the officers' mess demolished – the night sisters' house badly damaged – an ambulance and driver blown up], jumping up . . . the air so thick with smoke and the smell of cordite, that it was impossible to see more than a few inches ahead – to find out if the night sisters had been hurt as their house was some distance away. We could see the flames where we stood, and the planes diving down and machine-gunning but that didn't stop Miss West. In she rushed and later returned to say they were all right in spite of their house being half on top of them and they were already on their way up to join us and have some tea (which we all badly needed).[3]

Evelyn, clearly very frightened herself by now, was cheered when she heard Miss West and the CO praising the nurses' coolness under fire:

Miss West told me very proudly that the Colonel had praised the nursing staff for their courage during these critical days and asked her to name anyone who had shown outstanding bravery. She had replied 'that it was impossible to pick out any Sister – all had been splendid'. I am convinced that everyone there would wish to correct this reply and mention Miss West's wonderful calmness, cheerfulness and total lack of fear or thought for her own safety. She was an example to us all. When we thought we were not going to be evacuated, I comforted myself with the thought that Matron would be with us and it *was* a comforting thought. She would help us to pull through.

Meanwhile the terrible casualties continued to mount, flooding, like a grim parody of musical chairs, into an ever-decreasing number of hospitals. For such a brief campaign the Allied casualties were enormous – almost nine thousand dead, compared to three thousand five hundred for the Japanese. Olive Spedding, who had been a Matron in an up-country hospital, described the desperate situation. By now only three hospitals were still treating the wounded.

The wards were quickly filled to overflowing as one after another of the hospitals were hit, till eventually No. 20 (ours) Alexandra and BMH Johore were the only military hospitals functioning. No. 17 GHQ (which like ourselves had moved to Singapore) had been bombed out and evacuated, also an Indian General Hospital . . . had been bombed and burned out with fearful casualties . . . We had many shell-shocked patients, who were, I think, the most pathetic of all. When the din had worked up to a crescendo of shells whining overhead, bombs bursting and our A.A. guns banging away, one found them in all sorts of odd corners and it was difficult to prevent them running out into the open . . .[4]

Three days after the first attack the Allies had suffered a body blow when the Japanese air force sank two of the Royal Navy's most prized battleships responsible for defending Singapore, HMS *Repulse* and HMS *Prince of Wales*, with the loss of 840 lives. The terrible burns suffered by many of the 2,081 survivors were described by one QA with rare frankness as so bad 'some did not at all resemble human beings'.[5]

After that the fall of Singapore was just a matter of time. By the end of December the Japanese had reached Kota Bharu, halfway down the east coast. On 1 January they overran Kuantan. Ten days later Kuala Lumpur fell. On 30 January the causeway linking Singapore to the mainland was blown up and on the night of 8/9 February the enemy crossed the straits of Johore and established a beach-head north east of the city. Later that day they destroyed the airfield and the reservoirs that provided the island's water. Less than a week later, on 15 February, General Percival, Commander-in-Chief Malaya, surrendered. Before he did so he ordered the evacuation, not just of thousands of civilians, but military nurses too. The order to abandon patients was seen as unprecedented, but after what had happened in Hong Kong no one was taking chances.

Sister Hartley at the Alexandra Hospital expressed the general consternation. 'We felt as though the bottom had fallen out of our little world – the hospital was full to overflowing – everybody was working at top speed – our poor boys lying all over the floors and they coolly saying we must go. The faces of those poor boys watching us leave, saying "it's all up now".'

Matron (Olive) Spedding's reaction, too, was disbelief: 'On Friday Feb 13th, a day none of us will ever forget, my CO came with news so unexpected and so dire that at first it was difficult to grasp the meaning of it. We were to go – to go in half an hour's time and leave behind all our patients and our hopes of being able to help them.'

The last heavily overladen ships left Singapore on 12 and 13 February – which happened to be a Friday. Superstition was the last thing on anybody's mind. But the fate of those who sailed on the 13th was to differ tragically from their colleagues whose ship sailed a day earlier. It was a lottery where the fate of hundreds would be determined by a difference of twenty-four hours.

In the hospitals still functioning there was a state of near chaos regarding the evacuation of nursing staff. The docks were being strafed and there were not enough ships to take all the fleeing civilians. Orders were being countermanded almost as soon as they had been transmitted. At first nurses who wanted to get out were asked to volunteer. Then, because, with commendable courage, so many opted to stay on, names were chosen at random for immediate evacuation. Those who were selected were told to be ready with hand luggage to leave at any moment and about thirty left on 11 February, sailing the next day. They were the lucky ones. On the morning of Friday 13 February the order came through that all nursing staff must leave.

The remaining nurses at the Alexandra had in fact given up hope of escaping and were resigned to being captured. However the defending troops, determined to protect the women, pulled out all the stops and held up the Japanese just long enough for them to escape.

Evelyn Cowens with the doughty Matron Miss West was among the last to leave.

Miss Jones sent a message to say that 80 of us were to be ready to go to the docks (with hand luggage only). Before we had time to move off another message came with 'Everybody was to go to the hospital at once as the enemy had advanced and was almost at the hospital gates.' We went over dodging the machine gun bullets en route. We were now experts at throwing ourselves prone on the ground. We sat and waited to be handed over to the Japs but our troops pushed them back four miles and so gave us another chance to escape.[6]

77

It was an eight-mile hike from the Alexandra to the docks and the procession was under constant attack from machine guns and dive bombers. The roads were filled with hundreds of retreating troops and when the planes came over everyone took cover in the 'Singapore ditches' as the open sewers which lined the road were called, emerging with soaked and stinking clothing. Some took shelter in the Cricket Club in Singapore, but this proved no haven when the upper floor was blown away by a shell.

Eventually everyone reached the docks – where a scene of utter confusion awaited them.

Both Evelyn Cowans, who had admitted feeling braver when Matron was by her side, and Catherine Maudsley were among the lucky ones who got away from Singapore on Thursday 12 February. Evelyn describes the chaos that awaited them as they found the docks as they had never seen them before. 'Our next difficulty was to find the ship. The docks were on fire and no one knew the way. For nearly one hour we dashed about trying to find an entrance that was not burning and dodging the planes overhead. Finally we found it and scrambled on board . . .'

The ship they sailed on was the *Empire Star*, a modest Straits steamer designed for taking civilian passengers on short hops between the islands. She had twenty-four cabins and no lifebelts. On that trip she was carrying 2,500 passengers. The nurses, who had nothing with them – no food and no possessions – slept on bare boards in the hold with only tin hats and gas masks to act as pillows and between 8 a.m. and midday suffered constant air attacks from up to a hundred planes. The raids smashed all the lifeboats and killed twelve passengers. In addition several men were blown over the side. The ship was under constant attack and developed a fire in her stern, but the crew put the damage right as best they could and the *Empire Star* sailed doggedly on.

Evelyn Cowens was still wearing the stinking clothes she had been wearing when she took shelter in the sewer: 'For four hours we had raids, the last one consisted of 57 enemy planes which did a great deal of damage . . . the ship had seven direct hits . . . It was a terrifying experience; several times the ship pitched over to one side but managed to right herself and plod steadily on. After each lurch it was like sweet music to hear the throb of the engines . . .'

There was hardly any food aboard and the officers shared their meagre rations – tins of army biscuits and corned beef – with the nurses, who gratefully drank the tea – which was regularly brewed up in buckets – out of cigarette tins.

To the immense relief of everyone the ship eventually outran the Japanese and reached safety in Batavia (now the capital of Indonesia, Djakarta). Catherine Maudsley realised they owed their lives to the plucky Captain. 'Had it not been for the Captain and the staff of that Merchant ship we should never have reached Batavia.'

Catherine was put on an evacuee ship bound for Ceylon almost straightaway. Evelyn Cowens opted to stay at the Dutch Military Hospital nursing British troops. She was later offered a passage to Bombay on a troopship.

For their colleagues who had volunteered to stay on in Singapore the outcome was to be tragically different.

7

Shipwrecked

As the last QAs to leave Singapore scrambled aboard the heavily overladen vessel shipwreck was the last thing on their minds. In opting to stay with their patients until ordered to abandon them they had taken a huge risk. Now they were on their way to safety.

While still taking on passengers SS *Kuala* was attacked by wave after wave of enemy aircraft, killing dozens of passengers and a QA. The ship was carrying six hundred people, five hundred of whom were civilians. Half of these were women and children. Scores were injured by shrapnel fragments and flying glass. As the nurses did their best to bind up the bleeding wounds, with children screaming and the injured moaning, the atmosphere was one of utter panic.

There were about fifty nurses on board, including civilians and military nurses from the other services. The QAs included Miss Violet Maud Evelyn Jones, Principal Matron Malaya Command and Miss West, the indomitable Matron of the No. 1 Malayan General Hospital who had inspired the young QAs with her bravery under fire, and at least sixteen more.

Dorothy Garvin, the carefree Scots girl who so recently had baked oatcakes in the engine room of the ambulance train, was one of them. She embarked with her friend and fellow QA Lydia. A young officer offered them his camp bed on the officers' deck and so they had a reasonably comfortable night. When they awoke they found they were at anchor off an island alongside another smaller ship, HMS *Tien Kwang*, also carrying fleeing civilians. The Master of the *Kuala* had decided to sail at night when they were less visible to aircraft, and lie to during the day. They had just sent men ashore in boats to camouflage the ship with branches and thatch when the planes came over. The

Irene Anderson, who spent most of her service in India and the Far East, models the veil and scarlet-trimmed cape for which the QAs were famous. The veils were made of stiffly starched muslin, which was fine in India, where *dhobis* were on hand to wash and press them, but was a problem in tented hospitals, especially when water was scarce. As the war progressed the dress and veil was abandoned in favour of the more practical battledress.

◄ Meta Manson sailed to Aromanches in the aftermath of D-Day in the worst storm seen for a generation. Working in tents she followed the troops to Brussels where she saw some of the recently liberated prisoners from Belsen. She then transferred to India where she nursed the returning prisoners of the Japanese.

◄ Mary O'Rourke sailed to North Africa on the sister ship of the ill-fated *Strathallan* and had to set up her hospital with minimum equipment as most of it had been lost with the *Strathallan*. She followed the First Army up through Italy and got married in the thick of the fighting, only to find herself back at work, and separated from her husband, after a three-day honeymoon.

▲ Brenda McBryde wrote two of the best books on the QAs' wartime service. She too had had a brutal introduction to the savagery of war when she was sent, before being mobilised, to work in a plastic surgery unit caring for seriously disfigured pilots who had been injured in the Battle of Britain.

◄ Dorothea Chisholm was one of the few QAs who had seen serious injuries before she enlisted and was more prepared than some for casualties she witnessed in Normandy. She trained at Liverpool Royal Infirmary during the Blitz – a time of appalling loss of life. The iron self discipline and calm of the older medical staff while the hospital was being bombarded nightly (because of its proximity to the docks) impressed her deeply.

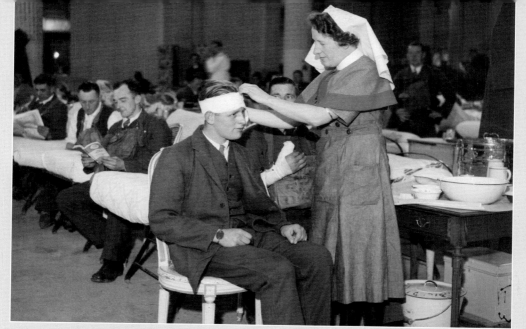

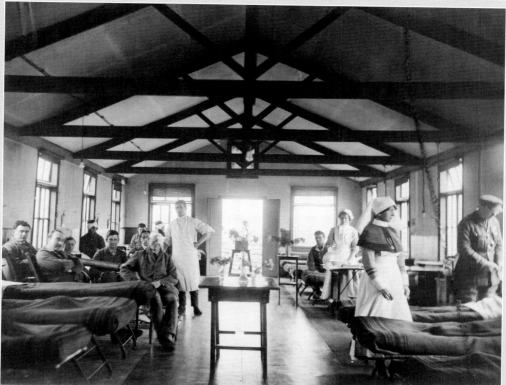

▲▲ A QA dresses a minor head wound for a member of the British Expeditionary Force in Number 8 General Hospital in Nantes, France, April 1940. Six weeks later Germany invaded France and by the third week in May the BEF and the QAs were in headlong retreat.

▲ Walking wounded being treated by a QA sister in 83 Dublin Hospital in Boulogne-sur-Mer. The speed of the German advance in the spring of 1940 took the BEF by surprise and on 25 May the Germans invaded Boulogne taking 5,000 British and French troops prisoner.

Margot Turner (left) and Daphne van Wart, both of whom were prisoners of the Japanese (Margot in the notoriously harsh camps in Sumatra), at a reunion of QA ex-POWs.

▲▲ British soldiers surrender to bayonet-wielding Japanese in the aftermath of the fall of Singapore in February 1942. The considerable number of QAs who had been working in Malaya and on the island were evacuated: many died when their ships were attacked by the Japanese, and most of those who survived shipwreck were taken prisoner. Very few made it to safety.

▲ Led by Lieutenant-General Arthur Percival, Commander of Allied forces in Singapore (far right) a surrender party from the British forces is escorted by a Japanese soldier to their Headquarters on 15 February 1942. The white flag is carried alongside the Union Jack. Learning that QAs had been raped and murdered when the Japanese invaded Hong Kong, General Percival was anxious to evacuate the nurses before the surrender.

These pictures offer a unique view of what it was like to survive the ordeal of shipwreck. One of the passengers aboard SS *Strathallan*, a converted liner transporting troops and nurses to North Africa in the aftermath of Operation Torch, was the American war photographer Margaret Bourke-White. The *Strathallan* was torpedoed just after midnight on 21 December 1942 near Oran in Algeria. The Royal Navy came to the rescue and, because the ship did not sink immediately, losses were relatively few.

◀ Glad to be alive. Still wearing their greatcoats two QAs beam out at the new day aboard HMS *Verity*, the Royal Navy destroyer which rescued them. The *Strathallan* was also carrying vital medical equipment for casualties from the Eighth Army in its bitter struggle with Rommel's Afrika Korps. 250 QAs were on board; many could not swim and five were lost.

▼ After many cold and anxious hours in lifeboats, where several of the nurses were repeatedly sick due to the oil they had swallowed, three QAs enjoy a welcome cup of tea brewed by a smiling British sailor.

QAs, American Army nurses and Merchant and Royal Navy
personnel aboard HMS *Verity*, the destroyer which rescued them
after their troopship was torpedoed. The coast of North Africa
can be seen in the background.

Hope returns. After a long night in lifeboats daybreak has finally arrived. The survivors are
making V signs and waving in excitement as a plane is spotted overhead which will tell the navy
of their position and lead to their eventual rescue. In the foreground, wearing a spotted headscarf,
is General Eisenhower's driver Kay Summersby, who was much admired by the troops.

◄ Molly Budge, who kept her camera with her throughout her five-year war service, enjoys a brief respite in her tent in the Egyptian desert in 1941. Matron dinned into trainees that uniform had to be immaculate and despite severe water rationing Molly still sports a dazzling white collar and veil. Entering tented wards while carrying a tray of medicines meant that QAs were endlessly having to refix their veils.

▼ Three QAs demonstrate the art of keeping their veils immaculate in the desert by using Army-issue folding canvas washstands. When they first saw these, the girls found them hugely comic. But they worked considerably better than their counterpart, the folding canvas bath, which had a tendency to collapse.

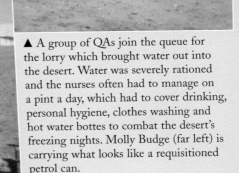

▲ A group of QAs join the queue for the lorry which brought water out into the desert. Water was severely rationed and the nurses often had to manage on a pint a day, which had to cover drinking, personal hygiene, clothes washing and hot water bottes to combat the desert's freezing nights. Molly Budge (far left) is carrying what looks like a requisitioned petrol can.

◄ Field Marshal Montgomery, commander of the Eighth Army, visits No. 2 General Hospital shortly after their capture of Tripoli at the beginning of 1943. Montgomery was exceptional among army top brass in expressing his appreciation of the work of the QAs.

women heard a warning shout to take cover and the ship was rocked by a massive explosion as the bridge suffered a direct hit and the boiler room caught fire. With the stricken vessel sinking fast the order came to abandon ship. There were only two lifeboats and not nearly enough lifebelts. Terrified passengers, some bleeding from serious injuries, distraught mothers with babies in their arms and screaming toddlers clutching their skirts, paralysed adults who couldn't swim – all were forced to jump from the blazing ship into the water where a fierce current was sweeping away from the island and out to the open sea.

They hung on to whatever they could – mattresses, chairs – anything that floated. An Australian Sister found her hand caught up in the hair of a Chinese girl who had lost a leg. And even as this helpless human flotsam clung to life the Japanese came swooping down and strafed them, hitting one of the lifeboats and catapulting the passengers back into the sea.

Dorothy Garvin abandoned the ship with Lydia.

> We were told just to jump overboard. There was simply nothing else for it. The officers started throwing everything wooden overboard. Lydia and I went down into the hold and down the ladder into the sea, but she was only really learning to swim and got frightened . . . We were both very nearly drowned . . . Paddy Clark (who did midder [midwifery] with me) was with us in the water. She was a very strong swimmer and managed to put Lydia on a raft. The great difficulty was a strong current sweeping round the ship and bearing out to sea. I honestly did not think I should ever make it, but I saw a lifeboat ahead of me . . . The second wave of bombers came over while we were still in the water . . . A lot of the good swimmers were all killed then and a lifeboat was hit.[1]

The ordeal was even worse for another QA, Sister Hartley, who, like Lydia, couldn't swim:

> Sisters McGregor and Ingham had left me sometime before and I never saw them again. I put my lifejacket on and went down the rope ladder and into the water, feeling not very brave as I had always been very much afraid of the sea . . . and then I saw Miss Oswald and some of our emergency sisters hanging onto a mattress

and . . . tried to make for it . . . then I found myself in a different part of the water and nobody near. Later on I saw Mrs Dunlop in the water and she appeared to be almost gone . . . but I came across a chair and tried to fix her hands to that and pull her with me, I not being a swimmer. We carried on like that for some time when I saw a small boat, which I immediately hailed and an Air Force boy swam out and took her to the boat. Then the current got me and I was carried away, but after a short time the same boy came out and helped me in.[2]

A member of the crew left a graphic picture of the physical and mental devastation caused by the sinking of the *Kuala*:

Between the islands floated boats and rafts laden with people; and here and there, upheld by his lifebelt, the lone swimmer was striving to make land. All around the rafts and swimmers were dis-membered limbs, dead fish and wreckage drifting with the currents; below in all probability, were the sharks; and above at intervals the winged machines of death. Among those who had escaped death from bombs or the sea there was not one who did not suffer from mutilations, wounds, sickness, hunger, cold, dirt, fear or loss and no one knew what the morrow would bring forth.[3]

At least eight QAs were killed on the *Kuala* and two more died later as a result of their wounds. The dead included Miss Jones, Miss West and Miss Winifred Russell, Matron of 17 GCH. Dorothy Garvin estimated that half the last batch of QAs to leave Singapore were killed. The nurses who managed to get into lifeboats did their best to tend the wounded but many were beyond help.

Dr Margaret Thompson was in the boat and a soldier boy . . . He had a head injury, fractured lower arm and fracture of lower leg . . . Dr herself was injured . . . but she was rowing as though nothing was wrong with her. A mother arrived with two children, one baby . . . as she was 'blue' [*sic*] I . . . smacked her hard and she was all right, and then my attention was called to Mrs Dunlop, but I saw I could do nothing . . . she died within five minutes of my getting into the boat. I then had to put her into the sea and then later the soldier also died . . . We now had about 35 people.

Another soldier with a large wound in his back died and also was put into the sea.[4]

The QAs who survived the raid on the ship and the subsequent massacre in the water included Olive Spedding, the up-country Matron, now seriously wounded, who had been so reluctant to abandon patients in Singapore; Sister Hartley, Helene Bell Murray, Sister Brand, who had a serious wound in the buttock from which she later died, Margot Turner, Beatrice le Blanc Smith, and Dorothy Garvin.

Thanking her good fortune in being a swimmer Dorothy eventually managed to get into one of the lifeboats and reach Pom Pong, the island where the crew of the *Kuala* had been collecting thatch to camouflage the ship.

A woman in the lifeboat was very seriously injured having been shot through the abdomen. Although her dress had been already ripped to ribbons by the sea and the rocks Dorothy used what was left of her skirt to make pads and bandages to try to stop the bleeding. When they eventually reached the island the land was too steep to carry the woman ashore so Dorothy and a VAD sat with her for about two hours on the rocks. Eventually a lifeboat took the VAD and the dying woman round to the other side of the island where there was a beach. Dorothy, who for decency's sake had been given a shirt by one of the men, started to try to swim and scramble round to the other side of the island. By now she was totally exhausted, but even now the enemy were still hunting them.

'It was here, while I was feeling really worn and scared, that I heard [John's] good Aberdeenshire voice saying "Here that curly-headed one is not getting on very well", so they waited for me and I held onto the other lad while they swam round. We just reached the shore when the planes came over and bombed again. I should never have the heart to shoot anything after being defenceless myself.'[5]

Of the nine hundred the *Kuala* and the *Tien Kwang* were carrying between them only five hundred survivors made it to the island – four hundred people perished in the sea, either through drowning or as a result of machine-gunning from the air.

There was no food on the island. They were so hungry that when a seagull dropped a piece of fish, they washed it in the sea and shared it out. Dorothy, whose determinedly positive 'survivor' attitude did not desert her even in this crisis, wryly described her stay on the island as 'very slimming'. She survived on a daily square inch of bully beef and a biscuit from the meagre rations which had survived the wreck. In the first few hours, as they tried to look after the injured as best they could, she had also been scantily clad, a detail, she notes with her characteristic humour, which at the time seemed irrelevant. 'I was given a boiler suit on the island as I lost my frock, some of it in the sea and on the rocks, and some as bandages. I'll never be shy again. Several of us were flying round in our knickers, just as if we were in stiffly starched caps and aprons at home.'

The water situation was critical. One barrel had been washed ashore and there was only one small spring on the island which was sufficient to provide half a mugful night and morning. They couldn't wash as the sea was covered in oil from the wrecks. A few first-aid kits which had been found in the lifeboats were all that was available to treat the injured.

But with so many nurses among the survivors it wasn't long before the men were put to work building beds and a mini tropical hospital, complete with duty rotas, was established. Dorothy Garvin threw herself into the work: 'I was lucky that I had automatically put myself on duty as the hospital staff were a grand crowd and our days were filled from dawn to dusk. We had about 20 stretcher cases (on real desert island beds made from canvas and the boughs of trees by the engineers). We got a lady doctor the second day . . . She went off in a lifeboat later with two Sisters to another small island without help.'

They even took turns at night duty, five Sisters lying next to each other on the ground using the one waterproof watch that had survived the shipwreck to wake the next one up after three-hour watches. None the less, with so many seriously injured people without access to medical facilities, conditions must have been dreadful. One survivor was haunted by the heart-rending moans of the injured. Many died and graves for them were dug on the island, with rough crosses erected on which their names were scratched.[6]

Compared to the Sisters who had sailed on the *Empire Star* on 12 February, all those who boarded the *Kuala* seemed unlucky. Now, against all the odds, some had survived. But Fate had not yet finished with those who had sailed on Friday the 13th. Before long, further ordeals would reduce those who finally made it to freedom to a tiny handful.

The hunger of the survivors was eased to some extent when Malays from a neighbouring island brought food and fruit. The day after the wreck a ship's boat was sailed over to a big island some way off with a telephone or telegraphic connection with Sumatra. The Dutch authorities were informed of the plight of the shipwrecked civilians, and the following night, with great bravery (as the straits were being constantly patrolled by Japanese fighter planes), they sent a small cargo ship, the *Tanjong Penang*. About twenty wounded men, 180 women and children, and most of the Sisters were put on board. It was decided that the Sisters who were off duty would go, while those who were on duty would stay with the patients who were too ill to be moved. It must have looked as if the people leaving were the lucky ones. After the boat's departure the island camp was down to about three hundred, of whom two hundred were troops.

Dorothy Garvin had had the opportunity of getting away on that first boat, but was concerned about an injured woman doctor who was marooned on the other side of the island and opted to stay on. 'I just did not want to go that night,' she wrote in a letter to her mother.

After two more days a small motor trawler turned up at night, sent by the Dutch Government to take off the remaining wounded and the nurses. In charge was an American wearing a Dutch naval officer's cap.

One of the Sisters who had agreed to go aboard the *Tanjong Penang* was a QA called Margot Turner, who had started her overseas service in an up-country hospital in Malaya. They embarked the passengers, many of whom had to be carried on, on the night of 16 February and sailed early the next day. Margot spent the day dressing wounds and handing out rations of food and water. The boat was crowded with survivors from other shipwrecks. All the patients and the women and children were placed in the hold, but as a reward for all their hard work the Captain allowed the Sisters to sleep on deck. They had just settled down at 9 p.m. when the deck was lit up by two dazzling searchlights. Without any warning there were two massive explosions as two shells hit the ship and the deck was suddenly covered with dead and mutilated bodies. Margot Turner reports:

I was lying next to Sister Beatrice le Blanc Smith and there were people dead and dying all round us. Beatrice got a nasty wound in the buttock . . . My first thought was for the women and children in the hold; but a VAD struggling up from there to the deck, her dress covered in blood, said that the hold had had the full force of one of the shells and was absolutely smashed. In any case I realised that there was nothing I could do as the ship was already at a steep angle and obviously just about to turn over. Beatrice and I just stepped into the sea and were very lucky not to be sucked down when the ship suddenly turned over and sank.[7]

Just before the ship went down the officers had managed to throw a few small rafts overboard and Beatrice and Margot got hold of two and tied them together. To experience two shipwrecks in less than a week must have been absolutely terrifying, but the fact that it was night time, that the ship was smaller than the *Kuala* and that it had received such a central blow, made the carnage far more harrowing. 'The cries and screams of the wounded, the helpless and the dying, were quite terrible.'

The two Sisters swam around and managed to pick up fourteen people, including six children, two of whom were babies under a year old. They arranged the rafts with people sitting back to back each holding a child in their lap. The remainder had to stay in the water, hanging on to the lifelines. Margot urged everyone not to let go but when dawn broke two had disappeared. Beatrice le Blanc Smith insisted on being one of the ones in the water, despite being gravely wounded. She died later that day.

The tropical sun, from which they had no protection, scorched them and every day brought more deaths.

There was only one other person on the raft whom I had ever met before . . . She died at the end of the first day; and on the second day the children went mad. We had a terrible time with them – and lost them all. I examined each of them with great care before committing their small bodies to the sea. The last one was a very small baby and it was difficult to know when it was dead. I thought 'this is some woman's precious child; I must not let it go until I know it's dead.' . . . One by one the other women had gone and on the second night Feb 19th I was left alone with a Mrs Barnett, whom I had never seen before.

On their third afternoon on the raft Margot and her companion began to see small islands and decided to try to brave the strong currents and paddle towards one, using pieces of driftwood. By now both women were extremely weak.

'Mrs Barnett let her paddle slip from her grasp and, before I could stop her, she had plunged into the sea after it . . . I was much too weak to swim after her. I called and strained my eyes to catch sight of her – but there was just nothing. I was now all alone.'

Margot stayed alive by eating seaweed and collecting tiny amounts of rain in the lid of her powder compact, which had miraculously survived two shipwrecks. She thought of her home and her family and she prayed.

On the afternoon of the fourth day she saw a ship. She wasn't strong enough to stand up and wave but she sat up and hoped the ship would see her. As it came closer she saw that it was a battleship, but her hopes that it would be the Royal Navy were dashed when she saw incredulous Japanese sailors peering down at this wasted young woman, burned dark brown by the sun.

The crew threw a rope down to her and told her to tie it round her waist, but she was too weak, so one of the sailors came down a rope ladder and tied it for her. Then she was hauled aboard. There was a doctor aboard who spoke English and who realised how fragile her condition was. Thirst had made Margot almost delirious, but to allow a person in her condition to drink too much at once could prove fatal, so he gave her some tea, a little drop of whisky and some bread and milk. He treated her painful sunburn, rigged up an awning on deck to protect her and gave her a shirt and trousers – the remains of her dress had been ripped off as she was hauled aboard on the end of the rope. Having let her sleep for a while, they roused her later the same night and told her they would put her ashore. She was carried ashore at Muntok on the island of Banka, off Sumatra in the Dutch East Indies.

It was only nine days since she had left Singapore and yet in that time Margot had seen and experienced more suffering than most people see in a lifetime. The memories never left her.

To anyone who has not experienced the sudden destruction of a ship at sea, crammed full of women and children, with no lifeboats and lifejackets only for the very few, it is difficult to imagine the sheer ghastliness of the scene. And if on top of all this there is machine-gunning of helpless people in the water, and the darkness of night, it becomes all the more horrible. Those who left the ship alive simply didn't know what to do – or who to try to help; and the wailing of helpless mothers looking for their children, and vice versa, is a sound the survivors are never likely to forget.

Having survived not one but two shipwrecks Margot must have thought her troubles were over. But Banka was already in Japanese hands and Margot was now the prisoner of an enemy whose reputation for inhumanity, particularly towards women, was just starting to become known.

All those at home who had relatives caught up in the fall of Singapore suffered agonies of worry as there was simply no news of those who did not reach their intended destinations. The facts about the shipwreck of the *Kuala* did not become generally known to the British public until four months later – on 17 June 1942 – when a Singapore-based British civilian wrote an article describing their escape and the eventual rescue of some of them by the Dutch and the Royal Navy.

Many families had to wait till the end of the war with Japan to find out whether their relatives had survived. But for the family of Beatrice le Blanc Smith fate had a particularly cruel trick in store. Beatrice, a young woman who in many ways typified the values of the QAs of the war generation – energetic, patriotic, self-sacrificing – had written her parents a letter from her hospital in up-country Malaya. It is the kind of letter any parent would be proud to receive.

My darling Dad and Mother,
. . . don't worry about me. Whatever may happen to me cannot but be for the best, and so far I seem to have been so well cared for that I see no reason why protection should suddenly cease, and whatever I may have to go through is all experience, and proves one's strength of character and fundamental beliefs. I have no fear for myself at the moment. I look on life as a great adventure with

the unexpected round every corner. Many people, finding themselves left with nothing, are learning life's true values . . . To hold life cheaply, and all one's worldly possessions of no account, may take some doing but it is the lesson many have to learn . . .

Waiting for the baptism of fire doesn't worry me much except for the usually empty feeling at the sound of planes and guns. One Sister has been through France, the Middle East and Greece – and I want to do likewise.

At last my existence here seems about to be justified, and the year of 'fun and games' preceding this was just the prelude and will be something to be remembered with a tolerant smile . . .[8]

Beatrice had written this letter on 1 January 1942. By the time her parents received it, on 1 May, their daughter had been dead for nearly three months.

The mystery and anxious speculation regarding the whereabouts of so many Sisters following the fall of Singapore prompted the Matron-in-Chief to issue a hard-hitting statement which today may seem somewhat heartless, but was doubtless the most pragmatic advice at the time.

'It is not War Office policy to encourage the next-of-kin of missing personnel in the Far East to entertain much hope that their relatives are alive; the grim facts of the Far East situation make it most unlikely that any large proportion of them have survived and it is no kindness to raise false hopes.'

The thousands who left Singapore in those two chaotic days in February fell into three groups: those who died at sea; those who were taken prisoner; and a small blessed minority who escaped both and made it to Ceylon or India. Blind fate decided who belonged in which group. 'Luck played an extraordinary part in deciding human fate in these waters at this particular stage of the war. Some people would arrive on one island, be picked up by some rickety old boat and get clean away from the Japs; others would appear to be in clover, and suddenly find themselves in prison.'[9]

If anyone were going to outwit the Japanese and escape to safety it seemed likely that it would be the QAs who left the island on the *Tanjong Penang*. Yet now, after inflicting so much suffering, fate decided to be kind to those who were left. On the fifth night an invasion barge arrived and took off all the remaining women and the wounded, with one Sister. The party numbered about forty or fifty and included fifteen seriously wounded, including Matron Spedding. The boat returned to the island a second time and brought off all the remaining people.

Dorothy Garvin was among the last to leave. The barge hit rocks on the way but bailed with a bucket and against all the odds managed to reach the east coast of Sumatra safely, where the welcoming Dutch fed and clothed them. But Sumatra was on the point of being overrun by the Japanese and there was a mad dash against time to get the refugees across the mountainous country to the west-coast port of Padang from where they were most likely to be shipped to safety. Gwen Dowling, an Australian army nurse who had been on the *Kuala*, described being taken by Australian troops in a motor boat up the mighty rushing Indragiri River so that she could pick up a train for Padang.

As the refugees poured into Padang it was by no means clear that they would be able to be evacuated as no ships were expected. But out of the blue two Royal Navy ships and one Australian naval ship, which had been taking part in the Java Sea battle, put in to refuel. They took all the refugees on board.

Dorothy Garvin was jubilant: 'Never shall I forget the excitement when the fleet came in and took a thousand of us off. God bless the Navy.'

Dorothy had a wonderful journey as there were only six women on the cruiser which had rescued her – all of whom had been on the *Kuala*. These included Helene Bell Murray, who had made her way to another town on the east coast of Sumatra before crossing to Penang, and Gwen Dowling, the Australian QA who had sped up the Indragiri river. Halfway on their journey they transferred to an Australian cruiser where the officers – not surprisingly – made the women just as welcome. Dorothy recalled with affection the lusty singsongs on the quarter deck. Most important, however, was the unfamiliar feeling that, in the bosom of the navy, she was safe. 'I honestly felt that even if we met with the whole Japanese fleet I was not caring as everything would be done well and in order.'

The lucky few arrived in Bombay on 5 March, three weeks after the fall of Singapore, and were granted rest and recreation after all their ordeals. There they met up with the other QAs who had left Singapore a day earlier on the *Empire Star* – women like Catherine Maudsley and Evelyn Cowens. Dressed in second-hand refugee clothes and with no possessions of any kind, Dorothy Garvin was positive, as usual. In a letter home she reflected on the effect her tribulations had had on her:

> What the Japs have not got of my belongings 'Old Davy' has . . . Do you know that when I travelled as a cabin passenger in luxury liners I never met with such kindness as I did as a refugee, without a cent and with only what I wore.
>
> . . . The Australian Red Cross have been very kind to us and gave us parcels with pyjamas and tooth-brushes, etc. . . . I have no money to buy uniform and things like a pen and watch till the army produces some or else gives us a permanent address so that I get some cabled. There are so many people in this state that I don't worry . . . It's amazing how you can do with nothing, and such a boon when travelling.[10]

But while Dorothy and the rest of the small handful of survivors were recovering in Bombay, other QAs who had survived shipwreck were about to sacrifice what they valued almost as much as life itself – their freedom.

Sister Hartley had managed to make it to land after the *Kuala* sank and, together with some of the injured, was rescued by a Chinese junk with a sympathetic crew who gave them food. They met up with other Sisters and RAMC people who were also fleeing Singapore and had eventually made it to Padang.

Padang fell to the Japanese on 17 March 1942 and from then on the Sisters and their patients were prisoners of war. On Banka island Margot Turner had met with the same fate, as had many others who had survived shipwreck.

As far as their families were concerned they simply disappeared off the face of the earth and the War Office was deluged with letters from distraught parents (including Margot Turner's mother) asking, 'What has happened to my daughter?' Little was known in Britain about the treatment of British prisoners of the Japanese for nearly two years until 1944 when Anthony Eden, then Foreign Secretary, made a statement in the House of Commons revealing the callousness and brutality they were enduring. This was followed a few weeks later by even more disturbing revelations by the Secretary of State for War about the horrific conditions that military prisoners were subjected to by the Japanese, particularly those forced to build the notorious Burma–Siam railway. Little emerged even then about the treatment of civilians and many in England must have assumed that defenceless women and children would be treated humanely.

It would take an International War Crimes tribunal to reveal just how tragically misplaced those assumptions had been.

8

The Disappeared

Some people seem to be marked out from birth as survivors and Margot Turner was one of them. But before long Margot was to meet another young nurse whose grim story of survival was even more incredible than her own. Vivian* Bullwinkel, a bubbly vivacious girl with a big smile, was a 26-year-old Australian nurse who had had to leave Singapore when the 2/10th Australian General Hospital was overrun by the Japanese. Like Margot she sailed on Friday the 13th on a ship which was destined to suffer the same fate as the *Kuala*. The *Vyner Brooke*, a small Royal Navy vessel with just one gun, had embarked about three hundred people, of whom sixty-five were Australian army nurses, and was headed for Java when it was attacked by Japanese planes in Singapore harbour. The attack holed all the lifeboats on one side of the ship. The next day the planes returned and scored a succession of direct hits which sank the *Vyner Brooke* within fifteen minutes.

The Australian Sisters stayed together clinging to rafts and whatever of the wreckage remained afloat while strong tides carried them helplessly this way and that. Finally they drifted into a river estuary and were washed up on a beach which turned out to be Banka island. A fire glowing in the darkness led them to other survivors of the *Vyner Brooke*, including Irene Drummond, the Australian Sisters' Matron. Numbers were increased when a lifeboat carrying British servicemen, survivors from a sea battle with the Japanese, arrived. By morning almost sixty men, women and children and twenty-two Australian Army Nursing Service (AANS) members were on the beach without food or water.

---

* The transcripts of the Tokyo War Crimes Trials list the spelling of Bullwinkel's first name as 'Vivien' but her name was usually written with an 'a'.

The next day a search party of five nurses, including Vivian, set out to ask local people for help, but by now the Japanese were in control of the island and the villagers, fearing reprisals, refused to help them.

By Monday 16 February there were about a hundred people, including children, who, through hunger and thirst, were by now crying constantly. The wounded lay on stretchers on the beach. An officer from the *Vyner Brooke* decided that as they had no means of looking after the helpless and no way of feeding anyone they should surrender to the Japanese. He agreed to walk to Muntok, the main town. While he was away Matron Drummond, in an unselfish gesture that was to have fatal consequences, suggested that the mothers and children should also start walking towards Muntok with the aim of surrendering. The officer returned with about twenty Japanese soldiers. Having separated the men from the women the Japanese divided the men into two and marched them at gunpoint along the beach and round a headland. The nurses heard the sound of round after round of gunfire and the Japanese soldiers reappeared. They then marched the other group off round the headland and again shots were heard. The Japanese returned and in front of the horrified nurses sat down on the beach and began cleaning the blood from their bayonets. The officer then told the nurses to walk towards the sea, shoving those who were reluctant. Twenty-two nurses, all wearing the Red Cross armbands, and one elderly civilian woman who had not wanted to be parted from her husband were forced into the sea until the water came up to their waists. At that point the Japanese machine-gunned them down.

'They just swept up and down the line and the girls fell one after the other. I was towards the end of the line and a bullet got me in the left loin and went straight through and came out towards the front,' Vivian told the War Crimes Tribunal in 1946. 'The conduct of the girls was most courageous. They all knew what was going to happen to them but no one panicked. They just marched ahead with their chins up. We waded into the surf and they fired on us.'

The force of the shot knocked Vivian, a non-swimmer, into the water but she did not pass out. The seawater she had swallowed made her want to vomit, but she knew she dared not show a sign of life. Somehow she managed to turn her head imperceptibly enough to gulp sufficient air to stay breathing until eventually the waves nudged her back to the shore again.

'I lay there 10 minutes and everything seemed quiet, I sat up and looked around and there was no sign of anybody. Then I got up and went into the jungle and lay down and either slept or was unconscious for a couple of days.'[1]

By Wednesday she had recovered sufficiently to drag herself to a freshwater spring close to the beach to slake her burning thirst. Here she discovered that although she was the only woman to have survived the massacre of the Australian Sisters, there was another survivor. A British private had been one of the stretcher cases whom the Japanese had murdered after they had shot the nurses. He had suffered shrapnel wounds before reaching the island and had been bayoneted in the chest, and left for dead. He was very ill, but the blade had not penetrated vital organs. The rest of the wounded still lay on their stretchers where they had been murdered. Many years after the war it emerged that two of the men who had been marched round the headland had also survived and one of them recalled finding the bodies of the other victims.

'It was quite horrible. All the male bodies had been piled on top of one another in one big heap. Then I went further along and found the bodies of the Autralian nurses and other women. They lay at intervals of a few hundred yards – in different positions and in different stages of undress. They had been shot and then bayoneted. It was a shocking sight.'[2]

Vivian Bullwinkel nursed the badly injured British soldier for about twelve days, begging food from women in the nearby village. When they thought they were both strong enough they decided to try to walk to Muntok, but on 28 February they were picked up by a Japanese officer in a passing car and taken to a prisoner-of-war camp. The British soldier was transferred to the camp hospital where not long afterwards he died from his injuries. Vivian was reunited with the rest of her Australian colleagues – fellow survivors of the *Vyner Brooke* sinking. Of the original sixty-five who had left Singapore there were thirty-two left. Twelve were presumed drowned, twenty-one had been shot and the rest were prisoners. Over eighty people had been killed on the beach.

Margot Turner was there when Vivian arrived at the camp and knew at once that she was hiding something. 'She walked quietly in through the door of the jail, clasping an army water bottle to her side. We could see at once why she was doing this – it was to hide a bullet hole in her uniform.'

Vivian Bullwinkel had not meant to tell anyone of her dangerous secret lest the Japanese, realising that there had been a witness to this particularly indefensible act of atrocity, would kill her. But the surviving nurses wanted to know what had happened to friends and colleagues they had last seen clinging to lifeboats, and under pressure from them she described the massacre on the beach. A decision was taken then that it would never be mentioned again until they were free.[3]

It is not hard to imagine how low Vivian's physical and emotional state must have been when she arrived at the camp. Wounded in body and shattered in spirit by the horror she had witnessed, she needed good food, a comfortable bed and above all to feel safe. The Japanese prison camp offered none of these things. Her fellow survivors found her a little cooked rice and a small amount of water. A sleeping space was made for her on a sloping concrete slab that served as a bed, but there was no bedding. But Vivian was a woman of formidable grit and no amount of bullying was going to break her spirit. Despite her ordeal, over the three and a half years of her captivity she recovered to play a full part in the bleak and often repellent duties demanded by the harshness and squalor of Japanese prisoner-of-war camps. A fellow internee describes how Vivian and another nurse earned 80 cents a day from the other prisoners for clearing the clogged lavatory drains. They had to make do with what was to hand and the task involved using half a coconut shell and carrying the human excreta half a mile into the jungle.[4]

Meanwhile in the same camp, which was filled with survivors of some sixty ships which had sunk or been captured in the vicinity of the Banka Straits, Margot Turner was making a slow and painful recovery. This process was not helped by the fact that she detested rice, which formed the basis of the twice-daily camp meals. Margot's first setback was the development of a potentially fatal condition which was a direct result of having been in the water for so long.

I began to get red patches on my legs which spread upwards and became very painful, keeping me awake at night. There was a naval doctor in the camp who had a look at them but could suggest nothing but an application of calamine. My legs got steadily worse and I realised perfectly well that I had some acute form of poisoning. One of the Civilian Sisters . . . who was looking after me, arranged for a Dr Kerr to have a look at me. He was an elderly Scotsman, who had been practising in Singapore for a number of years . . . he was quite convinced that I had deep-seated pus in both legs – what he called 'sea-water boils'.

They would have to be lanced at once and all he had to do it with was a blunt scalpel – and with this he opened up the patches and out poured the pus. Painful as these lancings were I realised quite well that they saved my life.[5]

A tragic footnote to this life-saving healing is that Dr Kerr later died in the men's camp.

After only a few weeks the camp at Muntok became too crowded and the inmates – civilian men, women and children – were moved across the Banka Straits to Palembang in Sumatra. Margot was one of three QAs in the camp, the other two being Molly Cooper, an Irish girl with whom she struck up a close friendship, and a married woman called Molly Watts Carter. They stayed behind to nurse the sick, but the Japanese were determined to reduce the size of the camp and the women and children continued to be moved in batches of about a hundred and fifty at a time. Margot was among the last to leave. She was still very ill and was transported to Palembang on a stretcher. Once she arrived at the camp, which comprised some seven hundred civilians, and included fifteen English missionaries, Margot was nursed by some Dutch nuns. At this camp the men were separated from the women and children. By now the Dutch, too, were interned, and the composition of the camp was two-thirds Dutch and one-third British. The women lived in small Dutch houses in dreadfully overcrowded conditions, sleeping twenty-five to thirty-five per house. Their meagre rations were boosted by the kindness of some Dutch people who had escaped internment and who with great courage brought a variety of comforts to the camp. As a direct result of their kindness the women ate green vegetables and a ration of pork on two occasions in the first month.

In that first camp the days of Margot and her fellow nurses were divided between nursing the sick, collecting rations, which meant carrying heavy sacks of rice, and cooking. This was done on smoky wood fires using logs the prisoners had to chop themselves. Compared with what was to come, however, this POW camp was five-star.

> We had plenty of rice then, so were able to make all kinds of fancy dishes; we were also able to buy extra things such as sugar, fruit, coconuts, coffee and curry stuffs . . . People who hadn't money, but had jewellery, could sell it for money. Others would work for other people to get money – chop wood, do washing etc. As in ordinary life, so in camp, there were always people who had plenty (mostly Dutch) and those who had nothing. But I think on the whole, those who had nothing were the happiest because they did not miss it so much when things got really bad.[6]

At Palembang there was a great deal of free time to fill and Margot whiled away the long hours playing bridge with homemade cards and mahjong using bits of wood they had found. Classes in French, Malay and Dutch were organised and an elderly British missionary, who was musically gifted, wrote down music from memory which was played at camp concerts. Margaret Dryburg, who had worked in the Far East for many years, composed the poignant 'Captives' Hymn' which Margot and her fellow prisoners sang every Sunday at the weekly camp service.[*]

It was in Palembang that Margot encountered the dreaded Tenko that remained one of the most loathed memories of all Japanese prisoners of war. This was the daily roll call that was called without warning and often required prisoners to stand to attention in the hottest part of the day and wait to be counted. The senior prisoner in each group had to bow from the waist and give the number of prisoners in her group. Margot detested having to bow to the Japanese. But one day when she failed to show the necessary deference a Japanese guard hit her in the face, knocking out one of her front teeth.

In October 1942 Margot and her friend Molly Cooper were offered

---

[*] The last verse reads: 'May the day of freedom dawn, Peace and Justice be reborn, Grant that nations loving Thee O'er the world may brothers be, Cleansed by suffering, know rebirth, See Thy Kingdom come on earth.' Sadly Margaret Dryburgh, who had been such an inspiration to her fellow prisoners, did not live to see her day of freedom. Worn out by years of poor diet, tropical disease and endless moves, she died in April 1945.

the opportunity of going to help nurse in a native hospital run by a
Dutch doctor some three miles from the camp. This was an unhoped-
for chance of freedom and the two women jumped at it. They were
allowed to go into the town and shop in the market and were even
permitted to visit the hospital where Allied POWs and internees were.
This meant that they could take them in little treats, do their shopping,
and even carry notes so that husbands and wives could keep in touch.
The next few months amounted to a charmed interlude. Margot and
Mary lived like free agents, doing the work they loved and going for
walks and shopping. But it wasn't to last. Things began to tighten up in
March when they were told the POW hospital was out of bounds. A
Japanese doctor took over the native hospital, discipline was increased
and whenever the girls went out they felt they were being followed.

Then, on 6 April, Margot came face to face with the brutality which
left its indelible mark on so many survivors of Japanese prison camps.
The Dutch doctor and the nurses who had worked for him, including
two civilian Sisters, were interrogated by the universally feared Kempei
Tai. The doctor was brutally beaten up, as was his wife who tried to
protect him. The next day they were all thrown into the local jail.
Margot and Mary shared a cell which was large enough for them to
walk four paces. The three others – the two civilian nurses and the wife
of the Dutch doctor – were on the other side of the jail. The women
went in just the clothes they stood up in, with no towel, no soap and no
covering. They slept on a rush mat on a stone slab on the floor.

Margot, who had already undergone the harshest of ordeals, described it as 'the longest six months of my life'.

'We were allowed out of the cell twice a day for about five minutes.
The sanitary arrangements can be left to the imagination. We had
two very meagre meals a day and sometimes either cold tea or water.
Our fellow prisoners were murderers and thieves, Malayan or Chinese . . . But they were very good to us . . . knowing that discovery
would mean some form of brutal punishment . . . they would sometimes pass through the bars to us some black coffee in a cigarette tin or
maybe a banana or a bit of cake . . .'[7]

Conditions for the women improved when they were let out to walk
for half an hour every day, but suddenly in mid July the numbers of

Japanese guards in the prison soared, unleashing a sadistic reign of terror.

'Terrible things then started to happen in the jail; the prisoners were beaten and tortured and many of them died as a result. The things we saw were so horrible that I still can't bear to think – much less talk – about them. We heard afterwards that Dr Holweg and Dr Teclecburg [Dutch doctors] were also imprisoned in the jail and were beaten unmercifully. I believe they both died . . .'

One day towards the end of September (1943), with no explanation, the Japanese asked them if they would like to return to the camp and Margot and Molly agreed.

Margot described her experience with a characteristic lack of self-pity. But the horror of that time had left its mark; the squalid living conditions, the lack of occupation, the claustrophobia and the terror of whether she would be the next victim of the Japanese torture sessions . . . Fellow prisoners at the camp witnessing their return were in no doubt as to what they'd endured. 'They looked dreadful – their eyes had a wild look in them, they had lost a lot of weight and had been treated very badly by the Japanese. But they were quite sane . . . though far from well. One of them had to go straight into the camp hospital, where she died some time later.'*

By the time Margot and Molly Cooper returned to the camp there had been a move and conditions were appreciably worse. Now five hundred women and children were to live where the men had been, in a cramped camp of specially constructed wooden huts – each hut housing sixty people – shut off totally from the outside world. 'The new camp had been constructed on swampy ground below sea level and it was thick with bugs, rats, fleas and mosquitoes . . . The whole area of the camp was only about a hundred yards long by forty yards wide . . . The actual space allowed per person was twenty-seven inches.'

In this camp not only did the women prisoners have to clean out the primitive stinking latrines, but without the men nearby the daily trucks of firewood ceased. The women had to chop wood every day, with a blunt axe, for cooking. Margot was in charge of the wood squad, which meant carrying huge logs into the camp every day and dividing them

---

* This was Molly Cooper, who died of the effects of starvation in the spring of 1945.

between the British and the Dutch kitchens. In addition the Japanese had cut off the supply of piped water and the prisoners had to go out in the heat of the day and collect their ration of water. They then had to carry it back up a steep hill to the camp.

With the men housed nearby the celebrations of Christmas 1942 had managed to be fairly cheerful. The British and Dutch in the men's camp had sent in some longed-for soap and even a piece of beef and some vegetables. With the sexes parted their second Christmas in captivity was a far more subdued affair. But if food for the body was absent, spiritual nourishment, in the form of Miss Dryburgh's memorised repertoire, was imbibed in abundance. One of the women, who was a good singer, had hit on the idea of creating an 'orchestra' without instruments. This choir was composed of women of over thirty nationalities. 'The effect of an orchestra was created by humming the four parts of soprano, second soprano, contralto and second contralto, representing the four stringed instruments, that is violin, viola, cello and double bass. This music was the most wonderful thing in our lives and I don't know what we should have done without it.'9

Perpetual hunger meant that the women had to become adaptable. Without saucepans they cooked in old tins. If they got sight of a banana they would cook the skin and eat that as well. Occasionally, says Margot, they managed to get live fish and had to kill, gut and scale them without proper knives. Once the Japanese brought in a dead monkey as the meat ration. Margot's verdict was that it made 'a very tasty stew'. There was untold rejoicing when a cockerel escaped from the house of one of the Japanese and was leapt upon by a dozen half-starved women. 'After a great struggle I eventually caught it, and it was killed, plucked and in the pot within minutes . . . we hoped that the guard would not do a round and look in the cooking pot, as he often did. Luck was with us and that evening about sixteen people had a very small taste of chicken.'

For the first six months of Margot's return life in the camp continued much as before but in April 1944 the administration of the camp was transferred from the civilian to the military and a new jumpiness could be detected among the Japanese. Captain Siki, the new Commandant, banned concerts and cut rations, warning that in the event of air raids the women would be expected to evacuate to a nearby rubber plantation.

Cut off from all news since the fall of Singapore in February 1942 the women could not know that in the Pacific war the fightback had begun. In fact Orde Wingate and his Chindits were cutting Japanese supply lines in Burma, while the Americans were preparing to recapture the Philippines and step up their bombing raids.

For those who still had their freedom it was the longed-for beginning of the end. D-Day was only two months off. But, ignorant of the turning tide, Margot Turner and her fellow women were about to enter a new hell. Under Commandant Siki life was to become grimmer than ever. Many of his victims, ground down by months of too much work and too little food, would not live to see freedom.

Siki insisted that the women be given injections against typhoid, dysentery and cholera and this, Margot believed, saved many lives. But in return he required inhuman amounts of labour. 'Working parties had to be organised to unload the rations, which were brought into the camp in military lorries. The sacks of rice, which formed the greater part of the supplies, would have taxed our strength severely even if we had been in good physical condition; but in our debilitated state the work of moving the sacks left us utterly exhausted.'[10]

Then Siki decided that as food was becoming scarce the prisoners should grow their own. 'The area we had to dig was the space in the centre of the camp, consisting of hard clay, and also some ground outside the camp. All the digging had to be done with heavy hoes which made little impression on the iron-hard ground and jarred the diggers horribly at every stroke. In addition we had to tidy up the roads outside the camp, including the gardens of the houses where the Japs were living, and clean their drains daily.'

The water supply in the camp was inadequate and the women often had just one small tin of water in which to wash their bodies and their clothes. The feeling that they could never get themselves clean, particularly when so much of their work involved cleaning latrines and drains, was deeply demoralising.

Siki did allow some of the prisoners to leave the camp to collect buckets of water from a hydrant about half a mile away. This was invariably done in the heat of the afternoon when most of the indigenous population would be resting. But he insisted that the prisoners' own need for water be left till last. First they had to fill the baths of the

Japanese houses, and then water the gardens in the camp, which were dry as a bone. This involved several trips to the hydrant and at the end of it all they would be lucky to bring one bucket of drinking water into the camp.

'All this heavy manual work went on – in a tropical climate – every day from 5 a.m. to 6 p.m., with a break of three hours in the middle of the day. The British prisoners protested strongly that many of our members were quite unfit to undertake this arduous labour, but all our protests were unavailing. This, more than any other single factor, accounted for the many deaths of prisoners in the following months.' It was at about this time that Siki instigated monthly weighings for the prisoners. By now few weighed more than seven stone.

The best way to remain healthy in the camp was to buy in extra rations. Many of the women had come in with jewellery – engagement and wedding rings, watches – and had been able to sell these in return for food. Through having been shipwrecked Margot was one of the poorest among the prisoners and, in order to get some money, she and a civilian nurse with whom she had become friendly took on the worst job, cleaning the camp latrines. 'The latrines were quite awful – just huge long drains, with wooden planks for seats; and the drains were full of maggots. Margot and I were paid ten dollars a week each for this filthy job – and my word we earned it!'" It was while she was engaged in this fulfilling work that Margot Turner celebrated her 34th birthday.*

In August 1944 an Allied air raid on a big oil refinery not far away brought cheer to the camp, as did the arrival, later in the month, of the first batch of letters they had received since being taken prisoner. There was none for Margot, but now at least the outside world knew where they were. On the same day that the letters arrived a British plane dived low over the town of Palembang and climbed quickly up into the clouds

---

* A fellow prisoner wrote her the following poem as a present which conveys some of Margot's inspiring leadership qualities:

> You are hauling great logs 'neath the noon-day sun
> And hungry and tired but the job must be done,
> Chopping and cooking and chunkelling too,
> No task too unpleasant, no toilers too few.
> Your calmness and courage and enduring power
> Have carried you through life's bitterest hour,
> So may the good Lord bless your birthday today,
> And fill you with joy as you go on your way.

again. The prisoners took this as an encouraging sign that their location was known.

By now air raids were a regular night-time feature and even Red Cross parcels were being delivered. But just as Margot's spirits were beginning to rise, Siki announced that the camp was to move back to Muntok on Banka island. The journey was, in Margot's words, one of 'unspeakable hardship and discomfort'. First open trucks, then an exhausting crossing in an overcrowded river boat, where, despite the intense heat, they were given little to eat or drink, and then the fearsome mile-long pier at Muntok, down which, two and a half years before, Margot had been carried by the Japanese doctor. Forced to carry their possessions down this gruelling walk many of the prisoners fainted.

At first this camp seemed an improvement. It was newly built and spotlessly clean. But the water supply in the wells ran out within 24 hours and the prisoners had to go and fetch their water from a creek about ten minutes' walk from the camp. At first this chore seemed attractive. The women had to walk through a delightful flower-filled stretch of jungle to reach the creek. And after the lack of water at Palembang, to be able to wash and bathe all over seemed a long-forgotten luxury. But their optimism was soon cut short. The women were expected to undertake the same amount of heavy labour as at Palembang. This involved sinking heavy posts to carry a barbed-wire fence round the hospital, while the increasing shortage of food meant long hours on the vegetable gardens. The climate in Muntok was difficult, with long humid days punctuated by cold nights. The will to survive of many prisoners, even of those with husbands and children, was starting to waver by now. Three years of hard labour and a starvation diet had already led to fifty deaths and now many prisoners went down with malaria, beriberi and dysentery, with no hope of a cure as there was no medicine to treat them. And then, just when it seemed things could not get any worse, a new scourge that defied Margot's medical knowledge appeared.

'It occurred suddenly and produced raging temperatures and unconsciousness followed by skin irritation. For want of a better name we called it "Banka Fever". My theory was that it originated from the creek, from which we obtained all our water.' At one time two hundred prisoners were ill with Banka fever. The only response from the

Japanese was to produce the occasional small bottle of quinine – to share between six hundred people. Many people did not survive their encounter with Banka fever, especially mothers, who went without food to see that their children had enough. The dead were carried to a small Chinese cemetery in the jungle. The women had to do everything to do with the funerals themselves, constructing makeshift coffins, digging graves in the iron-hard ground – without spades – and conducting the services. By January 1945 seventy-seven prisoners had been buried in the Chinese cemetery. Early in the next month the Australian nurses suffered their first loss. Sister Ray Rayment had failed to show the necessary subservience to a Japanese guard. She was made to stand outside in the ferocious sun all day and never recovered. Two other Australian Sisters died of a combination of malnutrition and illness soon afterwards. Of the sixty-five nurses evacuated on the *Vyner Brooke*, only twenty-four returned to Australia.

Harried by the Allies and determined to hide their prisoners, the Japanese announced that they would be leaving Muntok and once again travelling to Sumatra – this time to a place called Loebok Linggau on the southern side of the island. This trip, which lasted four days, was to prove the worst journey of all, as so many prisoners were ill. The women were taken to the pier in open trucks in pouring rain and one Dutch woman died as they were waiting to board the boat.

Margot Turner paints a vivid picture of this pathetic exodus and of the indifference of the Japanese to their suffering. 'Those who could walk started off, carrying their own baggage, along that interminably long pier. The more active people, chiefly the Sisters, had to act as stretcher-bearers, going up and down that pier many times, carrying and helping those who were too ill to walk . . . there were Japanese soldiers everywhere. They gave no help to the sick and weary file of women who staggered past them.'

Hygiene problems on the boat were appalling as many of the mothers and children had dysentery. Some Dutch nuns managed to procure bedpans and Margot and her fellow nurses had to clean them by lowering them down the steep side of the boat on ropes and hauling them back up again. One Englishwoman died on the boat. Once they reached Palembang the stretcher cases were loaded on to cattle trucks, with doors and windows closed (for fear of air raids) and left all night.

By morning six were dead. When they arrived at Loebok Linggau they were again made to wait all night on the train. When they were permitted to leave the train the next morning – 'the Japs swinging their bayonets round our legs to hurry us along' – many more of the stretcher cases had died.

Life in the new camp – a former rubber plantation – was harsher than ever and Margot was to lose some of her dearest friends here. Her close friend Molly Cooper, who had survived the horrors of the civilian jail at Palembang, died of beriberi and soon afterwards Miss Dryburgh, for whom the journey had been too much, joined her. Loebok Linggau was notorious all over Indonesia for the virulence of its malaria and many of the prisoners were suffering from beriberi as well. An added burden was the fact that the camp was at the top of a hill, while the kitchens, and the water supply, were down next to a creek. The people charged with carrying the supplies were just too weak to carry on.

> Out of sheer weakness scores of the prisoners died in the camp in these last months of captivity. Many of the children were in a terrible condition, some of them so badly affected by beriberi that they could hardly walk . . . Malnutrition was making itself felt to an increasing extent. Quite a lot of the time had to be spent in making patients eat. We would sit for hours trying to make them take even half a teaspoon every five minutes. If they refused to eat at all they very soon died. It was very grim and exhausting nursing – particularly as some of us Sisters were in need of nursing ourselves. On the long wooden benches which served as beds, the patients lay cheek by jowl. It was quite impossible to separate the dysentery case, or any other cases, and survival was largely a matter of luck.[12]

The callous indifference to sufferings of the Japanese guards continued to the end. Getting wood for cooking the daily rice was a major problem. The rice had to be cooked by 10 a.m. in a central kitchen and then reheated at midday and in the evening. There were plenty of dead rubber trees and fallen branches outside the perimeter of the camp but the prisoners were not allowed to retrieve them. The hated Tenko, which was such an effort for the weak and the sick, now took place twice a day.

Early in July another batch of letters arrived but they were up to two years old and so the prisoners had no idea that Germany had already surrendered. Though they did not know it, the war was nearly over.

III

AT SEA

9

Sailing the Seven Seas

The sea was the great bustling highway of the war and wherever the troops went the QAs went with them. When the Matron-in-Chief said her nurses were 'sailing the seven seas' she was not exaggerating. Some QAs spent much of their active service afloat, serving on hospital ships or employed on medical trooping duty, transporting troops to and from war zones. Most nurses who volunteered for overseas service could expect to spend up to three months on board ship. The presence of U-boats in the Mediterranean added weeks to the journey to the Middle East and India as ships had to sail the far longer route down the coast of Africa and round the Cape, before either entering the Red Sea to reach the Suez Canal, or sailing on across the Indian Ocean.

Security decreed that everything about departure remained top secret until the last minute. Nurses could only guess at the identity of the port from which they were embarking and were not told their destination until they were well underway. As the training period in the mobilisation unit drew to its close, speculation mounted that a departure date was imminent. Notice was minimal as Gladys Aikens found when her stay at Peebles came to an abrupt end.

'We had been awakened at 2 a.m. with orders to be ready to move in precisely one hour. We were well aware that the British Army waited for no stragglers; one hour later found us settled in a train . . . Because we couldn't see out of the train's blacked-out windows, we had no idea where we were going . . . After what seemed a long, tiresome journey, we arrived at a seaport. Those from Scotland amongst the crowd thought it might be a place known as Greenock.'[1]

The troopships sailed in large convoys, heavily escorted by an assortment of Royal Navy destroyers, cruisers and corvettes equipped with guns, depth charges and torpedoes. Some were even escorted by aircraft carriers. They usually departed at night. The adventure of arriving at the anonymous port and clambering aboard the gigantic darkened ships filled the nurses with a mixture of fear and excitement. They had heard that if one ship got hit the rest would keep going. There was to be no stopping to pick anyone up unless specific orders were given. Along with thousands of troops, mostly young and apprehensive like them, they boarded tenders and sailed out to the great ocean-going liners anchored offshore. One Sister described what must have indeed been a stirring sight to the Matron of the hospital she had just left.

> Never in our lives shall those who stayed up to see the last of Britain forget the night we left. In the morning the fog lifted and we slowly, but surely, went up the river, staying when we got to the mouth for the convoy to collect. A rumour went round . . . that we were to leave at midnight – and we did. A brilliant moonlit night and the bay full of boats, some waiting to go down the river, us to go out, and lots just waiting. They all had tiny lights forward and aft, and those about to move had pilot lights as well. From shore both sides of the river, beacons flashed signals, and from the naval boats and from us, as the commodore boat, answering signals.
>
> Then quite quietly the naval escort moved out . . . it was a flattering number, and made you feel really safe. They looked marvellous silhouetted against the shining water. After they had slipped through the boom we followed, with siren shrieking, and all the boats in the harbour gave answering hoots of farewell . . .[2]

The ships, which carried thousands of troops, were mostly requisitioned luxury liners accustomed to plying vast ocean routes, offering top-class service and every comfort to the discriminating traveller. In peace and war they presented a microcosm of British society. First-class passengers occupied the upper decks, dined at the captain's table, enjoyed cocktails at sundown and, in southern waters, danced to the latest dance band under the stars. Third-class and steerage passengers were confined to the bowels of the ship where the atmosphere grew rank and stifling as the ship sailed south. This fetid inferno was the domain of other ranks. As officers, QAs were given first-class accommodation, even though they had to double up in their cabins.

The numbers these ships carried were awesome: four thousand men, three hundred officers and between fifty and a hundred women was normal. Some ships carried as many as seven thousand men and seven hundred officers, all rendered more attractive by their uniform. Heavily outnumbered by male officers, the Sisters were the centre of attention and in great demand. Several anxious Matrons gave their girls quayside pep talks about the dangers of love affairs with married men. What these young women were witnessing, though no one gave it a thought at the time, was the twilight of the glamorous age of sea voyages. Without the war young women such as these would have been unlikely to venture up the gangplank of one of these grand vessels with their exotic-sounding names. A few years later progress would consign them to the breakers' yard.

Many QAs, looking down at the quarters of the other ranks below deck, felt very sorry for them, and probably even secretly guilty at their superior comfort. With the ships so overcrowded many did not even have bunks but slept rolled under blankets on the bare deck. When they neared the Equator and entered the South Atlantic temperatures soared and the men suffered greatly from the suffocating heat.

One of the great perks of being an officer was the superb food. After years of rationing, which bit more deeply as the war dragged on, the girls were amazed at the land flowing with milk and honey they found on board ship. Gwladys Aikens, sailing to North Africa aboard HMS *Strathallan*, was stunned by the five-star fare. 'We were starving. A piece of dry bread would have tasted excellent. But we must have looked somewhat incredulously at the three-course meals placed before us. In Britain we might have had one egg and one ounce of butter and very little meat, perhaps four ounces, to last us for a week. Here our menu included succulent steak and fish dishes, mouthwatering desserts, thick, crusty breads . . .'

Irene Anderson (later Leighton) from Northern Ireland still has a copy of the lavish Christmas-dinner menu served aboard the hospital ship HMS *Tairea* in 1945. It would do credit to the heartiest Georgian diner:

Hors d'œuvres variés
Consommé frappé Crème de tomate

Filets de poisson au beurre
Côtelettes d'Agneau Reforme
Céleri Villeroy
Dinde Chipolata
Choux-Fleurs à la Hollandaise
Petits Pois à la Menthe
Pommes rôtiés
Pouding de Noël
Pêches Melba
Canapés de Sardines
Dessert

With so many novice sailors aboard, seasickness marred many of these journeys. As the convoys headed out into the North Atlantic, skirting the northern fringes of Ireland, the weather got rough. Despite the lavish fare many QAs lost their appetite and remained confined to their bunks for days, feeling unspeakably ill.

Trying to work on a ship which was continually rolling was deeply frustrating, as one Sister new to medical trooping found. 'On the second night we were kept busy by the rolling ship. Forms and screens fell over and finally we had to abandon their use and leave them on the floor. Bottles in locked dispensary cupboards fell over and continued to roll till morning. In the kitchen a few plates were smashed and we soon found that on board is a place for everything and that place is the safest. It was some consolation to hear that there were considerable breakages in the galley staffed by regular seamen.'[3]

Audrey Hayward, who had waited for five months at a military hospital in Shaftesbury before embarking, shared a cabin with two other girls who were both desperately seasick for the first half of her journey. Like most of them Audrey had left Liverpool without knowing her final destination. 'One of the other QAs predicted it would be West Africa as the name of the ship was *Abosso* of the Elder Dempster line. She knew the line and said it only went to West Africa. The boat had a very shallow draft because it was constructed for going up rivers so she wasn't very stable. I didn't go to breakfast once.'[4]

The *Abosso*, which was carrying a thousand troops, met up with the rest of the convoy off the north-west coast of Ireland. They were a huge array of ships spread out over a wide area of sea . . . lots of merchant ships, destroyers, corvettes and cruisers. I could tell we were sailing north-west by the position of the sun although I didn't understand why . . . but of course we were heading for the mid Atlantic to turn south . . .'

Life on board ship may have been materially luxurious, for the officers at any rate, but all ranks faced the same danger on these sea journeys. The Battle of the Atlantic was raging and the danger of attack to convoys from U-boats or from the air was ever present. The embattled convoys were playing Russian roulette with a hidden enemy that at any time could blow a ship out of the sea without warning. No one knew whether their ship would be the unlucky one. Thousands of merchant ships and troop carriers were sunk in the course of the war and many QAs were killed or shipwrecked as a result. The nurses were not allowed to close their cabin doors at night in case the ship was torpedoed and the doors twisted, trapping them in a sinking or burning vessel, as happened on numerous occasions with tragic consequences.

On the *Abosso* (which the QAs were finally told by Matron *was* bound for West Africa), the whole ship's company religiously practised boat drill every day. As Audrey Hayward remembers: 'The summonses were different, according to whether it was an air attack or a possible U-boat. One was a bell, one was a klaxon. For an air attack there was a station we were to go to on the ship. In the case of a U-boat attack we were to go on deck.'

She says she felt excited, rather than frightened, by the risk. 'We felt we were having an adventure. Things back home in the Blitz were far worse.' Then one day risk became reality.

Suddenly we heard the signal for a possible air attack. I got up to go to Action Stations – not forgetting to get my tin hat and gas mask from the top of the wardrobe. The first bomb hit the water and the ship lurched violently. Then another one fell and the ship toppled the other way. A crew member next to me pulled on his life jacket and shouted, 'Get up, Miss. Get to Action Stations.' One of the other Sisters was absolutely green with seasickness but she still managed a joke. 'I've been praying so hard for those engines to stop . . . and now they have!' And the engines *had* stopped –

because they were damaged. The Captain made an announcement over the Tannoy. He said that two bombs had been dropped by a single plane inflicting limited damage and that no one had been hurt. There was damage to the engine and two fridges and the dining room and breakfast room was all smashed. But if we were prepared to remain on deck for 20 minutes bacon and egg sandwiches would be brought to us.

Audrey and her cabin mates found the emergency proved a surprisingly effective cure for seasickness. 'Those of us who had felt too ill to dress up till then got dressed immediately and went up on deck. There we found that the convoy had disappeared and we were on our own.'

This, coupled with the fact that there might well be a U-boat hunting them, brought home to them how vulnerable they were. 'We were the last ship in the convoy because we were mostly civilians.' However, the engineers managed to get the engines going again before nightfall and they soon caught up with the rest of the convoy.

The Captain sent a tannoy message: 'To everyone aboard the *Abosso*: well done.' A couple of days after that I went up on deck and found that the two cruisers had left but we still had the destroyer. 'That's good,' I thought, 'that must mean that we're safer now.'

There were U-boats around. Two or three times we were summoned up on deck and all the flood doors were closed as an emergency drill. We girls decided to have a panic bag with things we couldn't do without in in case we did have to take to the water. I kept my oil cloth bag tied under my clothes. This led to some teasing in the bar when the men would say 'Let the ladies pay'.

A few days later the QAs learned the real reason the cruisers had left the convoy. The supposedly invincible battleship *Bismarck*, pride of the German fleet, had been sunk in the Atlantic by the Royal Navy. 'The *Dorsetshire* was the name of one of the cruisers escorting us. The reason it had left us was that it had been summoned to join the battle. The *Dorsetshire* had fired the last salvo on the *Bismarck*.'

What they did not know, as they drank a toast to the Royal Navy's victory in the officers' bar that night, was that the *Bismarck* had been sunk in revenge for the sinking of the Royal Navy battleship HMS *Hood*, which had gone down with the loss of 1,415 lives and only three survivors.

The problems of seasickness receded as the ships sailed south, only to be succeeded by problems caused by the baking, breezeless heat. On one ship the officers gallantly swapped their lower deck dormitory for the nurses' sun-blasted cabins on the upper deck knowing they would be cooler as they sailed through the airless Red Sea. The men had a rough time and some captains rigged up funnels made of canvas to try to get some air down to the lower quarters. Most of the ships had a small hospital and the beds soon filled up. There were cases of pneumonia and many of the troops went down with a mystery condition which was like dysentery with flu-like symptoms.

'. . . it was thought by some to (be due to) the very cool nights. Men who had perspired profusely in the intense heat of the day slept on open decks or directly under air-shafts or fans with very little covering. Some admitted during the night certainly suffered acute spasms of abdominal pain or cramp, which was relieved by warmth.'[5]

Not all the troopships were adapted for hot climates, as one Naval Sister travelling with QAs lamented. There was always a shortage of fresh water, for drinking and washing, and on many ships it was only available between 7 and 8 a.m. The women were reduced to 'bird bathing'.

'The worst part was the lack of air conditioning, as our ship was a North Atlantic passenger liner in peacetime, and had no amenities for the tropics. There were no chairs, so we all sat out on the deck, using our rugs spread out and our life-jackets as a cushion, when we could all find enough space to spread ourselves out to this extent.'[6]

Nothing could be done that might attract the attention of the enemy. This ruled out the boisterous 'crossing the line' ceremony which was such a favourite on board in peacetime. They were not even allowed to toss orange peel overboard and no wireless, gramophone or singing on deck was allowed for fear of alerting U-boats. It also meant no sun awning which, through fear of sunstroke, drove the nurses into the much-ridiculed topees. 'Those who had not brought a topee were issued with Army ones . . . and very funny some of them looked too! One sister, being about 5 ft high, looked just like a mushroom!'[7]

The major challenge to the Captains of these huge, heavily over-loaded ships was to keep everybody occupied. Cabin fever was a serious risk, especially in the sticky heat which made people lethargic and irritable. The organisation required to maintain a programme of education and entertainment was extremely demanding. Because of the huge numbers every show that was put on had to be repeated. Happily, in those dynamic days before mass electronic entertainment, there was an impressive pool of talent available to draw on. One QA travelled on a ship which had aboard the organist at the Gaumont Cinema in Hammersmith. He improvised a band and gave concerts to the officers in the lounge or played in the saloon when one of the senior officers had a birthday. The men had concerts most evenings. The ships operated effectively as floating education institutes, gymnasia, theatres and concert halls combined.

For the QAs the day began at 7.30 a.m. with an hour's PE on deck before the sun became too hot. This was followed by several hours of lectures, on a wide variety of topics, including medicine and general culture and, for QAs bound for India, talks aimed at giving them a smattering of vital words in Urdu. There were deck-tennis tournaments and boxing matches for the men.

Phil Dyer, a QA travelling from Lagos to India with a Nigerian regiment, enjoyed the contribution made to entertainment on board by the exuberant Africans.

> Between men, boxing matches took place. The Africans were allowed to enter for the sport. Their antics were not in the least professional but their efforts caused great hilarity.
>
> ENSA [Entertainments National Service Association] rallied forth and gave us a superb evening's entertainment. It was repeated for the Africans and they derived a considerable amount of fascination from the various mysteries produced by the conjurer's act. Determined not to be outdone, they proceeded to give a demonstration of their Black Magic. Another source of entertainment they gave us was music. A brass band played by the Africans of the 35rd Nigerian Regiment. They played extremely well and it was quite fantastic to hear our English tunes played by the Africans.[8]

Nurses with their talent for organising were a boon to have on board.

One QA wrote to the Matron of her old hospital in a way that must have made her proud:

> Life in the boat could have been very boring had we not determined it should not be. We had 38 sisters on our particular ship, nearly eight to one in officers, and countless troops. We took it in turns, two on two days at a time, to be on duty in the hospital . . . I represented the sisters on the Entertainments Committee, and worked jolly hard. We had also a terrifically enterprising Sports Committee and Library Committee . . . we were lucky in having six professional actors and a cartoonist on board. Our main object was to entertain the troops . . . We got up a series of concerts, serious music, bridge, chess and whist drives. Everything you had prepared had to be offered at least seven times to ensure that all the men had a chance of seeing it, so that we always had 60–70 people working hard.[9]

This Sister particularly appreciated the intellectual stimulus. 'Every morning we had three lectures each lasting three quarters of an hour. This we found was a very wise movement on the part of OC troops – it kept you all away from each other. Lectures in Hindustani, medicine, and then one of general interest, such as travel, books, etc. These were of course the nicest . . . The many weeks on board, because of our many activities, flew.'[10]

Despite the heat the Sisters loved their time on board ship. As they glided past exotic shores they saw an unspoilt world, ignorant of high-rise blocks and multi-lane highways, that had remained largely unchanged for centuries.

> Sitting on deck sailing down the Suez Canal to the west a brilliant sun was setting casting off exquisite colourings which changed every second and from the south-east a full moon rising. To add to the enchantment a few camels plodded their way by the side of the canal without a sound.
>
> In the Red Sea, to the left of us was Arabia and from what we saw it appeared to be all desert. Occasionally we would see outlandish posts where British tommies were holding fort. Frantic exchanges of wavings took place while the fingers produced the Victory V sign.[11]

During the long weeks an intense spirit of camaraderie built up between the groups who had travelled all those miles together. Traditionally on the last night there was community singing on deck, in which the whole ship took part. The sound made by those thousands of voices all of whom knew the words of national favourites must have been something to hear. For a while afterwards, nothing felt quite right.

Phil Dyer took one last look at the *Dunnottar Castle* safely docked in its destination port of Bombay and felt a lump in her throat. Would any of them meet again? 'A deserted ship was a very depressing sight and everything appeared quite flat. What a change from the atmosphere of continual hilarity.'

10

The Cruel Sea

Life on the troopships was hectic and fun, but the heavily laden ships were extremely vulnerable to attack. The gaiety of the sing-songs and dances that whiled away the hours above the water contrasted brutally with the silent and invisible enemy that tracked them. Like the old Roman god Janus the sea had two faces, one smiling, the other fearsome. Of the 236 QAs who lost their lives during the war, more than half died at sea. British convoys carrying troops and supplies to the battle zones were sitting targets, and German U-boats lurked everywhere. So much Allied shipping was lost in the Mediterranean during the first years of the war that convoys took the long route via South Africa and the Cape to the Far East. But even here they were not safe. Later on in the war new danger appeared in the form of giant Japanese super-subs, whose armour-plated hulls shrugged off shells as a dog shakes off water droplets.

Hospital ships, which were conspicuously marked with red crosses, were protected from attack by the Geneva Convention, but many German and Japanese pilots and U-boat commanders ignored this stricture and ten were sunk during the war. However, QAs didn't always travel aboard hospital ships and many of the sinkings in which they were caught up were those of merchant ships transporting troops and civilians in addition to cargo.

The attacks often happened at night. Many nurses in those days couldn't swim. To have to jump thirty or more feet down into the black, oil-covered sea, with the fear of imminent explosions, was simply terrifying. Ships in wartime were always heavily overcrowded, so there were never enough lifejackets – or boats. If the ship was listing only half the lifeboats could be launched.

The atmosphere on a badly stricken ship was often one of animal panic – as people fought to get into the lifeboats, and rowed frantically to stop boats from being sucked down with the ship. The reports make harrowing reading: screaming people unable to open their cabin doors because the ship has twisted, lifeboats full of survivors being smashed to matchsticks by the ship's propeller, boats launched without bungs and the occupants drowned . . .

Worst of all, as we have seen, was the experience of the QAs on the heavily overcrowded ships full of mothers and children fleeing the Japanese after the fall of Singapore. Not only were they forced into the sea without lifejackets, but as they struggled to keep friends and loved ones afloat in the water the Japanese returned and systematically shot them.

To read the long pages of the nurses' Roll of Honour is very sad. Next to the brief description 'died at sea' the same dates appear again and again: 14 February 1942; 7 December 1942; 13 September 1943; 12 February 1944. The most haunting are 17 and 19 February 1942, for these deaths are of women who had been torpedoed after fleeing Singapore and had managed to survive for days on life rafts before dying from injury, starvation, heat exhaustion or simply despair.

In both the North and South Atlantic and in the Mediterranean 1942 was a bleak year for Allied shipping.

The first tragedy to involve QAs occurred towards the end of October off the coast of West Africa. A convoy of forty-four ships left Freetown in Sierra Leone. One of these was SS *Stentor*, carrying a number of civilians returning to England on leave, as well as nine QAs on their way home after a year's service with the 56th British General Hospital. The convoy's escort was lighter than usual as all available shipping was being diverted to take part in Operation Torch, the massed Allied invasion of North Africa due to take place a month later. It was to prove a dreadful journey. German Intelligence knew a seaborne invasion of Africa was in the offing, but believed it would take place at Dakar on the Ivory Coast. Because of this the waters off West Africa teemed with U-boats.[1]

The *Stentor* was the first in the convoy to be hit. On 27 October there was a huge explosion as a torpedo found the ship's highly inflammable cargo of manganese.

Joan Hunter-Bates (later Moore) and her friend Marjorie Lloyd were two of the QAs on board. Joan remembered:

> To get out onto the deck from the staircase I had to duck through a doorway of fire, for the bridge was ablaze. She was going down bows first and, as I struggled uphill to the stern, I was joined by 'Taffy' Davis, a Territorial Army Sister. When we found that our lifeboat had already been launched and that we would have to jump about thirty feet to reach it, Taffy went back to a boat amidships which had not yet been launched. I climbed onto the rail and jumped into the water. When I surfaced, covered in oil, the *Stentor* was no more and Taffy Davis was not seen again.[2]

Marjorie Lloyd's foot was caught in the ship's ropes when she jumped from the boat deck and she was hauled into a lifeboat with a twisted ankle as the ship went down. Yet when the corvette HMS *Woodruffe* came to the rescue under cover of darkness, Marjorie somehow managed to climb the scramble net. The sailor waiting on deck to heave on board the clinging figures was expecting a man's weight and flung her high into the air.

'My God,' he said, 'it's a woman.' He had almost tossed Sister Lloyd back into the sea.

'We must have smelt terrible for we were covered in palm oil (part of the ship's cargo) but we had a rub-down and were given some of the crew's clothes. I was a peculiar sight in the Captain's tropical shorts kept up by a bootlace, a pyjama top and long seaboot stockings. Then we learned that four of our fellow QAs were missing.'[3]

The crew of the corvette *Woodruffe*, the escort vessel, were glad to have the Sisters aboard. Many of the survivors they rescued were in a bad way and all they had on board in the way of medical personnel was a sickbay attendant.

One sailor who was on the *Woodruffe* that night says that they never saw the submarine *U-515* – but knew that it was in the midst of them. It attacked the convoy for seven days and seven nights, sinking eleven ships. William Bromage took part in the rescue that night: 'SS *Stentor* was the lead ship and a torpedo hit her on the starboard side killing many. The sea was aflame. We picked up a lot of badly burned men. We used mattresses to carry them on board, though when the mattresses folded as they were lifted the men were in agony.'[4]

An even worse tragedy occurred during the night of 6/7 December 1942 when a ship carrying 656 passengers – military personnel and civilians – was attacked by a U-boat and sunk west of the Azores. The SS *Ceramic* was the largest passenger ship on the Liverpool to Australia run and the civilians included mothers and children fleeing war-torn Britain for the safety of Australia. The *Ceramic* was also carrying twenty-six QA nurses who were to change ship at Durban en route for service in the Middle East. On 23 November the *Ceramic* left Liverpool in convoy, but early in December she left the convoy and continued her voyage alone. At 8 p.m. on the night of 6 December she was hit by a torpedo from a U-boat. Two more torpedoes followed, hitting the engine room. The vessel was plunged into darkness and the crew managed to launch eight lifeboats, all of which were filled to capacity.

The ship did not sink straightaway and after a few hours the U-boat attacked her again, firing two more torpedoes. This assault broke her in two and she sank within a matter of seconds. It was raining and the sea was very rough, causing the lifeboats to be swamped by the waves so that they needed to be constantly baled out. By daybreak the next morning the wind had increased to storm force and the rain turned to hail. Some lifeboats capsized, pitching people into the water with only their life-jackets to support them.

At about midday the U-boat surfaced near the survivors, searching for the ship's captain in order to interrogate him. As there was no sign of the captain two of the U-boat's crew threw a rope to one of the men in the water and took him on board for interrogation. The wind was now reaching typhoon force and the waves easily topped the conning-tower of the U-boat. A lookout from the submarine reported seeing a lifeboat whose occupants waved to him, but no attempts were made to save them. A British cruiser and a Portuguese destroyer which had been sent to look for survivors were beaten back by the storm. Apart from the serviceman who was taken prisoner, everyone died. Eric Munday, who was that survivor, was a 20-year-old sapper in the Royal Engineers when he sailed out of Liverpool aboard the *Ceramic* in the late autumn of 1942. Now in his eighties and living near Croydon to the south of London, Mr Munday remembers every detail of the sinking:

Four of us used to play solo every night when we came off watch. I had just arrived in the saloon that evening when suddenly there was a huge bang and the lights dimmed. We knew it was a U-boat attack. The ship began to list steeply and women who had children down below started screaming. The ship did not sink at first – it took two more torpedoes to sink her – but the Captain gave the order to abandon ship and they began lowering the lifeboats right away. It was pitch dark. There were too many in my lifeboat and it was dangerously low in the water. People who couldn't get in were hanging onto the sides. We fought to keep the boat into the wind so that she would pitch and toss instead of side rolling. The crew were not much help as they all panicked and there was a lot of shouting and yelling. By now, even though it was dark, we could see the *Ceramic* going down.[5]

Eric Munday spent much of the night rowing, in order to keep the lifeboat afloat, but the weather was worsening and the increasingly heavy seas turned it over, throwing him into the sea and forcing him to keep swimming. Daybreak revealed a tragic scene: 'There were lots of bodies in the sea and exhausted survivors clinging to bits of timber and wreckage scattered over the sea . . . I saw other lifeboats still afloat, one of which contained some of the nurses.'

In the fortnight they had been at sea Eric and his friends, who were not officers, had come to regard the nurses with affection. It was not just the cheering sight of their fetching white uniforms. The Sisters had pulled off quite a coup for those status-conscious times, by managing to bring officers and other ranks together for recreation. 'The British officers on board had arranged a dance, to which the nurses, who were also officers, were naturally invited. But Other Ranks were told that the saloon was out of bounds to them. That didn't go down at all well. We then held our own dance in our own quarters and invited the nurses, who accepted. They must have protested at this stuffiness to the powers-that-be because the next day the whole ship was thrown open to us.'

Eric never saw the nurses or his three card-playing friends again. As the rain lashed down and the seas grew mountainous the incredible happened; the diminutive *U-515* that had destroyed the 655-foot long, 18,500 ton *Ceramic*, surfaced. Unable to locate the captain of the

Ceramic, the U-boat commander ordered his crew to throw a line to the nearest survivor swimming frantically among the giant waves. It was Eric. He celebrated his 21st birthday on the U-boat and spent the rest of the war as a POW.*

As he was being hauled aboard the U-515 he had no idea that he would be the only survivor of 655 people. Today he says with sadness: 'I thought lots of them would make it. I heard repeated SOS calls made, both from the *Ceramic* and the U-boat. I thought there would be other ships in the vicinity. I had no idea, until after the war when I was released, that it had been a total loss.'

Just fourteen days after this tragedy, as we have seen in a previous chapter, the *Strathallan* was torpedoed off the coast of Algiers. The loss of life was relatively light but the ship was carrying all the equipment for a general hospital at a time when casualties in North Africa were very high.

To be rescued by the navy from a burning ship was harrowing, but a small handful of QAs experienced an even worse ordeal – surviving a sinking, only to find themselves alone on a vast deserted ocean, to all intents and purposes doomed to die of exposure. Sister J. H. Bates was on board SS *Oronsay* off the coast of West Africa, when it was attacked by a torpedo fired by a U-boat on 9 October 1942. Sister Bates trained at the Middlesex Hospital and joined the QAs in 1939. She was in her mid twenties, had been working in the Middle East and may have been on her way home. The inspirational behaviour of the nurse, a young woman with outstanding leadership qualities, has the power to move us still, some sixty years later:

> On October 9th 1942, I awoke suddenly at 5.30 a.m. and knew instantly that we had been hit by a torpedo. The engines had stopped, the ship was motionless and there was a strong smell of cordite. I jumped out of my bunk and, owing to the sharp list to starboard, felt as though I were standing on the porthole. The electric light had failed . . . For one minute or second I felt utter panic. Then I said: 'Don't be a fool', and found my thick jersey,

---

* Over the last few years Eric Munday has travelled to Germany several times for reunions with members of the U-boat crew who took him prisoner.

overcoat and some slippers. I had no time to tie laces, so slung my flat crepe shoes round my neck and put on my lifebelt. The smell was increasing and I was frightened of fire . . .[6]

The account illustrates chillingly the lottery of the lifeboats, only a fraction of which were usable in an emergency.

The lifeboat was well away from the side of the ship. They gave me a rope and swung me over but I slipped between the lifeboat and the ship. Just as I could hold on no longer, an AB [Able Seaman] caught me under the arms and pulled me into the boat. The others scrambled in after me . . . We then descended with a rush on to another boat, smashing ours. We jumped into the boat below and the men tried hard to row away, but we were completely jammed. The ship was listing badly and we felt she would fall on us. B. my husband, then my fiancé, who was Deputy Purser, could be heard in the distance, and the SMO [Senior Medical Officer] called to him to take me. I half swam, half clambered, over to his boat; the others came too. They rowed away from the ship for about 800 yards, but there were too many in her and she was seeping badly through her seams. I took my coat off and when the water was level with the gunwales B. said: 'When I say "Go", we'll go over the side and swim for it.' We slipped over quite gently, and as we did the men came over on top of us with a rush; one gave me a mighty hit with his fist on the forehead and got me under and another got B. round the neck and pulled him down. Luckily we were both pretty strong and we fought our way clear with mighty kicks. We decided to swim away and chance being picked up rather than go back to this boat . . .

Covered in oil which made her sick and wearing only her badly ripped nightdress, the nurse and her sweetheart swam for an hour in the shark-infested sea, convinced that they were going to die.

Eventually they were picked up by another lifeboat. Their ship was still floating but just after they were rescued, another torpedo, the fourth, hit the ship and she sank before their eyes. 'It was an amazing sight with the sun just rising. I could not have imagined the sea could be so deep. In a few minutes boilers and engines burst and the sea was covered with oil and wreckage.'

And then, just as with the *Ceramic*, the U-boat surfaced and the hunted found themselves face to face with the hunter.

'It was uncanny; you could feel the eyes of the crew. Visions of machine-gunning ran through our minds.'

The U-boat did not attack them, however. Instead they discovered that they were part of a large number of survivors, distributed among a fleet of thirteen lifeboats and two motor launches. Sister Bates was the only woman to survive. The Captain went round pulling survivors out of the sea and allocated them to different boats. They decided to form themselves into two mini 'armadas' each towed by a launch, with the Captain's armada towing eight and the one Sister Bates was in towing the remaining five. During the night the Captain's armada became separated from theirs and when day broke they were alone on a deserted ocean.

'We sailed as an armada for two nights, but the engine of the launch failed . . . and it was thought better for the other four lifeboats to leave us, so they cast us off . . .

'We, the lifeboat that is, now towed the launch. We consisted of 20 men in the launch, 53 men in the lifeboat. They were mostly ship's officers and crew, Australian airmen, English airmen, one Sergeant Gunner and a Sergeant of the RAMC.' There was a wireless set on the launch and every three hours they sent SOS messages. They occasionally heard the incongruous sound of dance music being broadcast from London, but no one answered their distress calls.

They believed that they were 500 miles off the coast of Freetown in Sierra Leone and decided that their best chance lay in rowing in an east-north-easterly direction. That way they estimated that they could make land in twenty-one days. If they rowed due east there was a strong chance they would have to cross the Gulf of Guinea before they reached land, a forty-day journey that they would never survive.

Day after day, under the blazing African sun, the men rowed from 6 a.m. to 10 p.m., each man rowing for an hour with a two-hour interval between shifts. They existed on two small meals a day from the boat's meagre rations – 2 ozs of water, a teaspoonful of Pamican ('a horrible but sustaining Bovril') two biscuits, three squares of chocolate and three Horlicks tablets. This was eaten at 7 a.m. and 6 p.m. with only water in the middle of the day. The Sister was in the bow of the boat and survived on half an hour's sleep in twenty-four as there was nowhere for her to lie down.

Without this extraordinarily self-disciplined young woman they might all have perished. She took charge of the men's well-being, using whatever was available to see that they were fit enough to row and, just as if she were running a hospital on land, holding a 'sick parade' every morning. Men who were ailing were given extra water rations and time to recover.

'The men came out in boils and it was agony for them to sit and row. I put a safety pin in iodine, let it dry and dug down and got the core out, every two hours soaked the place in salt water and in two days it healed. The sunburn on their chests and arms became septic; there was one little tube of Tannafax and I put a smear on and the next day treated it with two hourly salt water.'

Indeed their worst enemy was the sun. 'I had heard from survivors in Aden that the men got terrible feet from dangling them in the sea. B. forbade this, first because of sharks and second because of the sun . . . every half hour while the sun was out every man had a bucket of salt water poured over him. We had one heat exhaustion, completely pulseless, and we organised a team of men who kept throwing continuous buckets of water over him.'

As the days wore on the nurse became increasingly concerned about the mental state of some of the men. '. . . they were terribly irritable and argumentative and we thought they might panic. We hit on the plan that when they looked like cracking they had a little talk with me, and wept, and then B. "braced" them; but it was a bit harrowing when they discussed the best way to go over the side when the end came.'

They were all growing weaker. The men's thirst caused them to fantasise contantly about beer. Sister Bates admitted she had 'a few little weeps myself under the blanket at night'. A shark had been following them for days. She and her fiancé sat in the boat and tried to distract themselves from their hunger by talking about food, but they too were growing weaker. 'B. and I sat and planned menus, but at the end couldn't think coherently what we had said at the beginning of the sentence.'

Then, when the end seemed inevitable, Sister Bates turned round and saw a 'black matchstick' on the horizon. It was a Royal Navy corvette.

Despite the long days of anxiety, thirst and hunger, one further ordeal still awaited her. 'It was horrible going up the rope ladder to board her. Each sailor held a cigarette for us, but our hands shook so we couldn't light them. Our legs were terribly wobbly and we went down to the ward room and had tea and whisky.'

They had been at sea for twelve days. During that time the men had rowed 380 miles.

There are few acts of war more repellent than the killing of helpless, wounded men. Hospital ships were meant to be protected from attack, but many were sunk – some in broad daylight. These disasters inevitably involved QAs.

The first to go was HMS *Newfoundland*, which was hit and sunk by the Germans on 13 September 1943 amid the intense fighting in the days that followed landings at Salerno in Italy. At the time she had a hundred nurses on board and was to take casualties back to Bizerta in North Africa. Two other hospital ships came to help with the survivors: HMHC *St Andrew*, which picked up most of the nurses, and the HMS *Leinster*. Six QA nurses were killed, one in the most horrific circumstances. Some members of the ship's crew had smashed a porthole and many of the nurses escaped this way, but one QA, who was rather plump, stuck in the porthole. The ship was on fire behind her and she was burned to death.

Those who were rescued were taken to Salerno and landed under enemy artillery fire. A 19-year-old private in the Hampshire Regiment, who had gone ashore in the first wave of landings, was there when the rescued nurses came ashore. '[It] . . . was a very frightening experience for these poor women to go through. They were in great spirits and we had great admiration for these very brave nurses.'[7]

In January 1944 as troops and vehicles landed on the beaches at Anzio prior to the assault on Rome, German planes bombed shipping in Anzio Bay. The hospital carrier HMS *St David* was anchored in the bay, acting as a floating hospital. Each day doctors and orderlies would set out in water ambulances to pick up the wounded and take them back to the ship for treatment. On 23 January, in the early evening, a torpedo struck the ship, which began shipping water almost at once. Many of the staff and crew managed to plunge into the icy January sea but some who survived the initial sinking were killed when the ship capsized and her mast came down on one of the lifeboats. Two QAs were among the sixty people who lost their lives in this disaster.

Two more Sisters were among the 106 killed when HMHC *Amsterdam* was sunk by a German mine as she waited off the coast of France to transport casualties back to Southampton from the Normandy landings. Just as with the *St David* at Anzio, the RAMC would go ashore in the ship's LCAs (landing craft assault) to collect the wounded from field hospitals. It took three to four days to load the ship. By the evening of 6 August 1944 the ship was full and due to sail. At about 7 a.m. the next morning, when most people on the ship were still asleep, there was what one crew member remembers as a 'muffled explosion'. The lights went out, and the ship immediately began to list. The explosion broke the ship in two, with one portion listing one way and the other half the other. The ship's propellers, still turning, had lifted out of the water. The weather was foggy and several of the wounded men jumped into the sea which, to make things worse, was rough that day. The ship sank in eight minutes. One crew member who jumped seconds before the ship went down remembers the panic to get off the vessel:

> There was a sergeant in the medical corps standing there, ready to jump over the side. If he had he would almost certainly have hit the propellers and died . . . We found the sergeant a lifejacket and got him over the side to a ledge and then jumped into the water . . . I kept thinking to myself that I had to get away quickly in case I was sucked down with the ship . . .
>
> I could hear a lot of screaming and shouting. I looked around and could see some of the wounded soldiers jumping over the side, and there were two people stuck in portholes. I was told afterwards that they were nurses.[8]

The death toll included fifty-five wounded men and ten medical staff, of which two were QAs.

By far the worst disaster at sea for the QA corps occurred in the Indian Ocean in 1944. The sinking of the troopship SS *Khedive Ismael* on 12 February caused the third-biggest loss of life for a merchant ship in the whole of the Second World War. Out of a ship's company of 1,511, 1,297 were lost. The ship went down in just two minutes. The *Khedive Ismael* had sailed from the East African port of Mombasa and was headed for Ceylon, taking troops and supplies to support the Burma campaign. On board were hundreds of East African infantrymen or *askari* from the King's African Rifles, fighting for the Allied cause under the command of European officers and NCOs. She also carried nearly eighty servicewomen, forty of them QAs, on their way to India and Burma. Most of the other women were members of the Female Auxiliary Nursing Yeomanry Service (FANYS). Only 208 men and six women survived the disaster after being plunged into seas that were not only shark-infested but erupting all round them from the depth charges launched by the escorting destroyers to try to sink the submarine. The catastrophe marked the greatest loss of serving women in the history of the Commonwealth.

The ship, which was part of a convoy of five troopships escorted by a cruiser, was sunk by Japanese submarine *I-27*, a 357-foot long armour-plated leviathan which had been operating in the Indian Ocean since the summer of 1942. She had already sunk 65,000 tons of Allied shipping and the navy was determined to destroy her. The departure from Kenya had been quite spectacular, with a Royal Marine band playing on the cruiser, the crews of the warships lined up on deck and the sailing marked by the traditional raising and lowering of flags. But it had been marred by an incident that was to prove fatally prescient. The *askaris* who were to travel aboard the *Khedive Ismael* had been allowed to go to the cinema while waiting to embark and the film they had seen featured the sinking of ships at sea. Soldiers rather than sailors, they were never very happy at sea at the best of times. The film terrified them and they had to be ordered to board the ship by their officers.[9]

The *Khedive Ismael* was the sub's last victim and her sinking was the cause of one of the most bitter and audacious sea battles of the war. The ferocity of the depth-charge attack by the two destroyers escorting the convoy, HMS *Paladin* and HMS *Petard*, forced the submarine to the surface, whereupon *Paladin* rammed her, opening up a huge gash in her side in the process. *Petard* opened fire on the sub, but the non-armour-piercing shells were no match for the state-of-the-art sub's reinforced casing and failed to pierce her bodywork. The Japanese crew rushed to man the substantial 5.5 in guns on her deck but were quickly killed by the guns from the Royal Navy ships.

The seemingly invincible submarine was finally sunk after a dramatic two-and-a-half-hour torpedo bombardment by HMS *Petard*. In the hands of an inexperienced officer, six torpedoes, fired one by one, missed the target. It was only when the seventh and last torpedo was launched that a direct hit sent the monster to the bottom of the Indian Ocean.

The confused and terrified survivors were taken aboard HMS *Paladin*. The following day was a Sunday and the captain conducted the usual Sunday service on the quarter deck. They sang the navy's traditional hymn, 'Eternal Father, strong to save'. The chorus 'O hear us when we cry to Thee, / For those in peril on the sea' had a special poignancy for all who heard it that day.

IV

NORTH AFRICA AND THE MEDITERRANEAN

11

Flowers in the Desert

From the earliest days of the war Britain – initially alone – had been engaged in a bloody trial of strength with the Italians and Germans in North Africa. The struggle was to last three long years. The cost in lives was immense. Once again the QAs were in the thick of it.

Italy had entered the war in June 1940 and at this time had some 236,000 troops in Libya. British-controlled Egypt was the plum, for whoever ran Egypt controlled the entire Eastern Mediterranean. Emboldened by the decision of French North Africa to side, not with the Allies, but with Vichy France, Mussolini was impatient.

There were few roads in the desert and the supply route from the Libyan border to Alexandria lay through two British bases, Sidi Barrani and Mersa Matruh. The Italian commander Marshal Rodolpho Graziani was under intense pressure from Mussolini to advance, but was reluctant to engage what he deemed an inadequate force in a venture that risked his army outrunning its supply line. On 16 September the Italian 10th Army occupied Sidi Barrani, after the British 7th Armoured Division had been ordered to fall back before the advance. Instead of pressing on to Mersa Matruh, which lay 75 miles ahead, Graziani delayed his advance, preferring to equip Sidi Barrani so that it could serve as a forward supply base. The British attack on 9 December in which a force of 36,000 took on an enemy five times that size caught the Italians off guard. The British Armoured 7th Division and the Western Desert Force under the command of Lieutenant General Sir Richard O'Connor cut the Italian 10th Army in two and took 38,000 prisoners against 624 British dead. In the camps the POW cages were crammed – 'Five acres of officers, 200 acres of Other Ranks' – crowed a jubilant Winston Churchill.[1]

After that, the British chased the humiliated Italians back across Libya in a triumphant onslaught that won them Bardia, Benghazi and, on 21 January 1941, the greatest prize of all – Tobruk. The significance of Tobruk was that it was a deep-water port, and thus a far more efficient base for landing troops and supplies than the long and gruelling land route from Alexandria.

But the surging Allied tide was reversed when the following month the German Afrika Korps entered the fray under the command of General Erwin Rommel, who was to become one of the most acclaimed commanders of the Second World War. Rommel's brief was to finish the job the Italians had bungled – to wrest Egypt from the British. He almost succeeded. For the next two years the desert became the scene of some of the bloodiest fighting of the war as the two armies battled it out. At first Rommel seemed unstoppable, storming east and recapturing all the territory the Allies had taken from the Italians. He won back Tobruk in June 1942 after a vicious seven-month siege, and forced the British back inside the Egyptian border.

Rommel's advance was halted on 23 October 1942, just 60 miles from Alexandria at El Alamein, and the balance began to tilt in the Allies' favour. Key factors were the appointment of General Montgomery as commander of the British Eighth Army, increased air power and the supply by the United States of super-modern tanks and the latest long-range guns. Now it was Rommel's turn to fall back. Monty's Eighth Army, backed up by 1,200 aircraft, inflicted a catastrophic defeat on Rommel and his troops. The casualties were colossal. The Allies lost 13,560 men, of whom 4,610 were killed or missing; the Axis losses were twice that – twenty-five thousand killed and wounded and thirty thousand prisoners. What remained of Rommel's seemingly invincible Panzer army was now, like the Italians two years earlier, in full retreat westward. In less than a year Rommel would be driven back further, even, than his starting point at Tripoli, to Tunis, and, eventually, out of Africa altogether.

Throughout the three years of the North Africa campaign QAs followed the zigzagging Allied battle line, tending fearful casualties caused by the ever-present landmines or the repeated tank battles that were such a feature of the desert campaign, and sharing the same rugged conditions as the troops.

Molly Budge (later Jennings) served in North Africa for the entire three years of the campaign, beginning at El Tahag in Egypt and ending up 800 miles west in Tripoli. She sailed out of Southampton in the converted liner *Cameronia* in the spring of 1940. To avoid the danger of U-boats the ship took the long route round the north of Ireland, down the coast of Africa and then up into the Red Sea and through the Suez Canal to set up No. 2 General Hospital. On the journey Molly had palled up with three other young nurses. The high-spirited girls had dubbed their bunks 'Cabin X' and were determined to stay together. As the bone-shaking army transport deposited them at Tahag, the isolated desert destination which was the location of No. 2 General Hospital, the four took over a tent which instantly became known as Cabin X as well. Tahag was about 90 miles from Cairo and 20 miles west of Ismailia on the Suez Canal. When Molly and her fellow QAs arrived, the thousands of Allied troops billeted there awaiting Mussolini's invasion were in a state of acute readiness for war. The nurses were there to care for the 7th Armoured Division of the Eighth Army, which was made up of one Indian two and British divisions. Menaced by Italy's North African Empire from the south and west and from Vichy French-controlled Syria in the north, Egypt and the Suez Canal were now surrounded by enemies. There was no fighting when the nurses arrived and they spent the first four days getting used to the discomfort of life under canvas and setting up the wards.

'Our tents were already equipped with camp beds, folding chairs and canvas washbasins,' says Molly. 'Next to each bed was a rush mat and in the centre of each was a jerry pot upside down. The sight of them reduced us to fits of giggles, but the pots were just a foretaste of how primitive our living conditions would turn out to be.'[2] The girls had come equipped with bedrolls and army-issue 'Beatrice' stoves. These ran on paraffin which also fuelled their lamps. Like almost everything else in the desert, paraffin was in short supply and there was often not enough to fill all the lamps. The girls used their Beatrice stoves not just for warming up a bedtime drink and heating their freezing tents (desert nights were cold) but also for heating flat irons to press their uniforms. But in a climate in which the daytime temperature in summer could top 122° Fahrenheit (50° Celsius) the most difficult aspect was the lack of water:

Every so often a tanker would drive out into the desert where we were and deliver the water. We were only allowed two pints a day, one for drinking and one for washing. And this meant not just our bodies, but our uniforms too.

This was not easy as then the QAs were still wearing their traditional uniform of grey or white dresses and white veils. The girls fetched their water ration from the Mess in our camp kettles and became extremely resourceful at conserving water.

We kept clean by strip-washing our bodies in two halves. Then, when that was done, we poured the water back into our kettles and boiled it up again on the Beatrice stove for our hotwater bottles.

Everything that was needed to construct a field hospital came folded up in labelled packing cases on the backs of lorries and Molly and the other QAs spent four days turning a succession of huge empty tents into forty-bedded wards. The highly efficient system followed a time-hallowed formula. The folding bedframes were assembled in twos and then the bed 'sandwiches' would be unpacked. These were two mattresses, complete with pillows, sheets and blankets, which had been made up and sandwiched together at the base for speedy assembly on site. Old packing cases were commandeered as bedside lockers. Behind a screen at one end the Sister would have her Beatrice stove – every drop of water had to be boiled before use. An up-turned soapbox stood in as a medicine cupboard and the 'ward' was ready for action.

Within four days, however, the pleasing ritual of setting up was forgotten and casualties were pouring into the wards at the rate of forty at a time. In advance of the anticipated invasion by the Italians the British Armoured Division had begun to make daily raids across the Libyan frontier. Although the raids inflicted harsh punishment on the Italians, casualties on the British side were high as well and Molly was shocked by her first head-on encounter with the bloody reality of war.

The wounded came to us straight off the battlefield and we got them ready for theatre. Some were in a lot of pain. The injuries caused by shrapnel or landmines were horrific and we'd never seen battle injuries. We saw soldiers who were little more than boys with arms and legs blown off, terrible stomach wounds, head injuries . . . The worst sight was a soldier who had had his lower jaw blown off. There was nothing to support his tongue which just hung down. In the end the doctors had to do a makeshift operation which stitched his tongue muscle to his upper jaw. At the beginning it was really hard to cope with all this suffering.

She was equally unprepared for the mental damage inflicted by frontline action. 'There were also a lot of men whose nerves had gone, and these were very sad cases. All army hospitals have high numbers of psychiatric cases. They called it shell shock or Battle Fatigue syndrome. These men were absolutely exhausted. When the guns started up they would hide at the bottom of their beds.'

The young nurses did not have much opportunity to form relationships with the injured soldiers, since the average length of stay in a field hospital was only four days. As soon as the men were well enough to travel they were sent in convoys to Cairo and Palestine. But the memory of one soldier did stick in her mind.

We had Gurkhas in the 7th Armoured Division. Their speciality was crawling along the ground, right up to where the enemy – Germans or Italians – were standing in their slit trenches and slicing off protruding heads with their ultra-sharp knives which were called *kookris*. I nursed a badly wounded Gurkha – he had lost an arm and a leg below the knee. He was very down. They are a warrior race and he knew he would never be able to fight any more – or go home a hero because he was disabled – so he gave me his *kookri*. I wonder what his life was like after that.

Front-line nursing was not just a question of getting used to the emotional stress. For those QAs and medical staff who battled so heroically to care for the injured in desert hospitals in 1940 the most sinister enemy was the inhospitable desert itself. One Sister, who had just been posted to Alexandria, vividly evoked the hardship of this isolated life. 'Sand, sand, and more sand, tents and huts, palpitating heat and a feeling of lethargy and monotony hanging over everything. This I think is more trying than the greatest danger, the hardest work, than anything I have yet come up against.'[3]

The desert bred rats and flies and mosquitoes and scorpions by the hundreds, and poisonous spiders which hid in the girls' beds. 'Everyone going to the latrines carried a stick to beat off the rats . . . They built their nests in the short concrete walls constructed at the base of the tent sides and would scurry up the mosquito netting over the patients' beds. They developed a taste for plaster of paris, and nibbled away at any exposed piece they could find. Immobilised patients beat them off their plastered limbs with long poles. A Sister was attacked by a horde of the creatures as she went about the ward one night by the light of a torch.'[4]

For Molly Jennings the insects were the worst aspect of desert life:

> Sandflies used to get blown in from the desert by the wind and got into everything. Everyone carried some sort of fly swat to protect themselves. The Sergeant had sticks with real horsetails, which were very efficient, but we had to make do with ordinary fly swats. The patients' beds were netted to keep out the sandflies and this created real problems with the big Victorian veils we wore. The beds were quite low and parting the net while carrying a tray laden with food or medicines without your veil slipping off was quite tricky.
>
> There were horrible scorpions which used to hide in our beds. You always stripped them back before getting in at night to check. I collected tin lids and stole some paraffin from the Mess. I filled the lids with paraffin and then stood each of the four legs of my bed in them so that the scorpions drowned in the paraffin.[5]

Later in the North African campaign, tented wards were increasingly replaced by Nissen huts, but at this early stage tents were the norm, and in desert conditions the British army tent was a disaster. Everyone dreaded the *hamsean* or *kamsin*, the hot wind that howled in, with its cargo of fine gritty sand, from the central desert. During a sandstorm nurses said the sand could get into a hermetically sealed jar. The *hamsean* blew at 50 miles an hour, shredding tents, lifting the roofs off buildings, smashing glass and china and leaving a fine layer of sand on everything, so that brown blankets and white sheets were indistinguishable. While a sandstorm was blowing surgery was impossible – often for days at a stretch — and food inedible. One storm was so violent it broke the kingpole in Molly's tent.

The sand got into the pores of the skin, refusing to be dislodged by water, which accentuated the nurses' feeling of never being clean. Molly finally solved the problem when a troop from ENSA, the company that organised shows for troops in action, made a rare trip out into the desert. 'They gave me some of the cream they used to take their stage makeup off with. That got it out.'

Living conditions in a desert hospital were exceedingly spartan — at least for the British, who usually seemed to have inferior equipment to their neighbours, ally or foe. The Italians, veterans of desert living, had superior tents which didn't blow down. They didn't rely on pegs and ropes, which were never very solid in sand, but used well-dug-in poles inside and sandbags round the outside.

The food was basic and monotonous; dreary meals taken in the Mess tent on folding wooden chairs and tables, which revolved round two staples — corned beef and the universally detested fatty Maconochie's stew. Hard army biscuits, which reminded the nurses of dog biscuits, were broken up and mixed in as carbohydrate. There was no fruit, apart from dates, though cigarettes and alcohol were widely available.

'I smoked in those days — Craven A,' Molly recalls, 'and we usually had a bottle of whisky on the go.'

At this stage although there were plenty of Americans fighting in the desert, they did not yet have their own hospitals and were nursed by QAs. One American patient was appalled at the rough scratchy army blankets the nurses had to make do with and came back with some soft wool blankets for them.

Sheets, for the QAs, were just a memory. Molly used her ingenuity: 'In the absence of sheets we managed to get hold of several rolls of shroud material. We'd roll out our hairy army blanket, place shroud material on top to make a bottom sheet, then another layer of shroud material as a top sheet, topped by a second hairy army blanket. I hung onto my shroud material after the war ended and it turned out to be very useful. I dyed it and turned it into a perfectly serviceable pair of dining room curtains.'

Nursing in the desert meant not just battle casualties, but injuries inflicted by the pitiless, inescapable sun, which caused everyone to drip with perspiration and became a sinister enemy in its own right. In the early summer months if much outdoor work was being done in the area, between forty and fifty cases of heat exhaustion might need treatment in one afternoon. Milder cases were entrusted to orderlies who regularly showered the men with cold water, under the watchful eye of the Medical Officer, and usually recovered in a matter of hours, but more serious cases required more dramatic intervention.

> A man would collapse suddenly in a dehydrated condition. Sweating stopped, and the whole of the body's heat-regulating mechanism was thrown out of gear. Left untreated, a man's temperature would continue to rise to 108 and sometimes 110 degrees, taking him through convulsions and coma to death.
>
> To bring his temperature down when no air conditioning was available was no easy task. Treatment was immediate and intensive. Naked except for a covering sheet, he was placed on a bed beneath an electric fan. Ice was packed round his groins, armpits and spine, and he was doused from time to time with cold water. To reduce internal heat, he was given cold enemata and intravenous transfusions of saline and glucose. When he began to respond, his chilled body had to be gently rewarmed with most assiduous monitoring.[6]

Molly Jennings regularly treated soldiers for burns which were not the result of enemy action but caused by the sun heating the rails of the open lorries to such a temperature that anyone leaning against them on a long journey risked getting burned through their shirts.

One of the effects of severe heatstroke was that many of the men developed a sudden and severe type of dysentery, very difficult to nurse with such a restricted and monotonous diet. Molly hit on a solution when desert Bedouin tribesmen took up camp in the vicinity. Their travelling food supply included small hens which they packed into wicker cages when they travelled.

'I was always looking for diversions whenever there was a lull in the fighting and they were quite approachable. I thought a nice poached egg, with its binding properties, might help my dysentery patients. I knew Arabs liked tea so I carefully saved our old tea leaves, dried them and took them down to the Bedouin and bartered old tea leaves for fresh eggs.'

The Middle East was a hotbed of serious – and potentially fatal – infectious diseases and much of the nurses' time was taken up caring for soldiers with smallpox, diphtheria, typhoid fever, poliomyelitis. There was even the odd case of bubonic plague. This placed the nurses at considerable personal risk and many showed outstanding bravery in this area. Several were decorated for dangerous nursing.

The Matron of 63rd BGH (British General Hospital) at Helmieh, about 10 miles from Cairo, was deeply impressed by the courage shown by one of her nurses caring for a diphtheria patient. The man had had a tracheotomy, but was still having difficulty breathing.

> I hurried to the soldier's bedside, for it was obvious that a plug of mucous must be blocking the airway. I found Sister Anne Roberts . . . behind the screens, quite cool and calm.
>
> 'He's all right now, Matron,' she said.
>
> The man was indeed all right and breathing easily through his tracheotomy tube. On his locker was a bowl and a catheter. Sister Roberts had saved his life, and put her own in extreme danger by sucking out the plug of mucous from his throat through the catheter. God must have been watching over that brave woman, for she did not catch the disease.[7]

Trying to contain an outbreak of a serious disease in a primitive desert hospital was a perpetual challenge. The infected were nursed in tents isolated from all other patients and the nurses, who were vaccinated, also wore barrier clothing. In one hospital in North Africa a case of smallpox was being nursed in a tent pitched a mile from the rest of the hospital – yet three more patients in another ward contracted the disease. Puzzled and frustrated the commanding officer decided to visit the isolation tent to see if he could solve the mystery.

'His eye fell on a thin trail of ants crossing the tent floor. This was not an unusual sight in the desert, but these ants carried the dried crusts which dropped from the skin of the sick man. Here was the mode of transmission. The Isolation Tent was moved a further five miles from the rest of the hospital, and there were no more outbreaks of smallpox.'[8]

As the 7th Armoured Division continued to harry the Italians in the build-up to the anticipated invasion, the isolated desert life offered little in the way of diversions. But the nurses were young and inventive. ENSA rarely made it out to No. 2 BGH in those early days, so Molly and a group of officers set up their own theatrical company and put on a couple of plays. The girls had already discovered that the orderlies harboured all sorts of unexpected talents and one of them made Molly a costume out of a German parachute. Another, who they discovered had been a hairdresser in civilian life, was pressed into setting their hair.

The presence of women brought a poignant home-making touch to these arid field hospitals. One Sister describes how she made a garden in the sand. 'Every time a truck . . . comes up, you get them to bring you a present of a little mud – maybe it's only a seven pound jar, but that's enough to grow a flowering cactus. And you've no idea how nice those tented wards can look.'[9] Molly even acquired pets:

> I adopted two kittens whom I called Aristophanes and Mahitabel. I rolled up one of my stockings, turned it into a toy ball and tied it to the tent and the kittens would play with it for hours. One day someone brought me a big box containing a desert lizard which had been injured – he was about a foot and a half long. We called him Leonard and brought him grubs and nursed him back to health. I also had a pet chameleon which lived on a big twig on my desk and sometimes rode about on my cap.

The job of QAs based, like Molly, in field hospitals, was to get the soldiers fit for action again as soon as possible and to clear the beds for the next batch. The more seriously wounded were evacuated to base hospitals by hospital ship. It would be hard to exaggerate the heroic role these ships played in bringing thousands of wounded and exhausted men to safety. Throughout the war they doggedly plied their mercy journeys, often in conditions of extreme peril, taking stretchers on board over rough seas from blasted jetties, under attack from land, sea and air. Although their distinctive red crosses were supposed by international convention to make them immune from attack, ten were sunk in the course of the war. The ships were equipped with a full complement of nurses, many of whom remained with their ships for years. During the gruelling North African campaign, being posted to a hospital ship was one more way in which QAs found that the front line had come to them.

The hospital ship *Somersetshire* made so many journeys between Alexandria and Tobruk between December 1941 and March 1942 that she was affectionately dubbed The Old Tobruk Warrior by the men fighting in the western desert. The acting Matron described in a letter to the Matron-in-Chief the challenge of loading the wounded while under fire:

Owing to the depth of water required by the Hospital Ship *Somersetshire* . . . we were unable to anchor within a mile and a quarter of shore. This meant that the embarkation of the sick and wounded was a long and very tedious task. We only possessed two motor launches and these had to tow two or three lifeboats to and from the jetty. The jetty was somewhat damaged and in consequence each stretcher had to be lowered some four or five feet from the end of it into the lifeboat. Each lifeboat could take nine stretcher cases and two or three sitters.

. . . On our first visit to Tobruk we embarked about 540 very sick and badly wounded patients. There was constant bombardment throughout the day and we saw shells bursting on the foreshore and on the sand dunes, and also hitting the water. Unfortunately we were unable to finish embarking patients before nightfall and had to spend the night where we were. And what a night it was! Nearly eleven and a half hours of bombardment. We had arranged beforehand that half the nursing sisters and RAMC orderlies should go to bed at 9 p.m. until 2 a.m. and the remainder from 2 a.m. to 7 a.m. However, I don't think many of them went to bed at all, and certainly not to sleep; it was much too noisy. We were truly thankful to leave Tobruk at 7.30 the following morning, December 7th.

About 4 o'clock in the afternoon we suddenly heard four terrific explosions, followed by the rat-tat-tat of a machine gun. We appeared to 'shudder', but mercifully no harm was done. After circling round for a while the bomber flapped his wings and departed.[10]

The *Somersetshire* was in harbour at a time of great rejoicing – when the British wrested control of Tobruk from the Italians. Her reception reveals how rare the sight of a white woman was to the troops stationed in Africa.

> At Tobruk on the morning of the 16th [December] the OC asked me if I would like the honour of being the first woman ashore since the invasion. If so, I could go ashore that morning . . . and take two or three of the Sisters with me . . . we paid a visit to the Base Hospital. Everyone was very pleased to see us and on our way back to the jetty a lad of the Royal Tank Corps ran out of a shattered building and, touching me on the shoulder, said in a bewildered voice, 'You are a woman then; you are real!' He then stepped back and saluted, saying, 'Pardon me, but I thought I must have had "one over the eight" last night; I haven't seen a woman for over ten months.' . . . Several lorries, armoured cars, etc. were slowed down in order that the occupants could satisfy themselves that we were really 'women'.[11]

The rejoicing was short-lived, however, and within a few months Rommel was laying siege to the strategic port. Now there was more need than ever for the *Somersetshire*'s doughty presence and in five months she brought over six thousand patients out of Tobruk. The ship had to lie some way off because the harbour was choked with sunken Italian ships. This time patients were loaded 750 at a time and the process took two days, invariably over choppy seas and under constant shelling.

Mary Evans had been based on the *Somersetshire* throughout the siege of Tobruk, and witnessed her final hours. She recounts the story with the matter-of-factness the Sisters invariably displayed:

> Three times we were dive-bombed and machine-gunned; and we were finally torpedoed on Easter Tuesday in 1942. Luckily it happened as we were on our way into Tobruk, so no patients were on board. Six of the nursing orderlies and one Indian seaman lost their lives . . . and the rest of us were in the boats within five minutes of the ship being hit. After seven hours we were picked up by a Greek destroyer, the *Queen Olga*, and she circled our own ship the whole

of that night until tugs came out from Alexandria to escort her into port.[12]

While Molly Jennings tended wounded soldiers in the desert her colleagues at No. 6 BGH were tending, albeit reluctantly, a celebrity patient. Farouk, the King of Egypt, was well known to readers of the gossip columns in England, where photos of his huge bulk appeared regularly heading tales of excess. One day a flustered Lieutenant burst into the operating theatre and announced that King Farouk had been injured in a car accident and was demanding treatment. The theatre Sister, Violet Bath, was not the sort of woman to kow-tow to a man of Farouk's reputation. King or no king he had to be loaded on to a trolley. The only problem was that the trolleys were held together by butterfly nuts and bolts, for easy transportation.

> With great difficulty his massive body was heaved onto the trolley. A slow tearing sound came from beneath his frame and almost in slow motion he collapsed through the trolley and lay partly supported, arms stretched out.
> It took all our efforts to extricate him from a mess of twisted tubes and canvas. Then we got him wedged onto another trolley. I was walking alongside him . . . with his eunuchs trailing behind, when I felt his arm sliding up my arm higher and higher.
> 'Get him undressed,' I said to the orderlies.
> Two minutes later the orderly came back. The king was refusing to cooperate. Sister Bath stormed in.
> 'Here, prop up his back,' I said to the orderly. And I debagged him, the horrible man.[13]

Farouk had a suspected fracture of the pelvis but Sister Bath was outraged by the royal patient who dared to try and take over her hospital. 'He brought his own cooks who set up the kitchen outside the officers' ward. One of his eunuchs had to taste all the food first to make sure it was not poisoned. That weekend we had a concert in a large tent. Halfway through a messenger came in and announced "Will the cook go back to the officers' ward. Farouk wants his dinner." You can imagine the roars of laughter.'[14]

A striking defeat in the German struggle for control of the

Mediterranean was their inability to conquer the little island of Malta. The British colony withstood incessant pounding by the Italian and German air forces until the balance of power had shifted to the Allies. Once again British army nurses found themselves on the front line.

12

Under Siege in Malta

Things in the Mediterranean looked bleak for Britain in the autumn of 1941. America had not yet entered the war and Britain was battling Germany and Italy for control of a seaway that was crucial in maintaining supply lines to troops in Egypt and North Africa, as well as to the rest of the Empire. German U-boats had been inflicting heavy losses on British shipping in the area for months and towards the end of the year two sinkings marked the lowest ebb of the war. On 13 November a U-boat sank *Ark Royal,* one of the Royal Navy's most celebrated aircraft carriers, whose fighter-bombers played such a vital role in defending the convoys. Two weeks later the battleship HMS *Barham* was torpedoed, exploding with the loss of all 859 men. These ships had formed the backbone of Force K, dedicated to harrying Axis convoys taking supplies into North Africa. With Force K knocked out, and supposedly no one left to defend her, the Axis powers turned their firepower on Malta. With its magnificent harbour at Valetta, Malta, a British colony since 1800, was a prize of the utmost strategic importance.

What came to be known as the siege of Malta began the week before Christmas 1941. For the best part of a year waves of Italian and German bombers roared over the island, sometimes three times a day, pounding and strafing and reducing much of the colony to rubble. From 1 January to 24 July 1942 there was only one 24-hour period when no bombs fell on Malta. The principle targets were the naval base and the airfield, from which Spitfires flew out to engage in spectacular dogfights with invading Messerschmitts. Unfortunately the island's main military hospital stood on a hill overlooking the dockyard and for almost a year the Matron and her staff of QAs found themselves on the front line of a bloody and prolonged battle. It was an abrupt change from the life Malta had known. Imtarfa Military Hospital had admitted thirty casualties for the whole of 1940 and fifty-eight in 1941. Yet in the next month – January 1942 – 896 casualties were admitted, of whom 791 were still there at the end of the month. Many of the casualties were RAF, but even more were from the Royal Navy. As in the sieges of the Middle Ages supplies of everything began to dwindle – coal, vital for sterilising as well as keeping warm, medical supplies and food. As a result of the emergency the nurses abandoned their official roles and lent a hand wherever it was needed. QAs who were meant to be employed as theatre sisters found themselves acting as Casualty Clearing Station staff, treating wounded men on the battlefield and preparing them for surgery. One Sister tended the injuries of a South African pilot, loading him into an ambulance and bringing him up to the hospital herself. Other victims to whom the nurses gave vital first aid were a group of men who were wounded when a gun position just below the medical officers' mess received a direct hit.

At this time letters between Malta and Britain were taking up to two months to reach their destination. Notwithstanding this the Matron of the 1,200-bed Military Hospital at Imtarfa, Maud Buckingham, charted the progress of the siege in a series of vivid letters to the Matron-in-Chief, Dame Katherine Jones. Matron Buckingham, a veteran of the First World War, combines all the elements of a British Army officer during wartime. Her reports are controlled and matter-of-fact, dismissive of personal danger, and frequently tinged with a peculiarly British brand of gallows humour.

'The hospital is on top of a bare rocky plateau overlooking one of the aerodromes. In such a small island it was impossible to have all the hospitals out of range of military targets, and we suffered in consequence. The aerodrome was bombed heavily and regularly, day and night, in an effort to put it out of action completely. The army went to the help of the Air Force and infantry regiments filled in the craters on the runways almost as soon as they appeared. These men were without shelter of any kind and suffered many casualties.'[1]

Displaying the true Blitz spirit, which was able seemingly to make light of the worst horrors, Miss Buckingham explains how nursing staff arranged their time so that the bombers did not interfere too much with the working day. 'The enemy appeared at 7 a.m., midday and 6 p.m. We used to watch the first as we were scrambling to get dressed for breakfast; we spent the second raid in the theatre or the mess, according to whether we went to first or second lunch; and if there were several casualties to do during the afternoon we planned whether we would finish before "the six o'clock raid"; we usually made that raid an interlude for tea'.

The Italian planes usually flew in in a formation of five, which got them cheerfully dubbed 'The Frightful Five' by hospital staff. The Messerschmitts, on the other hand, used to 'play hide and seek up and down the blocks of the Barrack Hospital'.

The Messerschmitts became more circumspect when a squadron of Spitfires, heroes of the Battle of Britain, arrived on the island. They were given a rousing welcome by the beleaguered inhabitants.

'. . . The first time they went into action was rather more exciting than usual . . . because the fighters went in to attack the Ju. [Junker 88s] formations over the island . . . instead of turning over the hospital for their dive onto the aerodrome, they (the Jus) came straight on and a 1,000-pound bomb came down with a terrific swish, bounced once and came to rest leaning up against the mortuary wall! It was followed by a couple of 500-pounders which also failed to explode.'

The sole defenders of the island in the early stages of the siege were the pilots of four Sea Gladiator aircraft. These were biplanes specially adapted to land on aircraft carriers and had been brought to Malta in crates to resupply aircraft carrier squadrons at sea. Because of the emergency they were quickly assembled and flown by the RAF. The pilots of the planes, affectionately known as Faith, Hope and Charity, were regarded as celebrities. '. . . the pilots were very well known, especially one man called Taylor. He shot down an incredible number of planes and the Maltese announcer used to mention him by name over the local "news", thank him when he was successful and condole with him if he had failed to score.'

When a raid was on the planes flew so low the people on the ground could see every detail, including the bombs leaving their housing as they headed for the ground. One heavy raid occurred during the afternoon as Miss Buckingham was helping the surgeon with a patient who had sustained a head injury. 'I looked up at one extra heavy crash and saw a

JU.88 just outside the window! I remember clutching the patient's head and bracing myself for another crash, but nothing happened and the plane roared over the roof . . .'

The incredible fact is that facing this kind of sustained bombardment day after day some people got used to it. Miss Buckingham clearly had a sneaking regard for the British phlegm displayed by two orderlies during what must have been a terrifying experience.

> We had all been standing out on the balcony watching the raiders come in. Suddenly we knew that three bombs had left the planes too late to hit the aerodrome. We could see them shining in the bright sunlight, and we all lay down as flat as we could while hell was let loose around us. I was working with a naval sister at the time, and presently she passed me on her 'tummy' making for the door into the theatre . . . Head to feet we crawled under cover . . . to find two orderlies sitting comfortably under the colonel's desk having a quiet cigarette.

Even at a time of intense personal danger Miss Buckingham's wry sense of humour did not fail her. Describing a very bad raid in which two Sisters were badly injured and had to be dug out from beneath a layer of debris, she notes: 'Among all the wreckage of dust, water from broken pipes, glass, blocks of stone, and general muddle, a little motto still hung on the wall in Matron's damaged bedroom, triumphantly asserting, although a little askew, "Don't worry. It may not happen." '

Throughout the freezing winter the siege tightened its grip. Casualties poured in from the naval dockyard which was bombed repeatedly. There was great sadness on 10 January when the wounded from HMS *Illustrious* were brought in. *Illustrious*, an ultra-modern aircraft carrier with a proud history of defending Malta convoys, had been so badly damaged by German dive-bombers that she would remain out of action for nearly a year. The injured were operated on in a hastily converted cellar beneath the Barrack Hospital. The Sister-in-Charge, who had already done most of the conversion work herself, scrubbing floors, cleaning out cobwebs and whitewashing walls, worked for 48 hours without a break.

As the weeks went by supplies began to run out and the nurses were forced to improvise.

The really hard time was when fuel became very short; we only had steam for the autoclave* twice a week to do all the sterilising for the entire hospital of over 1,200 beds, as well as for the second theatre in the Barrack Hospital. Primus stoves were old to begin with, and we could get no new ones or spare parts. We were reduced to manufacturing primus 'prickers' from broken flyswats . . . When we could no longer have hot radiators because of the lack of coal, we used to try to take the chill off the big theatre with five oil stoves. I have seen Miss Albrecht [another Sister] black to the elbows after wrestling with one of them. Wicks were not obtainable, so we made them out of old blanket, and, of course, the fuel was adulterated and would not burn. As soon as the operation was about to begin we had to carry the stoves out and keep the patient as warm as possible with hot water bottles. This . . . was all in wintertime and it can be bitterly cold in Malta, especially at night when the *gregale* blows from the north . . .

The next thing to run low was medical supplies. 'We were rationed to one pint of spirit per week and one gallon of Dettol per month. Test-tubes, rubber gloves, catgut and some drugs, quick drying plaster bandages and X-ray films were all rationed monthly . . . Whenever there was a night raid the lights were sure to fail, and, when the emergency supply failed too, we carried on with hurricane lamps and torches.'

They even had to ration food, though Miss Buckingham makes light of it. 'We were a bit hungry for a time, and it was not very funny when it came to counting out the slices of bread for breakfast and tea, but we always had more to eat than the civilian population, which really did starve – one tin of bully beef per fortnight and 9 ounces of bread per day was their ration for a time.'

From February 1941 to November 1942 Maud Buckingham, like the dedicated army officer she was, kept a meticulous diary, noting without emotion the number of raids the island received in a day, the number of bombs dropped, the damage to property and the casualties. By April 1942 she is convinced that the enemy are including the hospital among its targets. On 25 May 1942 she notes that four 200 lb bombs fell 'at the

* A pressurised container used for sterilising medical equipment.

NE end of the football pitch'. The gymnasium, which had been turned into a sixty-bed ward, suffered a direct hit.

She records admissions for May as 549 and for June as 434. Her entry for 5 July 1942 reads: 'Blitz on Bk Hospital' and for July 13th 'Blitz 5 bombs outside Quarters (Sisters'). Mrs Hanublin severely injured and died later.'

From July she was no longer filling in her records of numbers of patients in and out. But the merciless pounding continued. The entry for 3 November, almost a year after the siege began, reads: 'Blitz on Mess. S [Sister] Miss Marchant S Miss Janneson injured. Roof of Mess. Top corridor and annexes. Sisters' rooms extensive damage – Annexes and staircase maids' quarters destroyed. Storerooms and annexes downstairs destroyed. Sisters' rooms and annexes downstairs extensive damage. Front staircase and halls up and downstairs, matron's sitting room badly damaged. Doors and windows downstairs destroyed – water main burst . . .'

In a letter to Dame Katherine Jones, Miss Buckingham describes the tragic circumstances under which, in the pitch black, one of the Sisters was injured: 'The upper corridor leading to the Sisters' bedrooms was almost completely destroyed, and the bedrooms and equipment badly damaged. One Sister walked from her room into space and received spinal injuries. Another Sister was saved from this fate by the timely use of a torch. Others were found under tables, wardrobes and beds, but apart from minor cuts and bruises, and a certain amount of shock, they were unharmed.'

A vital supply of food the Sisters had managed to secure was less fortunate. 'For several months prior to this mishap we had been keeping poultry and feeding them to the best of our ability . . . We had recently succeeded in completing a new hen house and run, but alas this was destroyed, together with the hens. . . . Our kitchen on this fateful morning was a grim study in dust and rubble, breakages and feathers!'

One night the hospital air-raid shelter received a direct hit, but miraculously no one was injured. A general hospital in another part of the island also received a direct hit, killing some RAMC doctors.

Despite the horror, which must have seemed unending, Maud Buckingham continued to think positively, stressing the low rate of casualties among hospital staff relative to the physical damage:

During the many raids on this little island it can easily be imagined that the hospital buildings and areas surrounding them did not escape damage, but it was truly remarkable how, on so many occasions, the staff escaped being killed or injured . . . In March 1941 a wing of the Isolation Block for women and children received a direct hit, but fortunately at this time all the patients were being nursed at the other end of the building, and although they received considerable shock from blast etc. no one was injured . . . On March 21st 1942 at about 3.15 p.m. the Sisters' Quarters of the Women's Hospital attached were almost completely demolished by bombs, but on this occasion all the nursing staff, including the Night Sister, were out of the building.

Necessity meant that, despite the rubble and dirt and destruction, even apparently ruined uniforms could be restored. 'The Sisters lost many of their personal belongings, but it was surprising how much they salvaged afterwards with the help of the RAMC and RE [Royal Engineers] personnel. Uniform coats, dresses, blouses, hats etc. were reclaimed, brushed, cleaned and put into use again. During these days of difficult transport it was impossible to obtain new clothes, but the Sisters managed to overcome this inconvenience . . .'

In the mayhem everything could be lost – or, just as improbably, preserved. 'One of the Sisters . . . had left a small basket of eggs in her room. She naturally did not expect to see them again, but . . . they were preserved safe . . . A tray had fallen over them, and although all around was chaos, the eggs were saved for breakfast!! On another occasion in this hospital a large piece of shell had pierced the ward wall and bounded to the other side of the ward, and the Sister on duty narrowly escaped being hit.'

It was, as their Maltese cook firmly believed, as if St Paul was watching over them.

Ever keen to demonstrate to the public at home the bravery and devotion to duty of her army nurses Dame Katherine Jones made a habit of asking Matrons involved in front-line fighting to describe their experiences. She was planning a book which would celebrate the achievements of these nurses who were facing challenges no nurse of any nation had ever faced before. (*Grey and Scarlet* would be published in 1944.) When asked for her memories of the siege of Malta, Maud Buckingham replied with characteristic verve:

> Cold dark miserable nights, when light and fuel were scarce and window panes missing, and the high winds of Malta played havoc with the dust, and one's tempers!
>
> . . . the Night Sisters trying to carry out their duties when battling with blackout rules, lack of hot water, light, fuel and equipment. The eternal wail of the siren and raids – the deafening noise of the guns. Laundry problems due to lack of water, soap and laundry facilities. Journeys to and from duty when raids were in progress. The welcome advent of bicycles for the Staff . . . The sad memory of our blitzed vines and the loss of our grapes. Vivid anxious moments at night during raids when one's thoughts would fly to the Night Sisters, VADs and orderlies on duty. Thrilling fights in the air, and times when the hospital compound looked like fairyland lit up with the lights from flares, tracer bullets and searchlights. Defence rations! And the strange dishes they produced.

One of the duties QAs took particularly seriously was writing to the families of dying soldiers giving them much-desired details. Even the chaos of the siege of Malta did not prevent the punctilious Miss Buckingham from performing a task which she knew meant so much to the bereaved. The letters of appreciation sent in reply are very moving. Helen Warrack wrote from Coventry on 20 September 1941: 'Dear Matron, your very kind letter arrived sometime ago. I was very thankful to know my son was able to get the cable we sent him. I know he got every care and I must thank you very much for your letter. It makes it so much easier to bear my sorrow when I knew just what had happened. The shipping Co had little news to tell . . .'

Dorothy Mackie wrote a heartbreaking letter on 10 March 1942 from Edinburgh about the death of her pilot son.

> Dear Matron
> Thank you very much for writing to me about my son's death. I was so thankful to know that he never regained consciousness after his crash and so did not endure any terrible suffering – he was always

such a splendid brave boy and I am pleased to know that he has been one of the defenders of Malta.

You must have seen so many sad cases – and we all think your island is simply wonderful. Withstanding all the continuing air attack. I shall hope, one day, when this cruel war is over to visit Malta and see where my boy is buried – my husband is in hospital in Durban suffering from shell shock. He was bombed in Singapore . . .[2]

The siege of Malta ended on 3 November 1942, but Maud Bucking-ham did not leave until the following July, by which time she had been on the island for three years.

As she left she was handed a duplicated slip of paper headed 'Security. *Your Duty*'.

1. You are leaving MALTA – others are not.
2. Wherever you go avoid all thoughtless talk concerning this island.
3. When relating your experiences confine yourself to events PRIOR to 1943. Any reference to present activities of any kind, land, sea or air is dangerous and expressly forbidden. Too many lives have already been *lost through CARELESS TALK*.

After all she had been through this was the last thing she needed. Malta was awarded the George Cross by the King for its valour and Matron Buckingham received the Royal Red Cross.

13

Operation Torch

In November 1942 the Allies launched Operation Torch, the first combined Anglo-American venture of the war. Its purpose was to conquer French North Africa, then in the hands of the Vichy French, and squeeze Rommel in a pincer movement from west and east. Sixty thousand Americans landed at Casablanca and Algiers, followed by the British First Army, whose brief was to go ashore at Algiers, capture the town and then turn east for an attack on Tunis. The operation, which embarked in a series of huge convoys from Liverpool and Glasgow, required the presence of scores more nurses. Mary English, a farmer's daughter from Northern Ireland, was one of them.

Mary spent her first days in Algeria shivering. She and more than twenty-five fellow QAs had docked in Algiers just before Christmas 1942 in the depths of a chilly North African winter. They arrived just one month after the massed Allied landings and were there to set up the 67th British General Hospital which was to care for the troops of the First Army. The nurses were shivering because Matron-in-Chief and her colleagues at the War Office were not aware of the extremes of the desert climate. The grey and scarlet QA uniform was designed for indoor nursing and was not suitable for year-round life under canvas. Mary and her fellow QAs disembarked from the *Arundel Castle*, the ship that had brought them out from England, with just two grey cotton dresses each.

The situation in North Africa was desperate that Christmas. The Allies had encountered stiff resistance from the Germans, the Italians and the Vichy French. There were battles going on all round Algiers, there was fierce fighting on the Algerian–Tunisian border and to the east the Egyptian campaign was still being bitterly fought. But initially Operation Torch had no hospital. The wounded were waiting on hospital ships for the hospital to open.

The plan was to open the hospital in Philippeville (now known as Skikda), a small resort and port built by the French 200 miles east of Algiers, which was nearer the front line. Speed was essential and after a few days in Algiers the QAs boarded the train for Philippeville. As the train chugged along Mary was shocked by her first sight of a battle zone.

'It was like a wilderness. The road had been destroyed by craters, the sides were littered with burnt out tanks and overturned lorries. The Arabs were so poor. They had nothing but rags for clothes."

At Constantine, they left the train and spent the night in a hotel whose luxurious marble floors would have spelled five-star luxury in peacetime. Now all the furniture had been destroyed and the dusty and weary Sisters found the marble chilly and unyielding as they undid their bedrolls on the bare floor and lay down for the night.

When at last they arrived at Philippeville Mary was delighted to find she and the other QAs were not going to be in tents, but had been allotted billets in a row of villas overlooking the Mediterranean that had once belonged to prosperous French colonials. 'The villas were really palatial, with electric light and running water, which lots of QAs in North Africa had to do without for years at a stretch. They had the ubiquitous marble floors, which made them very cold when we arrived, but were a boon in summer.'

The first thing the nurses did when they arrived at their hospital was to call on the Quartermaster to be fitted out in something warmer than their cotton dresses. It turned out that from now on they were to wear khaki battledress, like the men. 'Of course it didn't fit. The trousers were too big in the waist and too tight across our bottoms and having a front zip in the trousers struck us as very funny, but we were delighted to be warm at last.'

Setting up the hospital called for a great deal of ingenuity, as much of the equipment for the 67th was by then lying on the bed of the Mediterranean. It had been being transported on the sister ship of the *Arundel Castle*, the *Strathallan*, which had been torpedoed and sunk by a

German U-boat off the coast of Oran, about 200 miles west of Algiers on 21 December.

The *Strathallan* had been carrying 4,408 troops and 248 QAs, whose job was to set up other hospitals along the North African seaboard. Like the *Arundel Castle*, on which Mary English travelled, she was bound for Algiers. Although a torpedo went straight through the engine room and set it on fire, the ship did not sink until several hours later, by which time most people on board had been evacuated. Six of the crew, five QAs and a small number of passengers were killed.

The risk of attack by U-boats off the North African coast at that time was very real, yet the young nurses had been more concerned with drinking and flirting with the officers than with fear of shipwreck. One of them described the carefree atmosphere on board hours before disaster struck.

As we trudged out to boat drills daily we thought what a waste of our precious time. Then after a lovely voyage . . . we came to our last night. Early that morning, before 7 a.m., we had all arisen early to go out on deck to see The Rock [of Gibraltar] and the towns lit up on the Spanish coast. All day we had seen the mountains of Africa looming away on the horizon and then after a gay last night we were all packed and ready for the last stages and so to bed. We are naughty and go to bed not fully equipped for emergency, without our money belts on and some without slacks even.

Crash! 2.30 a.m.! We all know instantly what has happened. We feel for the lights. They won't function. The engines have stopped. We grope for our torches . . . And there we are grabbing our money and emergency bundles . . . and proceeding to boat stations . . . It does not seem possible that although the ship is listing that we can possibly desert ship and take to boats. But there are the boats already being lowered and we climb into boats, are lowered and are off. This . . . is the worst time. Leaving some people behind and struggling to get away from the ship without capsizing. This is not as easy as it sounds. Lifeboats are the worst thing possible for seasickness. We are all pretty sick, something hit me on the head, nearly knocked me out and I am sick continuously during the night in the lifeboat. We pick up people from the rafts all during the night, mostly men and a few Sisters. We do the best we can for the exhausted ones. All around us depth charges keep our boat rocking. Our own destroyer in convoy cannot pick us up . . . I imagine drifting out in the Atlantic for days . . . Someone keeps talking about food and we try to sing but we are all too sick.[2]

The fate of the QAs who drowned emerged later when the units were reunited. 'Their boat is turned into the water. Some swim to rafts and help those who cannot swim, some swim straight to destroyers complete with tin hats and some even respirators and gloves and curlers.'[3]

The people in lifeboats were picked up the following morning by a destroyer and the young women, relieved to be alive, sat on the sunny deck and sang carols with naval officers.

It later transpired that not everyone had left the stricken ship. As the torpedo hit, two QAs, Olive Stewardson and Julie Kerr, remembered that there were five stretcher cases in the sickbay on the lower deck. They got the men ready and helped lower them into lifeboats. They were about to leave themselves when the badly burned crew from the engine room were brought into the sickbay for treatment. Despite the fact that the ship was now listing heavily the nurses stayed to tend the injured men. More men were carried in and three other women passengers came to help. They worked all through the night. All on board were eventually lifted to safety before the *Strathallan* sank. For their courage and dedication to duty Sister Stewardson and Sister Kerr were awarded the Royal Red Cross,* two of only 216 QAs out of a total force of over ten thousand to receive this distinction.

To be willing to sacrifice your own life for others as these two QAs had been commands the highest admiration. Not everyone felt up to it. Gwladys Aikens was on board the *Strathallan* and, when, she heard the call for volunteers to go down to the hospital and take care of the patients, decided to put herself first. Her forensic account of a choice

---

* The Royal Red Cross was created by Queen Victoria on St George's Day 1883. The Royal Warrant stated that the Decoration was to be conferred 'upon any ladies, whether subject or foreign persons, who may be recommended by our Secretary of State for War for special exertion in providing for the nursing of sick and wounded soldiers and sailors of Our Army and Navy.' Florence Nightingale was one of first recipients of the RRC.

that few people are called upon to make in a lifetime is compelling. In total darkness and with the ship listing crazily, she was on her way up to the boat deck.

> We had just about reached the outside and I could smell the familiar salt spray mingled with a burning smell . . . From behind me someone called for volunteer nurses to go down with the patients in the ship's hospital . . .
>
> 'Go down?' I thought. The ship was actually going down – this was no dream. How could I run away and leave those people helpless, probably to die slowly without any chance of survival? How would they go? Just sink below the water as it quickly flooded the floors, rising higher and higher swallowing everything in sight?
>
> I just couldn't go back. I felt so guilty and knew that there were others behind me who would go back to the hospital to hold hands and weep with the patients. I wished that I hadn't heard that call, but I hoped that God above would forgive me and understand my strong desire to go on with my life. I wasn't ready to die, not yet. If that happened in battle, so be it, I had resigned myself to that possibility. But not now, not yet. I kept moving on, finally ascending the last step. I was on deck at last.[4]

A few months later Mary English and her fellow QAs were working round the clock at the 67th BGH in Philippeville. It was a tented hospital pitched on the land behind their row of villas. Everything was makeshift because of the loss of the *Strathallan*. There were no desks – Mary's was a box – but the soldiers were very good at making things and chairs were knocked up from any available bits of wood. Fighting was very heavy with wounded pouring in all through the day and night and the Sisters dressing twenty wounds at a stretch. From Christmas Eve 1942 to the fall of Tunis nearly five months later the 67th worked flat out as a Casualty Clearing Station, with as many as three men occupying one bed in the space of twenty-four hours, before being transported to base hospitals. Four hundred wounded Italian and German POWs were nursed in tents surrounded by a barbed-wire compound. 'We saw all kinds of battle injuries – gun shot wounds, fractures, lots of burns and many cases of shattered nerves and battle exhaustion.'[5] Many of the young American troops who had come over as part of Operation Torch had had very little preparation and went to pieces. 'When a bombing raid began, or even when a plane flew low overhead, they would leave their beds and run screaming in terror into the woods behind the hospital. We used to have to send orderlies to coax them back. It was the first time they had been exposed to battle conditions and they were incoherent with fright.'

Still new to army protocol, Mary soon learnt that nothing gets in the way of morning inspection. 'Every casualty had a locker by his bed, usually made out of a box, and everything on that locker had to be neatly folded in a particular way. If the patient was in bed he would have his blue convalescence trousers, his uniform, his facecloth, shaving kit and wash things on the locker. If he was walking wounded he would be wearing the blue trousers, so his pyjamas and battledress would be on his locker. Whether we were being bombed or overwhelmed with casualties, we Sisters inspected those lockers for tidiness at 10 o'clock every morning.'

The Sisters' Mess was in a large villa that looked out over the Mediterranean and which had belonged to high-ranking French colonial family. The cooking, however, did not live up to the elegant setting. 'We had tea and coffee and plenty of dates and figs. We could buy oranges from the Arabs in exchange for cigarettes, but our staple meal, day after day, was Maconochie, which we ate with hard dry Army biscuits.'

Because of its siting close to the front line the 67th operated as a transit station. The aim was to get the men on their feet again as fast as possible. The hospital had a plentiful supply of drugs, including penicillin, which was not yet available to civilians on the home front. The operating theatre performed minor surgery but there were no facilities for major surgery. As Mary recounts:

> We did amputations and set fractures. Fracture cases were con-
> valescent for between six and eight weeks before they were fit for
> action again as there was no physiotherapy in desert hospitals in
> those days. We had a lot of gunshot injuries – shattered arms and
> legs. Many men lost hands or legs through amputation as a result of
> gangrene. Any casualty needing complex medical attention would

be nursed until he was fit to travel and repatriated via hospital ship to a base hospital in England or Gibraltar. An injury such as a serious chest wound could not be cared for properly in Africa. It was always either too hot or too cold and there wasn't much hygiene. The hospital ships were very well equipped and bang up to date.

In addition to nursing casualties the men suffered various Third World diseases and at one stage there was an outbreak of smallpox which meant that the Sisters needed to set up an isolation compound.

North Africa for troops and nurses meant hard work in spartan conditions. The women had left the world of fashionable clothes and make-up far behind them. They were always in uniform – grey cotton dresses or drill trousers with bush shirts, according to the season. They didn't have stockings and regarded a new cake of soap as a luxury. Yet, despite the ever-presence of death and danger – or maybe because of it – their time off was hectic socially.

We swam in the Mediterranean in the summer and we used to hold a mess night once a week when the Home Sister would put out a bottle of whisky and a bottle of gin and we could invite our friends in. There were all kinds of Army units in our immediate vicinity – there was an SAS camp about four miles away and an RAF Spitfire base close by. We knew lots of Spitfire pilots. They had a wonderful uniform and always looked dashing and glamorous. When they flew over the hospital they would dip down low in greeting and we would wave. We were the only women in the place. There were usually only four or five of us off duty at any one time and when we went out in the evening we were outnumbered by men by a hundred to one. Some of the men we met when we were out had been patients. There was a club in Philippeville which had been a French casino before the war but had been taken over by the British Army. It was always easy for us Sisters to get a lift in in a jeep.

Winston Churchill's son Randolph, an intelligence officer, was based at Philippeville with the SAS. Mary saw him one night in an Algerian café in Philippeville sitting on his own with just one colleague, perhaps a bodyguard. 'The others pointed him out. They didn't have much respect for him. The feeling was that his father had foisted him on the SAS and that he wasn't expected to distinguish himself in the service.'

The Americans had joined the North African campaign as part of Operation Torch. They had a base near Philippeville and were predictably keen to entertain the tiny handful of women in the area. The British troops regarded them with disdain, maintaining they were too mollycoddled to be good fighters, but the girls found their invitations hard to resist. 'There was a cork forest behind our hospital and the Americans used to invite two or three of us over for picnics. We looked forward to these invitations as the Americans had far better food than us. They didn't eat tinned stew. They had sausages and fresh meat.'

Mary maintains that a lot of the British resentment was the result of envy – 'the Americans had everything – not just stockings, but plenty of beer. We even used to watch films with them . . . The poor old British Army couldn't keep up.'

The girls were regularly invited to British Mess nights too. 'The SAS chaps used to come to those. They were really wild characters, great fun as well as brave and tough. They used to tell us some of their adventures – how they went out in small boats and landed behind enemy lines in Sicily and Greece.' Colonel Sterling was their CO. 'He was a great prankster. He spoke German and he used to go up to the German POWs and pass himself off as a fellow German.'

The atmosphere on these evenings was one of almost frenzied gaiety, in which what would seem tragic in more normal times could seem funny. 'One night we were sitting at a table with a chap who was on crutches. He'd had his leg amputated and he got a bit tiddly. He completely forgot he hadn't got two legs and when he stood up he fell over. Everyone howled with laughter, including him.'

But despite the gaiety nobody was fooling themselves.

The risks were high and many of those who were based in Philippeville were killed. We were all on edge because people were young and falling in love, and yet death was an everyday occurrence. You'd ask after an SAS man you usually saw and they'd say, 'Jack? He didn't make it.' It was the same with the Spitfire pilots. You'd ask after someone who was missing from the table and his friend would say lightly, 'Roger? I'm afraid he bought it.' That was the expression they used. I had a boyfriend who was a Spitfire pilot while I was in Philippeville. He was brave and fun – but he was killed the following year in Anzio.

13

Life of Comradeship

While Mary English was getting the wounded back on their feet in Philippeville, Sylvia Skimming had come out to North Africa as a Welfare Officer with the Red Cross. She was attached to the 93rd British General Hospital, one of four big base hospitals situated about eight miles out of the now liberated Algiers. The 93rd had 2,500 beds, including five hundred for German and Italian POWs, and it took Skimming a week to get round to each patient. Her job was to provide the wounded troops arriving from the battlefield with small comforts – face flannels, soap, a shaving kit – as well as writing letters and providing books and other entertainment for the long-term bed-bound.

Skimming was billeted with the QAs throughout her time in Africa and wrote a graphic account of how the nurses lived. Winter in North Africa was characterised by bitter cold and torrential rain, which turned the sand into a sea of sticky clinging mud. By this stage of the war the Matron-in-Chief had reluctantly sanctioned the abandoning of the impractical grey cotton dresses in favour of battledress as the winter uniform for those nursing in the field. However, the QAs were still desperately under-equipped. Dame Katherine Jones, on a lightning tour of hospitals in North Africa in 1943, commented on the clothes shortages, noting that one American chief nurse she met was wearing men's shoes.

Skimming, too, was surprised to find how under-equipped the Sisters were. 'The camp was built unfortunately on very muddy sand and I remember on several occasions my boots getting so clogged up that my feet became too heavy to lift, and I had to wait outside a ward until one of the patients came and removed the mud with a stick. Very few of the Sisters had boots, and their thin little black shoes were worn out in a few weeks.'[1]

The climate was impossible. In winter it was bitterly cold, especially at night, and in summer sweat-soaked clothes meant endless clothes washing. Skimming, who was equipped by the munificent Red Cross, changed her clothes three times a day in the summer, but the QAs had had no replacement uniforms since they arrived and 'were getting very ragged and shabby'. Miss Jones may have suggested that American nurses were as under-equipped as British nurses, but this was not the general view. An American medical team was attached to the 93rd and the nurses' uniform was a source of much envy by the QAs. 'Their working dresses were all made of non-creasing cotton so that they never needed ironing, and they had very smart going-out frocks, designed purposely for a hot climate. Our Sisters had very nice white drill frocks, but were very impractical for life in a tent, and after a few hours in a sandy "fifteen-hundredweight" [lorry] on the way to a dance they were filthy.'[2]

Water was scarce and the nurses missed hot baths. Cold showers were available and were fine in summer but the bitter cold meant that the girls avoided them in winter. Desert storms continued to blow down the hopelessly impractical British tent, the pegs and guy ropes of which were never designed to hold in soft sand. One blew down the Sisters' tents and some of the tented wards and the unfortunate patients had to be 'carted into every available hut'. In the rainy season everything became damp overnight, so the women slept with their uniforms under the bedclothes. 'It was very difficult to undress while keeping one's boots on as there wasn't a single dry patch anywhere. Some of the girls had tarpaulins on their floors, which made things a little better, though when they had walked in and out several times in their muddy boots, the floor was almost as muddy as ours . . . We had to keep our trunks raised from the ground on bricks . . .'[3]

The 93rd was lucky in having flushing lavatories, but the next-door hospital, where ninety Sisters shared eight lavatories, was less lucky. 'Not only did they not pull, but in the summer water was severely rationed, and there was only water for them once every 24 hours.'

The army day kicked off at 6.30 a.m. with a batman who went round banging on each tent with a stick and shouting 'wakey wakey'. After this was breakfast, which was served in three sittings, 7, 7.30 and 8 a.m. Matron and the night Sisters went to the later sitting. The army diet was monotonous – a bleak round of bully beef, spam, tinned salmon and sardines and dehydrated vegetables – and most of them lost weight. There was no fresh butter or milk, but oranges and eggs relieved the monotony. Breakfast was the favourite meal – 'lovely slabs of golden-brown bread fried crisply, and eggs . . .' Dinner was eaten in a long tent lit by two small hurricane lamps. The girls used to take it in turns to strike matches to see what they were eating.

There was little privacy for the Sisters, corralled as they were in the midst of a camp of several thousand men and surrounded by barbed wire 'to prevent the Arabs getting in to steal', but in the end the women became less fearful of being spied on, while the men obviously welcomed the splash of feminine colour provided by the nurses.

> My tent was in a most unfortunate position. At one side were ward tents, so the men could see in if the flaps were up, and at the other side the cook-house, so the batmen had a good view from that side. So I practically lived in the dark, though in the end we got to feel the batmen as faithful friends, who were used to anything. We got quite used to hanging our scanties out to dry within full view of the entire hospital, and I often used to wonder what the men thought of the sight of dozens of women in various-hued gaudy dressing gowns carrying buckets of water![4]

If there was a lull in the fighting the Sisters had their off time between 2 and 5 p.m., or between 5 and 8 p.m. If they were off in the afternoon they would sleep, but the North African summer heated the tents like ovens and sleep was hard. The night Sisters, who all shared one large tent, had a particularly difficult time. 'Plagued by heat, flies and "Arab noises" . . . (they) found it hard to sleep at all.'

At this stage the majority of the patients in the 93rd were housed in thirty huge tents which each held thirty-six people.

The hospital was still being built when Skimming arrived and casualties were so heavy that some patients with minor conditions, such as skin complaints, had to sleep on stretchers on the muddy ground. All through 1943 the fighting was intense and injured men continued to pour in to the

93rd. The state of the exhausted victims, who had been obliged to travel for days, was pitiful.

> Towards the middle of October we began to receive, nightly, small convoys of transferred surgical walking cases passed on from CCS [Casualty Clearing Stations] and Base Hospitals nearer to the northern coast. These men travelled by ordinary passenger trains, often taking twelve to eighteen hours for the journey and making at least two changes en route. Seating accommodation was very limited and after the first train they seldom managed to get a seat. On receipt of a signal at the hospital, a medical officer and orderlies took trucks to meet the train at our nearest halt and so brought up the men the last three miles of their journey. In the reception room, each patient, after being allocated to his ward, was issued with a complete hospital kit and then, under the guidance of a waiting orderly, he was taken to his place.

Because of air raids this entire operation was often carried out in total darkness. 'Bread and hot soup were provided by the cookhouse, but if the alert was long and fires had to be damped down, the exhausted men were often fast asleep before the orderly could get it along to them.'

The more seriously injured travelled by hospital trains, and one of Skimming's duties was to go and meet these trains and give the weary men tea and sandwiches before they were taken to the hospital. Most had been travelling for three days. 'They had probably hardly been washed since they were picked up on the battlefield, certainly never shaved, just operated on and fixed up for the journey, and then pushed off onto the first train, so that the forward hospitals had room for the next batch.'

The only cheering part of this operation was the stretcher-bearers, usually Italian prisoners of war. 'They were in teams of three to a stretcher . . . They wore very brief tropical shorts, more like bathing-pants, and they carried the stretchers on their shoulders. They walked beautifully with perfect rhythm of movement, almost like ballet dancers.'

Medical training and iron discipline belong together and in the midst of the chaos of war the hospitals were havens of organisation, where each member of the team knew his or her job and did it promptly.

As an outsider, Skimming marvelled at the efficiency of the army machine.

> Each ambulance was unloaded and the men laid in rows on the steps of the hospital. A doctor looked them over, and a sergeant had a list of the empty beds in each ward, and as the MO graded them medical or surgical cases, so the sergeant chalked the ward number on the stretcher. Then someone else would take their particulars for hospital records and they would be carried off to their wards. Once in the ward, the up patients helped the orderlies undress them, and cups of tea were handed round. Severe surgical cases were taken to the theatre, the others washed and allowed to sleep, which was what they all seemed to need most. Later the MO would make a thorough examination of each new patient and describe his treatment.

The major problem for the base hospitals was what to do with those who were making a good recovery in order that sufficient empty beds would be available for the next lot of casualties. At that time there was no air evacuation and the long-term incapacitated were supposed to go home to the UK on hospital ships. German U-boats, however, were still sinking high numbers of British ships in the Mediterranean and hospital ships were few and far between. This meant there were often as many as ninety to one hundred patients waiting to go home. 'Our allocation on the ship might be twenty with luck, and, by the time the next ship arrived, the numbers would have gone up again, and very often more urgent cases would have arrived and those who were making good progress would lose their priority on the list.'

Nurses are trained not to react emotionally to the suffering to which they minister. Although the younger QAs had never tended battle wounds before volunteering for overseas service, it is a curious fact that very few of them remember much about the appalling injuries they tended. 'It's as if we've blotted it out,' as one former QA put it.

Sylvia Skimming had not had a medical training and found seeing so much young life wiped out or mutilated very hard to deal with. 'Sometimes I would go and hide myself in despair at the sight of so much suffering. They were all so young and it seemed so dreadful that their lives should be a long weary round of fighting and discomfort, often ending in death.'

The 93rd had a Facio-Maxillo ward, and she found visiting these patients deeply upsetting.

> I never got used to visiting this ward. It was imperative not to let the man see by any change of expression on one's own face that one was shaken by their appearance. Sometimes a face would be so disfigured that one wondered where the surgeon would begin. They were all amazingly brave . . . We would keep these patients until their faces had been built up again. They were anxious themselves not to go home too soon – they did not wish their people to see them until they looked better.

It seems a miracle that despite the hard work and the discomfort, the girls managed to enjoy themselves. But they were young and, despite the meagre rations, full of vitality. They went on washing their hair, even if the sand never really came out of it; they put on their lipstick, if they still had any, in front of pocket mirrors in dimly lit tents (many QAs didn't see themselves in a full-length mirror for years on end). They even went for walks in the countryside round the hospital. On the other side of the valley to the hospital was an Arab village of wattle-and-daub huts built round a circular white mosque, where Arab women in colourful robes, accompanied by hordes of dirty children, gawped at the white girls. Incongruously the horror of war seemed to make little impact on the indigenous people there. For them life went on much as it always had. In spring wonderful wild flowers covered the area, one field being full of wild gladioli which the Red Cross girls picked to decorate the wards.

Forced intimacy led to an irrepressible camaraderie. Sylvia Skimming was invited to a girls' 'party' that sounds like a midnight feast from Enid Blyton's *Malory Towers*. 'Their tent was pitched in the middle of a water-course and a river of water ran right through the centre, so it was very difficult to keep things dry. Everything reeked of damp, and no matter how good the tent, after a few hours' rain it invariably started leaking. So we sat in our Wellington boots and waterproof cloaks . . . The scene was lit by two hurricane lamps and there was the constant hiss of two Primus stoves.' The girls tucked into a feast of fried eggs, bread and spam with the *pièce de résistance* – ration chocolate melted and allowed to harden on army biscuits.

Social life was extremely important both to troops and nurses, but Matron, usually less in demand than her young charges, could be a killjoy. The QAs with the 93rd had a bar in their Mess tent which was open every evening between 6 and 8 p.m. They were allowed to invite male officers, but the visitors had to be gone by 9 p.m. Women were in extremely short supply in North Africa and nurses were regularly invited out to dances by other units, but as the deadline for returning to camp was 11 p.m., and the destination was often an hour's drive away, it was hardly worth going.

Sylvia Skimming describes one dance where at 10.30 p.m. promptly, to the fury of the officers who had gone to a lot of trouble to put on a good party, 'Matron got up and swept us all out.' The nurses, the youngest of whom was in her mid twenties, bitterly resented this heavy hand, but Matron held all the cards. Anyone who did arrive back after hours had her name taken by the sentry who would report to the Colonel. He would send the name of the offender to Matron, who would then summon the miscreant to explain herself. The preferred form of punishment, which all QAs dreaded, was to be 'posted'. Any nurse who had transgressed would, at a few days' notice, be sent hundreds of miles away, losing her friends and being parted from her current love interest.

Skimming found this boarding-school attitude widespread in army nursing. 'Only one hospital I served in was reasonable on this subject. She [the Matron] was young, and her maxim was, "Your time off is your own; if you keep late hours so consistently that you are unable to do your work properly, then I shall reprimand you for failing in your duty."'

It was just over six months after the Operation Torch landings that final victory in North Africa was achieved with the capture of Tunis in May 1943. Virtually the entire Axis army was captured with nearly a quarter of a million prisoners. Only a few hundred escaped.

But for the British and Americans, the costs were high. Some fifty thousand troops were killed or wounded.

When Tunis finally fell to the Allies the nurses soon felt it in the hospital. Casualties slackened off, and for the first time in months they had empty beds. The immediate effect was that air raids on Algiers ceased and a huge gun, not far from the hospital, fell silent. The Sisters put away their tin hats. Hundreds of German casualties poured into the hospital and thousands were taken prisoner. The atmosphere was euphoric, with French and Arabs making the Victory sign to the QAs in the streets. Everyone was cheered by the sight of 'mile after mile of Hitler's beaten army being marched down to the docks to be shipped to America and Canada'. The word among the war-weary patients of the 93rd was, 'It will be over by Christmas.'

As the hospitals in Algiers were no longer needed, Sylvia Skimming and some QAs were moved forward to the 67th at the port of Philippeville, where Mary English was stationed.

By now bulldozers were levelling the sand and Nissen huts were being put up to replace the tents. The Nissen wards were long and narrow, with a ward of about forty beds at each end, a kitchen and offices in the centre and a couple of single-bed wards for the very ill. This was Skimming's first experience of a forward hospital and it reminded her of a self-sufficient medieval town sprung up in the desert. 'Besides all the doctors, sisters, orderlies, cooks, there were the hospital staff, the quartermaster's stores, the pack stores, the steward's stores, a cobbler, a tailor, and last, but not least, the masseuses . . . We also had a little French boy of about fifteen years who was the barber. He pitched his tent in the middle of the camp and was busy all day and every day.'

They were still very busy as Allied troops were already in Sicily and the 67th acted as a Casualty Clearing Station for them. The wounded came over either by hospital ship or in air ambulances – large white planes marked with a red cross. They would circle round the hospital twice which was the signal for ambulances to go to the airfield.

As soon as hospitals were set up in Sicily only patients who were fit to travel came to Algeria and now they arrived freshly washed and bandaged. The change was a reflection of the way German power in the southern Mediterranean was ebbing away.

At the 67th Skimming encountered the same warm female camaraderie as she had in Algiers. 'We borrowed each others' things, did each others' washing and ironing, scrubbed each others' backs or entertained each others' friends if the Sister, whom they had arrived to see, was still on duty.'

Now, with the air raids over and the front line moved beyond the sea, the atmosphere was more relaxed. There was an entire division 'resting' round them and the girls could go to a party every night. There were picnic suppers on the beach and moonlit bathing in a romantic phosphorescent sea. There was no curfew and the girls slept out on their balconies because of the heat. It was a happy time. 'We were a few minutes' walk from the mess, and I can see myself now slipping on my camis and a dress and running down the road to breakfast, always late! The sea sparkled and danced and the beach lay golden and deserted at my feet. In the distance Philippeville, a town of white houses and red roofs, glittered in the morning sun.'

The 67th closed down on Christmas Day 1943, almost a year to the day since it had first opened. The entire hospital was moved to the new theatre of war in Italy. Remaining patients were put on a hospital train and sent to Algiers and the nursing team was broken up. With characteristic army efficiency it took only four days to dismantle it. The men took down the tents first, leaving the sand littered with packing cases, piles of beds and equipment covered with tarpaulin. The nurses hadn't finished packing when their tents went, leaving their furniture standing incongruously on the sand.

Their sailing for Italy was postponed for a month due to the sinking of the hospital ship HMS *St David* at Anzio and the lack of another in which to transport the Sisters. Eventually, however, the time came to leave. As Sylvia Skimming sailed past the beach where she and the nurses had shared such happy times with soldiers little older than them she reflected on the strange contrasts of war:

At one moment the beach seemed thronged with brown bodies as I had seen it so often, dashing into the sea with screams of delight; resting on the golden sand which was no more golden than they. I wished so much that those at home could have seen them as I saw them. It seemed to me that however terrible war is, this life of movement and adventure, of comradeship and of self-sufficiency, is how we were meant to live. I thought of all the things in England we deem indispensable and how happily we had lived all year without them. I had seen one cinema and one show in a year; had one bath and never been inside a house which had rugs and curtains and furniture. Never once been able to unpack; never turned on a tap and seen hot water come out. But we had all learned such a lot. The true values of life. We had . . . discarded all the paraphernalia with which we surround ourselves in any civilised country and found how unnecessary it all is to true happiness. Our lives consisted of work and plenty of it; our play had been lying in the sun, dancing, bathing and talking.

In stressing that even in war there are good times Sylvia Skimming was being honest. But it would be a wearily long time before any of them lay in the sun again.

15

Swept off their Feet

Nurses training in civilian hospitals lived a nun-like existence, their virtue guarded noon and night by Matron, usually a spinster of middle years, who viewed men as second only to Lucifer himself in the hierarchy of evil.

Joining the QAs was doing one's patriotic duty, but it also afforded thousands of women in the prime of life – most were in their early twenties – the opportunity to spread their wings and free themselves from the authority figures who had dictated their lives thus far. From being vestals cloistered away, they were suddenly like children in a sweet shop – surrounded by men: men, young and single and fighting fit; men, older and married (though not always owning up to the fact) but missing female company. Whether in the desert of North Africa, on the Burma frontier or pushing across France after the Normandy landings, there were only ever a handful of nurses compared with the thousands of fighting troops who surrounded them. When it came to dances they were outnumbered by hundreds to one. Even the plainest nurse had a choice of partners.

The sexual tension in these huge complexes was intense, but the rules of the mating game in British society in the 1940s were far more formal than they are today. On top of that, the army itself took an extremely tough line on illicit sex.* Men and women didn't automatically address each other by first names at the outset, let alone kiss on the first date. Compared to the worldly-wise teenagers of today these girls were extraordinarily innocent. Many a trainee midwife expressed shock at

---

* VD was regarded as a 'self-inflicted injury' and soldiers admitted for treatment had their pay stopped for the duration of their treatment.

discovering where the baby emerged from. One QA describes kissing a young officer goodnight, noticing something hard pressing against her and complaining, 'You might at least take your pipe out of your pocket.' 'And I was a midwife. I delivered babies!'

For women there was the stigma of being thought 'easy'. The moral and the pragmatic walked hand in hand. There was virtually no contraception and a pregnancy outside wedlock was a social disaster – for the woman, for the baby, who was invariably taken away for adoption, and even for the woman's parents. 'Nice girls didn't' was what I was invariably told when I asked former QAs about their courting rituals. The facts bear them out. Right up to the 1950s the majority of brides were virgins on their wedding night. Society's solution to an unexpected pregnancy was a shotgun wedding – but what if the man was married already? A Matron on a ship full of QAs posted to Hong Kong warned her girls against having affairs with married men. To modern ears she may sound as if she is exceeding her authority, but Matron knew that not all officers are gentlemen. The penalties, if such an affair got to the ears of the authorities, were draconian, particularly for the woman. The best would be an instant posting – to somewhere far away and uncongenial. If she was pregnant she would be sent home in disgrace and very probably expelled from the profession.

Fighting back against all these strictures was human nature and the heightened atmosphere. The energy and tension created by war, the knowledge that two people who have just met and feel instant attraction may never meet again, that tomorrow we may all die . . . incites people to break rules. Many QAs met their husbands while on active service and got married then and there in the midst of the fighting. Inevitably, despite the strict Christian upbringing most QAs had received, there were casualties of passion too.

The romances began straightaway – at mobilisation units where newly enlisted troops and nurses spent several weeks waiting to be posted, on ships that often took five or six weeks to reach their destination and, of course, in the hospital units where they worked.

Mary English, who spent her service with the British Eighth Army, first in North Africa and then in Italy, had met the man she was destined to marry on a blind date on London's Park Lane, before the war had started.

They used to hold tea dances at the Grosvenor House hotel. I was doing my fever training in Fulham and a friend asked me to make up a foursome. John was already in the Army – he was a Lieutenant in the Royal Artillery Regiment. We hit it off straightaway and then he was called up. When I joined up he didn't know where I was, but we kept in touch and we had a code we used to try to keep each other posted as to where we might end up. I went to Algiers and he went to Egypt. He went to Sicily and by an amazing coincidence we met up again in Foggia, when he was brought into my hospital suffering from jaundice. I'd always felt he was the one but I got to know him better in hospital and we decided to get married on the spot.[1]

Mary's honeymoon was three days spent at a small coastal resort just north of Foggia.

Later, as her unit moved up to Rimini, she got some more leave. Her husband had been posted to Greece and she decided to surprise him. 'I was friendly with several pilots and I managed to hitch one flight down to Bari, and another one from Bari to Greece. Then I took a bus to Athens. John was amazed to see me.'

Mary's ingenuity in getting to see her husband so impressed her colleagues that it made headlines in the Eighth Army newspaper of 16 December 1944. Under the headline 'Two Eyes of Grey Were Her Passport to Athens' an *Eighth Army News* reporter wrote:

Mary English, married in Italy last May to a young Lieutenant in the Gunners, is an Irish colleen with big grey eyes and a way of getting what she wants. A Sister in an Eighth Army hospital she heard that her husband was in Athens and made up her mind that she was going to see him.

By all the rules it seemed impossible – but few things are impossible to an Irish girl with big grey eyes and a lot of initiative. She hitch-hiked from the Eighth Army front to Greece, took a bus to Athens and telephoned her astonished husband.

While the ELAS [left-wing insurgents pushing for a Communist government] were marching and singing in the streets of the Greek capital, she spent four happy days with her husband,

slipping back to Italy just in time to avoid the rising and to report
for duty at the end of her seven days' leave.

Sarah McNeece's boyfriend, a pilot who flew Catalina flying boats,
was so determined to marry her he lied to his CO to get wedding leave –
without even having proposed to his bride. 'I had met Harry in England
at the hospital where I was doing my training. His mother worked there
part-time for the WVS [Women's Voluntary Service] and when his
father had a bad accident he was given compassionate leave to visit him.
He was playing the piano at a leaving do for one of the nurses when I
first saw him.'[2]

He invited her to a dance the next day and they began corresponding.
By now Sarah had joined the QAs. By a happy coincidence she was
posted to India where Harry was based. 'He waited for every boat that
arrived in Calcutta that day, but we missed each other. Then suddenly,
not long after I had arrived at my hospital, I received a telegram from
him. It said: "Get your wedding dress. We're getting married." I was
stunned. I hadn't really got as far as marriage – he'd never brought it up
before. But if I said "no" he would get into terrible trouble with his
CO, so I decided to go ahead with it.'

Sarah's wedding dress and her bridesmaids' dresses were all made
from parachute silk. The honeymoon was one night and they did not
even spend it together. 'I was very naïve. When I discovered what was
planned I was petrified. I stayed in bed alone and poor Harry spent the
night on the flat roof.'

Despite the inauspicious beginning, the marriage proved a long and
happy one – Sarah and Harry were married for forty-eight years. The
parachute wedding dress proved just as durable. 'After the war I had it
shortened and made a bolero jacket from the cut-off bit. I dyed the dress
red and the jacket black and used it as an evening dress.'

The authorities were obliged to accept legitimate relationships. But the
strict army code which delineated officers from other ranks for almost all
activities bar actual fighting meant that QAs, who were all gazetted,
were strenuously discouraged from socialising with NCOs, still less
falling in love with them.

Betty Biggs camped in a very remote part of Libya, just behind the line of Monty's Eighth Army, recalls how her forbidden love, for a chemist* in her unit, was kindled:

> There was an occasion when the Sergeants of Number 4 organised a dance, and Matron graciously gave us permission to attend. Sgt Geoff Cole was there, and somehow or other, we spent most of the evening together. He was a very courteous and attentive host and escorted me 'home' afterwards. Very tentatively he suggested we might meet again and I knew that I wanted to see him. We arranged to go for a picnic when next our off-duties coincided. We were breaking all the rules. If Matron discovered I was getting friendly with a sergeant we should both be in trouble.[3]

Betty found the reticence and modesty of her Sergeant a pleasant change from the 'brash, conceited and arrogant' officers, many of whom, she felt, regarded the QAs as there 'for their amusement'.

The news got around that a Sergeant and a Sister were getting very friendly and attempts were made to nip the romance in the bud by posting Sergeant Cole to a Field Ambulance unit at the front line. But they continued to meet at the YMCA in Ismailia, which had been an Egyptian prince's palace. They took leave together and visited what was then called Palestine, now Israel. On the last day of their leave Geoff proposed and Betty happily accepted. 'We knew there would be obstacles ahead and that it might be many months or even years before we could get married, but being engaged made us feel more secure of a future together.'

Matron was cool with her congratulations, but the Colonel gave the pair his blessing. After the wedding at Moascar Garrison Church in Ismailia, on 23 August 1944, the pair were parted again when Sergeant Cole was posted to Italy. But true love was not to be so easily outdone and he was soon back in Egypt, having arranged his return by exchanging his posting with a fellow dispenser who wished to stay in Italy with his Italian girlfriend. When Sergeant Cole was posted to Damascus, Betty successfully applied for a transfer to the Little Cedars of Lebanon Hospital in Beirut, about 80 miles away. Pregnancy put an end to Betty

---

* Dispensing chemists, though men with high educational qualifications, were not commissioned in the army, a situation felt by many to be anomalous.

Cole's war service. This time Sergeant Cole could not follow. His baby daughter was three months old by the time the couple were reunited.

Occasionally the presence of lusty fighting men desperate for female company turned the heads of older career nurses lacking the worldliness of some of their younger, prettier colleagues. This happened when Betty Cole's unit were in Barce, an isolated Bedouin village in Libya. 'One of our older colleagues fell hopelessly in love with a Captain responsible for policing the civilian population in and around Barce . . . and she was completely under his spell. From being a staid, prim and proper, old-maidish type, she blossomed into a happy, outgoing and far more tolerant person.'

The Captain was a womaniser and soon began paying court to a younger, more attractive nurse. 'It took a week or two for our older colleague to realise what was happening, but when she understood she had been cast aside she was completely devastated . . . The younger girl happened to be a friend of mine, and one evening after work, the rejected Sister knocked on my door in a very distressed state. She urged me to exert any influence to stop her seeing the Captain.'

Sister Biggs worked in the Sisters' Mess and her first task of the day was to knock on each door and make sure the nurses were ready for duty. 'Getting no response from the rejected Sister's room I went in and, to my horror, found she had taken an overdose of tablets and was deeply unconscious. Matron and the Chief Medical Officer were hastily summoned . . . Eventually, against her will, she revived. When she was strong enough to travel she was flown back to England. The affair was quickly hushed up . . .'

The older Sister was not the only nurse in Libya to experience the army's 'disappearing machine'.

> Another sister . . . had some very strange habits. To all intents and purposes she was a respectable, hard-working girl, but she struck us as being rather odd . . . she had a penchant for men!! She pursued them all, from the highest ranking officer to the humblest private! Of course it didn't take too long for this little quirk of hers to reveal itself and she too was quickly flown home. I suppose it was the unnatural conditions under which we were living, and the fact that

we were 50 women in a world of thousands of men that caused a
few of us to stray.

The appearance of the Americans changed the rules of romantic
engagement. Products of a new, less hierarchical society not accustomed
to regarding women as 'ladies', but more as fellow citizens, they were
strikingly (some say shockingly) less formal in every aspect of their
behaviour than the British. That included sex. Crucially, unlike the
British troops, they had condoms.

Mary English, based in Philippeville, Algeria, had an American unit
close by her tented hospital and was regularly invited to barbecues,
where the menu featured fresh meat, an unheard-of luxury in the British
Army, ice-cold beer and even film shows.

'I thought of myself as semi-engaged, so I was never romantically
involved with Americans. But a close friend of mine got very friendly
with an American officer. We weren't as frank in our conversations as
young people are today, but I suspected, from the way she talked, that
she was probably sleeping with him. I was very worried for her, but she
was all right. But another of our girls got pregnant in Italy. That was a
double disgrace as the man was a sergeant – not even an officer.'

A major problem was that men on the lookout for love did not always
admit that they were married. Irene Anderson, who was posted to India,
said it could be a real source of heartache.

I was very cautious about getting involved. It was very much a case
of here today and gone tomorrow. The lads were posted to Burma
and when were we going to see them again? There was a Welsh
fellow who was a lovely dancer. I really liked him, but one evening a
fellow officer told me he was a married man, so that was it. One
Irish girl I had met at Campbell College in Ireland before being
posted was demobbed after it came out that she had been big-
amously married. She came close to a nervous breakdown – and he
was allowed to remain in the Army.[4]

The fact that the nurses were less worldly than today's young women
sometimes left them vulnerable to unscrupulous lechers.

Mary Davies had been posted straight to India and found the new freedom of living independently of Matron and Home Sister had its own perils.

> The men were always trying to ply you with drink. I had led quite a sheltered life. I had started out neither drinking nor smoking – I got round it by trying to sit next to a plant and tipping my drink into it. I was proposed to while I was in India and had a less honourable proposition made to me by the Colonel.
>
> It was while I was in Dacca and I was given a weekend's leave to go to Calcutta. The Colonel heard I was going and said he was also going to Calcutta and would escort me to the train. I was to stay in the Lady Mary Herbert Club and he was staying at the Grand Hotel. He invited me to have dinner with him and I accepted. Only as dinner was nearing its end did I discover that he expected me to sleep with him. I was absolutely stunned. He was a married man and no way would I have done such a thing.[5]

The QAs who became pregnant were the real victims of the sexual lottery of wartime. In some ways British society had evolved little since the days of Jane Austen. Many believed their man would stand by them only to learn in their hour of need that he already had a wife. Fairness didn't come into it. Whatever their transgressions the men could not be spared from the front.

One of the QAs in Betty Biggs' unit became pregnant. 'We thought it strange she should wish to stay on night duty, and whenever we saw her she was wrapped in her cloak, but I still find it hard to believe that surrounded by 50 trained nurses, most of us midwives, she was able to keep it a secret. Her baby was born in Jerusalem where she had gone on leave, and she never returned to our unit.'[6]

Audrey Hayward spent nearly two years working in a home where unmarried ATS (Auxiliary Territorial Service) and WAAF (Women's Auxiliary Air Force) women had their babies.

> We didn't have any QAs in while I was there, but there were QAs who got pregnant when I was serving in India. They had their babies in hospitals out there and then went home. It was regarded by the authorities as a scandal but everyone I knew felt very sorry

for them. Because of the culture that applied then it was a tragedy for them.

They were not allowed to keep their babies and there was a lot of misery and upset. I remember the parents of one girl who had got into trouble coming in to visit her and having to tell her that her baby was going to be adopted. She was inconsolable.[7]

The treatment meted out to women who got caught out in the name of love seems unutterably harsh by today's standards. But then sanctions performed a vital role. The Allies' number one requirement was a plentiful supply of fit healthy men and fit healthy women to nurse them when they were hurt. There was a war to be fought.

V
EUROPE

16

'The QAs are here'

With the Germans roundly defeated in North Africa the Allies now turned their attention to Italy. After the success of the landings in Sicily in the autumn of 1943 the objective was to wrest Rome from a German force believed to be demoralised by the surrender of Italy to the Allies on 8 September 1943.

But in Field Marshal Kesselring, Commander-in-Chief of German forces in Italy, the Allies encountered an enemy every bit as able as Rommel had been in the desert. That and the country's rugged terrain, which the Germans commanded, combined to make the liberation of Italy a far bloodier and more prolonged campaign than anyone anticipated. The plan had been to distract Kesselring from the areas round Rome by a major attack to the south mounted by the US Fifth and the British Eighth Army. This was to clear the way for a surprise landing at Anzio, a small port 37 miles south of Rome, by a combined British and US force. Their brief was to create a bridgehead and then storm on to Rome cutting the Germans off from their supply line before Kesselring could plug the gap.

The bold initiative did not go to plan. The US commander lingered too long at Anzio and gave the Germans time to regroup. The route to Rome now lay, the Allied command reasoned, through Cassino, a small town dominated by a fourteenth-century hilltop monastery whose name has entered World War Two legend. The failure of the Anzio operation led directly to one of the longest and bloodiest stand-offs of the war, the Battle of Monte Cassino. It took the Allies nearly four months to capture the monastery. On one day – 15 March 1944 – 775 aircraft dropped 1,250 tons of bombs on Cassino and the countryside round it. A defiant German force used everything they had to repulse their assailants – guns, anti-personnel landmines, which inflicted dreadful injuries, flamethrowers . . . In the end the Allies' superior air power and the fact that Kesselring was forced to call for reinforcements from the troops defending Anzio created the longed-for gap and the US troops burst through. On 4 June 1944 Rome fell to the Allies.

But the price in human life had been colossal. By the end over 22,000 Americans, more than 2,200 British, nearly eight thousand French and approaching four hundred Italians had been killed, wounded or were missing.

Mary English and Sylvia Skimming both sailed to Italy from North Africa at the end of 1943, Mary as a QA and Sylvia to continue her work as a Welfare Officer with the Red Cross. Mary and another QA from Philippeville, Virginia Buck, docked at Táranto, a port on Italy's 'heel', and the two spent the best part of the next year following the British First Army* as it fought its way slowly and bloodily up through the country almost as far north as Venice.

Now instead of being part of a large general hospital, the nurses were allocated to Casualty Clearing Stations – small, flexible units, staffed by four or five Sisters, based about eight miles behind the lines. Italy's mountainous geography meant that this war was fought by small units, all intent on dislodging the enemy from the commanding heights, and Casualty Clearing Stations were highly manoeuvrable. The wounded were picked up and given basic first-aid treatment on the battlefield by Red Cross orderlies and were brought to the CCS by ambulance. These mobile stations offered a fairly basic medical service – soldiers needing major operations being transferred to base hospitals in Bari on Italy's Adriatic coast, or Naples.

People today think of Italy as a welcoming holiday destination, a land of warm sun, good food and soft wine. In the winter of 1943–4 it was very different. The weather was unusually cold and wet and the troops, based in the lowlands, endured mud and rain to rival the grim Flanders battlefields twenty-five years earlier. The Italians, though delighted that their country had changed sides, were starving as the Germans skinned

---

* During the course of the Italian campaign the British First and Eighth Army became one force.

the land, taking everything edible and drinkable with them to punish their turncoat former allies.

Mary and Virginia spent their first night in Italy in what had been a five-star hotel in Táranto, now stripped of everything except its marble floors. The next day they moved into a former school surrounded by vineyards in the little village of Trinitapoli, about five miles north-west of Barletta. Conditions were basic, but at least, unlike the locals, they were not starving. Part of the First Army, they travelled with cooks and so, if nothing else, there was always chai and Maconochie stew and army biscuits. 'The only thing that never let us down was the chai wagon,' says Mary. 'It was a huge machine heated by an oil flame and topped by giant urns into which everything – water, tea, milk and sugar – went simultaneously. We had our tin mugs with us all the time.'

The nurses were stoical about their conditions, but Sylvia Skimming was appalled at the state of the billets the army allocated them that first night.

> We were told to go to a block of flats . . . it sounded all right, but we were over-optimistic: it was awful. It *was* a block of flats – but it was completely empty! Marble floors, enormous windows, and not one stick of furniture. No heating and only a few lights in some of the rooms . . . Our batmen as usual did marvels. They got some kind of a Tommy cooker going, and we sat down to a meal of the inevitable bully, bread and cups of tea. We sorted ourselves out into rooms, and got our possessions together. Then Matron came in and told us, 'They're trying to get your beds off tonight, but it may not be possible.' I don't think I have ever felt more cold or miserable. A few of us were lucky enough to have rugs, and we sat for hours in our greatcoats in the dark, huddled together for warmth, but feeling frozen. At last, however, at midnight, our beds arrived, and the poor batmen staggered up and downstairs with them. Never have we unpacked and put them up so quickly. I had luckily kept my Primus with me and a kettle, and I made our dormitory hot water bottles.[1]

Skimming spent much of her year in Italy based in Naples and was indignant at the army's choice of billets for the Sisters.

They lived in appalling discomfort, sleeping thirty in a room, with the usual lack of furniture and no amenities . . . their dressing tables were the usual converted packing cases, with all the rest of their possessions in trunks under their beds. They lived in this fashion for a year, in a civilised country we had conquered! Nobody who hasn't experienced it, can imagine the horror of living like that. Nurses are on duty at different times, and one could never be alone for a minute, night or day, and, when trying to snatch a half an hour's rest . . . there would be constant coming and going and no peace at all. They had one small room with a dozen chairs as their mess and very little was done to better conditions for them.

Mary English was more concerned about the plight of the villagers, charming, warm-hearted people, whose gaunt, skeletal bodies bore witness to the pillaged land. 'There wasn't even any decent wine left. The Germans had taken it all with them. They did the same in Greece. We used to be woken at 4 a.m. by the rumble of cart wheels as farmers left the village to go out into the countryside and see if they could find anything to eat.'[2]

As the Italians were fighting alongside the Allies, the sisters now had an Italian batman. He used to offer the girls bunches of grapes – the only food the Germans had left. In gratitude the Sisters organised a party for all the non-medical Italian staff who worked for them in the CCS. They were amazed at the way they threw themselves on the food.

The Americans were a major force in the Italian campaign and one of their first successes, after a fierce and prolonged battle, was to wrest control of Foggia airport from the Germans. It was from here that the massive B-17, B-25 and B-26 bombers took off on the devastating raids which a few months later would reduce the town of Cassino and its ancient monastery to a heap of rubble.

But in the early evening of 2 December 1943, just as night was falling on the port of Bari on Italy's east coast, the Americans unwittingly became the agents of a humanitarian disaster the details of which were so shocking they were hushed up for over fifty years.

There were more than thirty ships in the harbour that night, unloading war supplies. The war had moved further up the coast by then and the Allies' guard was down. Bari was not very well defended and the radar installation, intended to give early warning of approaching aircraft, was out of action. A lone aircraft was seen overhead and many assumed it was an Allied plane. It was, in fact, a German reconnaissance plane. At 7.30 the first German Ju 88 bombers arrived, taking everyone by surprise as they roared in over the harbour at 150 feet. The raid was a catastrophe for the Allies. Seventeen ships were sunk and a vital port destroyed.

But worst of all were the terrible, inexplicable injuries and the slow agonising deaths. Gwladys Aikens, who had survived the sinking of the *Strathallan*, was nursing in the hospital at Bari and worked through the night as the casualties poured in.

> The aftermath of the explosion was almost too pathetic and grim to describe. Only a few hours after dawn following the raid we began to realise that most of our patients had been contaminated by something beyond all imagination.
>
> I first noticed it when one or two of my patients went to the sink looking for a drink of water. This was odd because drinks had already been taken as usual after supper. Suddenly there were more looking for water and we could hardly control them. They were complaining of intense heat, began stripping their clothes off. Patients confined to bed were trying desperately to rip their dressing and bandages off.[3]

Because they did not know what they were dealing with nobody knew how to treat the men.

> There were blisters as big as balloons and heavy with fluid on these young bodies. We were not sure whether the staff was at risk as we did not know what that fluid contained, although we tried to get tests done we were never informed of the results.
>
> We did everything humanly possible – draining the blisters, constant intravenous and eventually mild sedatives, but it was no good. It was horrible to see these boys so young and in so much obvious pain. We could not even give them strong sedatives since we were not quite sure how they would react.

Medical Officers tried to contact the War Office in London for advice on an antidote, but met with no cooperation. The nurses were distraught. 'Despite our ministrations, we were at a loss to battle this poison and we could not save the majority of the wounded; almost a thousand men died in one night and just as many in the aftermath . . . We tried to help make their last hours as painless as possible. Most of them were conscious throughout their ordeal and were so confused about their injuries. Their eyes asked us questions we could not answer.'

At the time, preposterous though it seemed, Gwladys and the other nurses suspected they were dealing with mustard gas. It had, after all, been outlawed by both sides after the First World War because of its horrific effects.

Thirty years after the war, as she was preparing to write a memoir of her life as a QA, Gwladys Aikens became increasingly determined to find out what had killed those young men. She asked the War Office in London for details of the Bari raid but her request drew a blank. It was as if she had imagined the whole thing. When, ten years ago, she revisited Bari and made a special pilgrimage to the British War Cemetery, the vital evidence was missing.

There were no graves corresponding to the date of the raid.

'Where were those men? . . . Easily 1,000 dead, more like 2,000, and there was not even a memorial.'

In the end it was a specialist shipping magazine that gave her the answer. The fifty-year secrecy blackout expired in 1993 and the magazine had picked up on the newly released information. Under the headline 'Mustard Gas Horror at Bari' it revealed that one of the ships moored in Bari harbour, a US Liberty ship* named *John Harvey*, had been carrying a top-secret cargo of two thousand 100 pound mustard bombs. The article described the nightmare:

> Moments later there was another huge explosion. The *John Harvey* had blown up. The ship had broken loose from her mooring and

* Liberty ships were emergency cargo ships built during the war to a British design by American shipbuilders to counteract the losses caused by U-boat raids in the Atlantic and maintain vital supply lines. Between 1941 and 1945 2,751 Liberty ships were built, totally outstripping the German Navy Chief Admiral Donitz's most pessimistic prediction. The emergency gave birth to new technology which broke all speed records. Prefabricated hulls were lifted on to keels with cranes and welding replaced time-consuming riveting. The fastest-built Liberty ship was built in four and a half days. A third of the shipbuilding force that built the ships was women. Liberty ships brought not just food and supplies to sustain a blockaded Britain, but most of the supplies that made possible the invasion of Europe in 1944. The missions they undertook across what was the most dangerous stretch of water in the world played a significant part in the ultimate Allied victory.

begun drifting across the harbour as the crew and medical experts on board tried to stop the flames reaching the cargo. The ship bore down on the tanker USS *Pumper* and just when it was feared the burning ship would inevitably hit the tanker the *John Harvey* blew up. She disappeared completely. There were no survivors among those on board – chemical specialists all died in this explosion. There was no one to warn the port authorities . . .

The report confirmed that the survivors died in agony. 'It was worse for those who had been rescued from the water, covered in oil, for the oily slime covering the surface of the water had absorbed large quantities of the mustard. For many of these men it might be several hours before their oil-soaked clothes had been removed during which time the mustard had gone to work.'*

As the Allies continued to meet stiff resistance north of Foggia and indeed right up the Adriatic coast, Mary English's unit moved down to the small old-fashioned port of Barletta. Then, as the final preparations for the assault on Rome began, they moved across country. At the time of the ill-fated landings at Anzio at the end of January 1944 and throughout the bitter fighting round Cassino, Mary's hospital was sited in a cornfield just south of the town.

The casualties throughout the first few months of 1944 were very heavy. An officer with the RAMC describes how all the medical staff at the Casualty Clearing Station at Anzio 'dug in' for safety. 'The motto was dig or die and the formula is – two shovel lengths long, one broad and one deep, making a grave-like cavity where one slept and dived for protection when off duty. We all became expert divers. Before I left, everyone and everything had been dug in, personnel, operating tents, ward tents and even the ambulances, safe from all except a direct hit.'[5]

Mary's unit received heavy casualties. 'We had bad head injuries, a lot of shell shock cases and dreadful burns. Lads who had been trapped in tanks had terribly badly burned legs.' The head injuries were sent back to base hospitals in Bari or Naples. The burns victims were treated with

---

* The mustard gas had been brought from the United States to back up President Roosevelt's promise that if poison gas was used against American troops, he would reply in kind. Its presence in Bari was top-secret. It was meant to have been unloaded by the time the raid happened but the port authorities did not give the *John Harvey* priority, expecting it to wait its turn. The ship's Captain was unable to discuss the reason for the urgency.[4]

Vaseline gauze which was left on for five days to enable the new skin to grow. Mary and her friend Virginia went through Cassino exactly one week after the Germans left. 'The devastation was total. There was nothing left of the town except piles and piles of stones and one incongruous little sign saying "Hotel".'

As they neared Rome, just a few miles behind the front line, the desperate battle was continuing – a situation one weary eyewitness described as 'shells, bombs and machine gun fire for 24 hours a day, seven days a week'.

> We were camped about eight miles away from Rome and we could hear constant gunfire. At that time the soldiers came to us straight off the battlefield. They were so exhausted, they almost couldn't move. The drivers from the Royal Army Service Corps also suffered from exhaustion. They were driving hundreds of miles in a stretch of duty, transporting war materials up to the front line and ferrying endless casualties to the CCS. They would come to us nearly dropping on their feet. We would just put them into bed. They weren't hungry or thirsty. They just wanted to sleep. We put them to bed and they slept – often for 24 hours. As soon as they were rested they'd be off again.[6]

Nurses like Mary English saw themselves as having a job to do and getting on with it. Even with hindsight they don't judge themselves to have been particularly brave or heroic. However, the sight of British nurses on the battlefield, a sight that had never been seen before, clearly achieved its aim of boosting the morale of the troops. The same RAMC officer who described the 'digging in' procedure at Anzio, paid a moving tribute to the pluck of the army nurses in those grim conditions in a graphic letter home to his wife:

> Imagine a ten acre field surrounded by pine woods and scrub oak and packed with the tents of a Casualty Clearing Station where the wounded were brought in night and day in an endless bloody procession – men shattered in nerve and mutilated in body – but not out of the battle (one was never out of the battle on the beach-head). The whistle of a shell, the pit pit pit of the machine gun

bullet and the horrid scream of the dive bomber is a super-hell to a helpless man on a stretcher.

But what is this? Those funny figures in battledress. They can't be RAMC orderlies (and a woman in battledress can look funny). God bless 'em, the QAs are here! Our own women are with us. Up go the drooping tails! They must not see how near we were to the dread-edge of panic! They're taking it too! And calmly they took it and proudly they hid their fear; a shaking hand was held, a joke cracked – the raid is passed (until the next one), a gruesome moment is over and the bloody, mucky work goes on. The sickly smell of blood, the bravely stifled groans, the dim lights – only a Hogarth could paint it, the setting of the epic conduct of these women. What a tribute to the discipline of hospital training! . . . No more strategically intelligent order was ever given than that which sent the QAs to the beachhead. And they were of all our races and had their national characteristics – English more reserved, Scots more rugged, Welsh fatalistic, Irish demonstrative . . . but they all gave of their finest, stirred to their maternal depths by many of the helpless men they served.[7]

He ends by saying with moving simplicity: 'To work for those women with my tail up in the dirt was the most satisfying thing I ever did in my life.'

Rome finally fell on 4 June 1944. Hitching a lift from some Americans days later Mary English found a silent city of empty shops and starving people. Kesselring's decision to proclaim it an open city had been scrupulously respected and the only sign of war damage Mary could find was one small window in the Vatican. She travelled in with her friend Virginia. Both being Catholic they looked up the Irish College and befriended the priests there. They too were starving, their habits hanging loose on their emaciated frames, and the Sisters took them tins of bully beef.

They went to the Vatican and saw the Pope, Pius XII, who invited service personnel into St Peter's after the Allies took over Rome. 'If you were in uniform he would come up and shake hands with you. He preached a sermon of welcome from the pulpit in St Peter's.'

The Irish fathers told the girls that while the Germans still occupied Rome the Vatican used to hide escaped British POWs and said they used to visit them. 'When the POWS needed to move, the Irish fathers would go to the Vatican and dress the British soldiers up as Italian civilians, right under the noses of the Germans. One night they were all nearly caught. One of the priests was with a group of escaped British prisoners, all dressed as Italians, including the officer, and the sound of hobnailed boots was heard on the paving stones. Italian civilians didn't wear hobnailed boots. "Pick your feet up," the priest hissed, just as a German patrol came into view. Luckily they got away with it.'[8]

Even though Rome had been regained, the Germans would resist ferociously every step of the Allied advance and the conquest of Italy would not be accomplished for almost another year. Mary's unit stopped briefly at Orvieto and then moved on to Perugia where she met up with more QAs. The beautiful city had been left largely undamaged by war and the QAs moved into a former school. The huge number of casualties from Monte Cassino meant that they worked round the clock with no off-time and often little sleep. They tended appalling injuries, and saw men suffering agonies.

There were dreadful burns which took ages to dress. There was one lad from a tank both of whose legs were very badly burned from the thighs to the feet. His uniform had melted into the wound and we had to cut the cloth away. We had big basins of saline and we used swabs to soak the cloth free of the flesh. Then we used forceps to pick out any bits of foreign matter that remained in the wound. It was very slow to do and agonisingly painful for the victim. I remember a driver who was in terrible pain from burns when his lorry was hit and had exploded. Naturally we gave painkillers, usually codeine, but occasionally morphine. After that we used Dettol as a disinfectant. With bad burns we used to grind up four or five sulphonamide tablets till they were a fine powder and sprinkle that on the burn. Septicaemia was the big risk with burns so you had to prevent infection at all costs. When the wound was perfectly clean we would put on a dressing of Vaseline gauze. Our surgeon believed that if you prevented air from getting into the burn you helped the new skin to grow so we left the dressing in place for about five days at a time. After that the wound would be a bit putrid, very smelly and full of pus, but when you cleaned it with salt and water you would see new skin growing. After the war some skin specialists disagreed. They insisted that the dressing be changed every day, which was what you did with wounds. That was awful as every time you changed the dressing you tore off the skin. After the war I even saw burns left to 'heal' in the air.

The soldiers who were burned suffered absolute agonies and it was very upsetting to see. But they were incredibly brave and uncomplaining. The British were particularly stoical and the Irish troops used to be able to crack jokes. Many soldiers had burst eardrums as a result of the colossal noise of the guns and shells and there were a lot of bad head injuries. They had to be treated in base hospitals in Naples and Malta.

Being constantly on the move meant ever fewer creature comforts. The camp beds the girls had with them when they landed had long since got lost en route and all they had now was a bedroll and a toothbrush. There was still very little food and they were always hungry. 'The only thing there was in abundance was grapes and you couldn't fill up on them. Once the cooks got hold of some flour and tried to make fresh bread which we hadn't had for months, but most of the time it was just army biscuits.'

In Perugia Mary found herself nursing many of the Indian and Gurkha troops who had played such a heroic role in the battle of Monte Cassino. 'We had two wards of Sikhs and one of Gurkhas. The Gurkhas had climbed right up Monte Cassino behind enemy lines and killed a lot of Germans by creeping up behind them and slitting their throats with their *kookris*. They used to sit around in the ward cleaning these *kookris* and took delight in telling us how many Germans they'd killed. They were lovely chaps, very appreciative of everything we did for them.'

The advantage of nursing these troops was that, in deference to their culture, they had their own cooks, a separate team for Muslims and Hindus. 'Their food was far tastier than ours. They used to make lovely curries, with proper spices, and sometimes they would let us have the odd titbit.'

It was at Perugia that the Sisters, used to the unquestioning obedience of British and Indian troops, had their first encounter with the more free-wheeling Australians. 'Tidiness and discipline were ingrained in our troops. Spare uniform, blue trousers for the up patients and towels had to be folded on lockers in a particular way and there was an inspection at 10 a.m. every morning. The Tommies would have theirs absolutely perfect but the Australians were a disaster. Their lockers were always a jumble and it didn't matter how much we remonstrated, they were always untidy.'

It was not long before the line moved on again, forcing back the Germans, who had been ordered not to retreat, mile by painful mile. The QAs took over a big school in Rimini, situated on the main road overlooking the Adriatic, turning the high-ceilinged classrooms into wards. Once known as the pearl of the Adriatic, the town had been blown to pieces. About five or six miles outside the town at San Marino there had been a devastating tank battle that had gone on for hours. Once again horrific casualties poured into the converted school. In addition to the dreadful burns which often penetrated right down to the bone, men whose tanks had been blown up by mines came in blinded, jaws and genitals blown off, skulls smashed, limbs severed. The noise made by a direct hit on a tank blew out the men's eardrums and the hospitals were full of deaf soldiers queuing up for ear drops.

For the Sisters, conditions became ever more uncomfortable. 'We hadn't had a bath in ages but we still had our canvas washbasin and we were forever trying to keep clean by sponging ourselves down in these washbasins. We had two pairs of pants each and we were always washing our undies. Virginia and I were running out of clothes and in Rimini we went to the Quartermaster to try to get another shirt each. We were both tiny and the problem was always trying to get something that didn't swamp us.'

It was in Rimini that Mary experienced what was for her the most direct personal tragedy of the war. She had been to church with a Sister she had recently met, a regular QA, who, like her, was a Catholic.

The padre who had preached the sermon was a crusty old chap and he had warned us, rather gloomily, we thought, that we should never miss going to Mass as in war you never knew when you were going to die. That very evening, as my friend was walking along the main road from her living quarters to the hospital for the start of her night duty, she was knocked down and killed by one of the huge lorries the Americans drove. She was only 30. We were all terribly upset. The roads in Italy were very narrow and full of craters and potholes and there was an unending traffic of tanks and lorries which were always in a hurry. There were a lot of casualties through road accidents during the war.

The Italian campaign was to continue to carve its arduous route northwards for many more long months – the Germans in Italy did not surrender until April 1945. But there was a new feeling of optimism in the air. Talk of a second front was rife.

Sylvia Skimming, stationed at the base hospital in Naples, rejoiced at the sight of Naples harbour filled with American and Royal Navy ships. The quayside was packed with crates of stores and ammunition and Italians were helping load the ships. 'The Germans did not discover this and there were no air raids on the harbour for the entire week.'

The emphasis of the fighting was shifting northwards and the QAs were to follow.

Many of the anecdotes about the behaviour of the Americans during the war are unflattering. Their detractors depict them as undisciplined and brash, lacking the respect for hierarchy that characterised the British Tommy and crude in their social interaction with women. But the Americans played a huge part in the liberation of Italy, showing as much courage and grit as any other national group and being slain in equal numbers. Those who liked them emphasise their warmth and humanity. This story reflects both views.

Mourning Miss Mac

We stood with our hats off and thought about Sister Mac. We had not seen her for a couple of months, but the days when she took care of us in Ward 4D East, in the British General Hospital in Naples seemed very close this afternoon. A pale, slender girl, with dark hair and eyes, she was very conscious of the two pips on her shoulder.

The British call their nurses 'Sister', but it is not a term of familiarity.

Miss Mac liked discipline and order. That was why she had such a hard time with Ward 4, where American Field Service volunteer ambulance drivers stayed when they were sick. We were unruly, untidy and sometimes a little impolite, which she could not understand at all. Some of us were there long enough to get to know her pretty well.

'The Dean'

Bernie, who had been in bed for six weeks, was 'Dean' of the ward. I was there nearly as long. The atmosphere of the place was that of a club, and chief business was teasing Miss Mac.

We never called her by her real name. Sometimes we called her 'Beautiful', which made her blush quickest of all.

That was a remarkable thing about Miss Mac – she blushed faster and more violently than any woman we ever saw. It became a game with us. Somebody would compliment her on her hairdo, or ask her if she had a date that night, or refer to her as 'The Dean's Girl', and immediately her skin would glow like a cloud with the sun rising behind it.

Her worst days were those on which the colonel inspected the wards. She could not believe that Wally could really want to light a cigar just at the crucial moment. She would rush about opening windows and getting the smoke out of the room.

Christmas Eve

On Christmas Eve somebody got hold of a bottle of brandy. We made milk punch in a hospital bucket, and lured her in for the party.

One of the boys had received a Christmas stocking from home, and we turned it into a present for Miss Mac. We put in some cigarettes, candy, a cake of toilet soap, and a little jar of cleansing cream, which somebody had been carrying around. Wally put in one of his cigars, and we filled up the rest with oranges and nuts.

That day, when she opened her drawer there it was, bulging and red, with a card saying, 'Merry Christmas, Miss Mac.'

She picked it up and slowly turned to face us, the blood rushed to the roots of her hair. She opened her mouth just once, but nothing came out, and she ran from the room.

But when she came back her hand was specially gentle as she took our pulses and tucked in the sheets.

Salute

That was about three months ago.

The day before yesterday the Germans raided Naples, and bombs fell on the hospital.

So this afternoon those of us who could get there stood with our hats off and thought about Miss Mac. Her coffin looked incredibly small as they lowered it into the ground.

At the end all the officers of the hospital stood one by one before the grave and saluted. You could not help thinking how that would have made her blush.

'The Dean' cried more than the rest of us, which was only natural because she had taken care of him the longest.[9]

17

'Come and see what we are part of'

By the start of 1944 it was clear that something big was in the offing. Now it was not so much *if* there was to be an invasion of Europe, as *when*.

The largest transport armada ever assembled – 4,126 vessels – lay in the ports of southern England, manned by two hundred thousand sailors. Nearly three million troops were at the ready. A D-Day strike force of nine hundred armoured vehicles and six hundred guns together with 13,743 aircraft had been earmarked.

Dorothea Chisholm was one of hundreds of QAs who were sent to mobilising units up and down the country to be prepared for the epic drama that was D-Day. Many of these girls were newly qualified and had not yet seen active service. The Sergeants whose job it was to get them fit had their work cut out.

Dorothea and fifty other QAs were sent to Peebles, near Edinburgh, to be put through their paces. Most were raw recruits, but some Sisters were back in Britain after serving in North Africa.

'The idea was that a Commando sergeant would get us fit enough to be able to join Monty's force. It was a very cold winter. We went for cross-country runs in the snow, over the hills and beside the Tweed, we vaulted over gates . . . we did drill and PE . . . I was very sporty, having swum for my hospital swimming team so I loved it, but not all the girls felt like me.'[1] There were also lectures to prepare them for the unfamiliar experience of working alongside male orderlies and for the need for flexibility when working in a field hospital.

Dorothea had joined the QAs at the end of 1943 and had been working in a babies' hospital in Liverpool while she waited to be called up. Like most of the girls she found the army equipment she was issued with faintly comical – 'A canvas valise, canvas wash stand, canvas bed, canvas bucket, even a folding canvas bath – all packed in a big tin trunk printed with our name and number.' But she loved the smart uniform for which each girl was personally measured at Hector Powe, the best tailors in Edinburgh. By this stage of the war the distinctive grey and scarlet uniform had been abandoned. From now on the girls would either wear battledress, complete with boots and gaiters, or, for dress occasions, a suit, worn with shirt and tie, made of the best khaki barathea.

The atmosphere at the training camp was one of high spirits as the young girls, liberated from the iron rule of their hospital Matron after four years of training, came into daily and unfettered contact with the three hundred men and twenty-five doctors – all destined, after the invasion, to become Number 6 General Hospital British Liberation Army. The girls were billeted in Nissen huts hastily put up on the hotel's tennis courts and had their meals in the hotel dining room – much better food than they had been used to as civilians.

At last they were being treated as adults, a feeling heightened by their new officer status. 'In pre-war days we had been known merely as nursing sisters, but now we were all commissioned. We were all lieutenants with two pips on our shoulders.' This gave them entry to the Officers' Club in Edinburgh where, to the southern girls' amusement, the men wore kilts for dancing. Dorothea, who came from a strictly teetotal family, even developed a taste for beer.

Their training complete, they were posted to their mobilisation unit outside Carmarthen in South Wales to remain on standby. There was no work to do and the army did its best to keep the young people occupied. There were regular games of hockey and rounders, treasure hunts and hikes. They went swimming in the river and drank in the pubs of Carmarthen. The RAMC officers held dances in their Mess and, because of the shortage of women, the army waived its usual 'no fraternising' rule. By special dispensation QAs were allowed to visit the Sergeants' Mess and attend the Other Ranks dance.

The byzantine reasonings of the army over traditions of rank was a puzzle to the newly commissioned Dorothea, who had become friendly with a highly educated man who was one of the chemists attached to No. 6 Hospital. 'One of the bones of contention was that the chemists were never made officers. They were always sergeants. I was friendly with one chap. His brother was a Major but he was unable to qualify as an officer.'

Time dragged as they waited for the off. No one said anything officially. And yet it was clear that something was happening.

'Suddenly half our doctors and fifty of the men disappeared. We were all waiting for news of a second front and of course they had all gone off on D-Day. They had gone over in tank landing craft to bring back the wounded. Just as suddenly they were all back, but no one talked.'

Soon orders came that they were to move again. This time their destination was Goodwood House in West Sussex which had been given over to the Army by its owner, the Duke of Richmond, because it was near Southampton, which was to be their embarkation point.

The girls slept in the attic, which had been the servants' bedroom, and ate in the ballroom. The grand stone staircase resounded to the tramp tramp of army boots. Once more the girls were swept into a round of parties. 'The RAF were camped in tents on the nearby race track. They always had the best bands so we had wonderful music to dance to while we were at Goodwood. Swing bands were coming in then so we had the pick of the latest tunes.'

While at Peebles Dorothea had fallen for a young Captain, who was married. 'It was all very innocent. We just enjoyed being with each other. Wherever we were sent we always looked out for each other and managed to keep in touch.'

They spent hours exploring the wonderful grounds of Goodwood House. 'Once after a dance we had gone for a walk in the grounds, which of course were pitch black because of the blackout, and I fell in a slit trench. My chap had a 2.2 and he showed me how to shoot a rabbit. I'd never fired a gun and to our horror, as I fired my shot, the Goodwood House gamekeeper appeared. I hid the rabbit behind my back as he gave me a severe dressing down.'

With no warning the idyll was over. They were told they were moving the next day.

There wasn't much to pack as we had very few personal belongings. Our luggage was taken ahead in trucks by the men. We knew we were going to France but that's all. Our journey took us to the countryside behind Portsmouth and as we got nearer the coast we

QAs and RAMC members sunbathe beside a lake in Denmark in April 1945. They had been ordered to take a week's rest and recreation after liberating Bergen-Belsen concentration camp. Molly Budge is seen on the extreme right with cigarette.

Allied troops and QAs enjoy a Sunday afternoon tea dance in the compound of No. 2 General Hospital in Tripoli in 1943.

◀ War wedding: Sister Jane Hitchcock at her wedding in the Officers' Mess in el Quassasin, Egypt on 9 May 1942. Jane was one of Molly Budge's tent mates. The bride sports her QA veil rather than the more conventional lace, since troops and QAs on active service had no clothes other than their uniforms.

The wonders of parachute silk. Sarah McNeece (below) marries Harry Saville in the Baptist Church in Dacca on 30 April 1945. All of Sarah's bridesmaids (right) were QAs and all wore dresses made of parachute silk. The silk was very strong and Sarah kept hers for years afterwards, turning it into a cocktail dress by dyeing it and using the material in the skirt to make a bolero jacket.

► A QA helps a weary-looking injured soldier drink in a tented field hospital in Italy. The QA top brass has not yet acquiesced to demands that military nurses wear battledress and the veils were constantly getting pulled off by guy ropes and tent flaps.

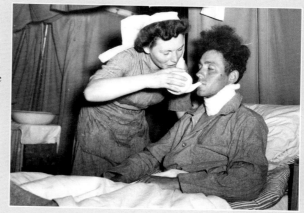

► QA nurses who have sailed to France in the aftermath of D-Day waiting to be allocated to tented hospitals close to the front line in the Normandy countryside. There were so many of these hospitals lining the road between Caen and Bayeux that the area was known as 'Harley Street'. By now the QAs have swapped their dresses for the less ladylike and more practical battledress, a development their patron, Queen Mary, deplored.

▼ QA nurses assist RAMC orderlies in transporting a casualty from operating tent to recovery ward at 78th General Hospital, Bayeux, 20 June 1944.

▲ A historic photograph taken by Molly Budge as the British medical staff leave Belsen. Molly is riding on an army lorry. Her picture shows contaminated huts burning after being set on fire by flame-throwers. The task of tending to the victims of the concentration camp was so onerous that the staff were prescribed stimulants to stay awake longer without succumbing to fatigue.

Two QAs nurse a frail Russian Jewish prisoner who survived the horrors of Belsen. Getting the prisoners to eat was tricky as they could not abandon their habit of hiding and hoarding half of whatever they were given.

A kind face at last. The infamous Changi jail in Singapore, where 3,000 British and Australian servicemen were interned, was liberated in September 1945. Eight hundred and fifty men died there of disease and malnutrition. This survivor enjoying a cup of tea looks on keenly as QAs dispense food such as he has not seen for three and a half years. What the prisoners, fed up with a diet of watery rice, wanted most was bread.

◀ A Ghurka band gives SS *Tairea* an exuberant welcome at the docks in Madras in September 1945 The hospital ship, which had a heroic war record, was bringing the first liberated prisoners of war back from Hong Kong. In the foreground the gangplank is ready to disembark the patients while a fleet of ambulance waits to take them to hospitals.

▼ Irene Anderson enjoys a cooling bath at the back of her all-women residential compound in India. Note the Lux soapflakes favoured by the India *dhobis* for their laundering.

▲ The medical staff of SS *Tairea*: in the centre, adorned with flower garlands, sits the Commanding Officer Colonel Gibson. Irene Anderson is in the front row, far left.

◀ Irene Anderson wearing the dress uniform of the QAs with her QA Reserve badge in evidence.

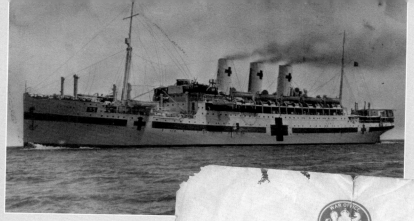

▲ HMHS *Tairea*. This one-time passenger ship was over 20 years old when the war began and was one of a fleet of hospital ships which performed heroic tasks throughout the war, taking wounded men off, often in the thick of battle, and taking them to base hospitals. The old ship would make eight return trips bringing thousands of POWs out of Hong Kong, Singapore Burma and Malaya to be nursed back to health in India

▶ Irene Anderson's release papers. Like many younger QAs who enlisted after the war began Irene was obliged to stay on for some time after war ended. She worked in hospitals in Italy where the people were starving and many injuries were the result of fights over food.

Madam, *Sister I. Anderson. Q.A.I.M.N.S.R.*

Now that the time has come for your release from active military duty, I am commanded by the Army Council to express to you their thanks for the valuable services which you have rendered in the service of your country at a time of grave national emergency.

At the end of the emergency you will relinquish your commission, and at that time a notification will appear in the London Gazette (Supplement), granting you also the honorary rank of Sister. Meanwhile, you have permission to use that rank with effect from the date of your release.

The War Office
A.M.D.4.
20 JAN 1947
Initials *L. M. B. S.*

I am, Madam,

Your obedient Servant,

Lic. B.B.Bird.

◀ A plaque presented to the CO of medical staff aboard HMHS *Tairea* by the officers and Sisters under his command. The plaque lists all the locations of the ship's service between August 1940, when she set out from Bombay on her first mission as a hospital ship to when she brought the last prisoners back to Madras from Port Swettenham on 2 December 1954. During the war she crossed the Equator 32 times, sailed 214,310 miles and treated 35,010 patients.

Dame Katherine Jones who, for most of the war, was the Matron-in-Chief of the QAIMNS. A career army nurse, Dame Katherine's somewhat stern looks belie a warm and sympathetic nature. She missed no opportunity to talk up the achievements of the QAs to a seemingly indifferent public and campaigned vociferously, though unsuccessfully, for equal pay for QAs with male officers of the same rank.

passed trucks and tanks hidden in the copses and woods that lined the roads. Eventually we reached a camp and were told to go to the Mess for a meal. We sat on the ground to eat and everyone threw their change into the centre and said 'let's drink it away'.

The following evening, in full battle gear and tin hats, the unit was embarked in three troopships, the men occupying two and the sisters in the third. They all carried a bag containing a box with 24 hours of emergency rations. 'This included solid cubes of tea milk and sugar combined which were revolting. There were also things made of oats, a bit like a flapjack, a billy can and a little tin containing rock-hard chocolate. Also included were four cigarettes which we could swap for flapjacks if we didn't smoke, and four pieces of lavatory paper. I think we were allowed to take a comb and a lipstick and hankies.' Some girls, worried about the primitive nature of the life they were about to embark on, had brought packets and packets of sanitary towels in their truck, but in the event there was never a shortage. 'In fact you were entitled to government-issue sanitary towels.'

The nurses embarked in daylight and worked out that they must be somewhere off Portsmouth, though no one would confirm this. They lay off the coast of England until nightfall. The women were under strict instructions not to undress and to sleep with their tin hats slung round their necks. Only their boots could be removed. The bunks were made of metal and extremely uncomfortable and Dorothea couldn't sleep.

'I went up on deck. I like the sea so I wasn't scared, just excited. The adrenalin was really flowing by then. We didn't know where we were as it was all secret. By the time we disembarked at Arromanches in Normandy it was daylight. As we neared the amazing floating harbour* I looked over the side of the ship and saw dead bodies floating in the water, all bloated by the sea.'

When the ship docked they walked down a gangplank on to the floating pontoons which formed the Mulberry harbour. The pontoons were topped with planks of wood which had not been nailed down so

---

* The Mulberry harbour was an unprecedented engineering feat which had been put together specially for the D-Day landings. Two artificial harbours, each made up of six miles of flexible steel roadways that floated on steel or concrete pontoons, had been towed across the Channel to create a harbour able to handle 7,000 tons of vehicles and goods each day.

they had to watch their footing. There was no shooting as they landed but the air was still heavy with the smell of cordite and there was an intense feeling of bustle and activity. As soon as the men waiting by the lorries which were to take them to their hospital saw the QAs there was a cheer – 'Come and look at this. There are *girls* coming over.'

Audrey Hayward sailed to France three weeks after D-Day to join 29th General Hospital, also scheduled to operate among the Normandy apple orchards outside Bayeux. There was no prior announcement. 'The only notice we got was when the men loaded the valises and announced: "We're moving."'[2]

She spent her last night in England in the New Forest. 'Once we knew we were being mobilised we were isolated. We couldn't write letters or receive phone calls. As we drove along we could see tanks hidden in the trees lining the road – some had lines with washing hanging from them. By this time we knew we were waiting to be mobilised to France.'

Despite being in tents, they ate excellent food off crested china. 'We were told that it was Monty's express wish that the troops being mobilised for D-Day were to have the best.'

Before they embarked they were all given a small amount of what was known as BLA (British Liberation Army) money in notes. This was to be their spending money in France, its value backed by the Allies, thus avoiding the need to use the currency of the German occupation which could well collapse.

Audrey was not a good sailor and, even though the sea was calm, spent the night below deck on her metal bunk. It is something she now regrets.

'One of the Sisters called me in the morning and said, "Come and see what we are part of." And there was Mulberry harbour. We were surrounded by what looked like a guard of honour – hundreds of ships bringing supplies to the troops in Arromanches. We went ashore in DUKWs.* Tanks were being unloaded from the ships. We were then

---

* Amphibious landing vehicles that you could paddle right in until they ran aground, when they became lorries and drove up the beach.

loaded on to the back of a lorry and taken to where our hospital was to be.'

Audrey says she felt overwhelmed that first day in France. 'On the way to Bayeux we passed a field full of gliders which had brought over the airborne troops. The gliders and the sight of all that magnificent array of ships unloading troops and weapons and provisions in the bay moved me deeply. I felt full of amazement and pride that the Allies had been able to do this.'

The pleasant feeling that she was part of a liberating army was abruptly punctured as they entered the ruined town of Bayeux and a French woman wearing black spat down at them from a balcony. 'I was so upset, but the men told me not to take it to heart as the country people had been treated fairly well by the Germans. The entire place was devastated and when I thought about that woman's reaction later I could understand. She was just fed up with the war.'

Meta Kelly had watched the airborne wing of the invasion from her mobilisation unit in Angmering, West Sussex, where she was wait- ing with the rest of what was to become the 75th British General Hospital.

'On the evening of the 5th we heard a noise in the sky and looked up. The sky was filled with planes and gliders. They kept on coming. It was a proud and unforgettable sight. We looked at each other and said: "This must be it. We'll be off soon." '[3]

Meta's crossing was very different from Audrey Hayward's. Ignor- ing bad weather they sailed from Portsmouth in the troopship *Invicta* on 19 June. The army weren't expecting women on board and had to create a makeshift cabin for them next to the mess, using hammocks. Meta, who in 1944 was a tiny girl of 26 (she just topped 5 feet), says: 'I had had no training in how to get into a hammock and every time I got in I fell out the other side. The others were all in stitches, and though they managed to subdue their hammocks without much difficulty, I couldn't get the knack and so had to sleep on the floor.'

Unbeknown to Meta, that crossing was to go down in the history of the Second World War as one of the worst ever seen in the English Channel. The seas were so heavy that the crossing, which should have taken a day, took three days and nights. The girls, in full battledress, including boots and gaiters, had been ordered not to undress, in case of emergency, and were not even able to wash. 'The only thing we were allowed to take off at night were our boots – mine were size three.'

Most of the girls were very seasick and, Meta feels, probably very scared. None of them had ever left Britain before and many had never been on a boat. She says, however, that they kept their feelings secret. 'We were very afraid of showing fear. In those days there was greater emphasis on self-control. The big question was: "How can I cope without showing fear? I'm a nurse. I'm here to help people." '

The epic journey came to an end and the girls, up on deck, were stunned by what the dawning day revealed. 'The skies were filled with aircraft and the sea, as far as the horizon, was filled with grey vessels of all shapes and sizes, all battling against the wind and the mountainous seas and all unable to make it.'

By the time they got nearer the French coast the storm had died down a little, although the sea was still too choppy for the ships to come alongside. Motor boats came out to the ship and long ladders, tricky things to negotiate, were lowered over the side. 'It was the first time I'd climbed down a rope ladder and we were pretty laden. We had our tin helmets on, our gas masks round our necks and our kit bags, containing ground sheet and unbreakable plate and cutlery on our backs, but the men shouted, "Let's be having you," and helped us.'

They reached land as a fierce battle for the key city of Caen was getting underway.

> It was a scene of complete devastation – ruined buildings all around, burned-out tanks strewn across the beach and everywhere signs that a terrible battle had taken place there. Groups of soldiers, members of the Pioneer Corps, were working at clearing the beach of wreckage. They were very cheerful and as soon as they saw us they all shouted, 'What's happening in England? Have you brought any newspapers? Did you bring any white bread with you?' There was terrifyingly loud gunfire all the time we were landing and it sounded as if the Germans were really close.
>
> The gunfire and shells continued through the night with the constant sound of planes overhead. We were very tired after the

awful crossing but we were overjoyed to be able to take our clothes off for the first time in three days – the bliss of getting our socks off dwarfed our fear of the guns.

18

Operating in the Orchards

The first weeks in Normandy plunged the young QAs abruptly into the reality of war. The Allied attempts to broaden the foothold achieved by the D-Day landings met with unexpectedly stout resistance and injured and mutilated troops – British, American and Canadian – poured into the hastily erected tented hospitals in their thousands. Many were victims of the extensive minefields laid by Rommel, who had been charged by Hitler with improving defences along the north European coastline. In the intensity and confusion of those first desperate weeks, many were, tragically, victims of 'friendly' fire. With the German C-in-C Field Marshal von Kluge under express orders from Hitler not to retreat in the face of the Allied advance, many nurses found themselves far nearer the front line than they expected. By the end of July 10,641 US troops had been killed and 51,387 wounded, and 34,700 men of the British Second Army were killed, wounded or missing. Duty rotas and off-time went out of the window as the nurses tended the endless convoys of stretchers.

Most of the hospitals that nursed the D-Day troops were situated among the apple orchards for which Normandy is famous, on the road between Bayeux and Caen. The 29th, to which Audrey Hayward was attached, was one of the first, but as the Allies consolidated their position, so many hospitals sprang up, either side of the road, that the area became known as Harley Street. The discomforts of life under canvas were increased when torrential rain, which began soon after they arrived, turned the tarpaulin on the ward floors into a sticky layer of mud.

'When we got to our hospital the officers and other ranks were already there,' Audrey Hayward remembers. 'The orderlies had got the tents up and the Pioneer Corps had set up the operating theatre. The French orchards were full of bumps and rabbit holes, but the operating table has to be level, so they used to lay a large concrete float in the middle of the theatre and place two operating tables on it side by side. The surgeons used to work back to back.'[1]

The plan had been for the 29th to act as a 1,200-bed base hospital, well behind an advancing front line, but because of the fierce German resistance, first at Caen and later at Falaise, the Allies were unable to move on as quickly as planned. The hospital ended up operating as an ultra-busy six-hundred-bed casualty station, taking the wounded straight from the front.

Audrey spent the first few days unpacking the famous army bed 'sandwiches' while the engineers set up the generator which gave light to the surgeons in the theatre – at this stage the wards had to rely on hurricane lamps. From the beginning Audrey could hear the booming of gunfire in the not too far distance. Noisier was the anti-aircraft gun positioned in a lane at the back of their field. One night a huge piece of shrapnel came down on her tent, but slid off without causing damage.

'The whole operation was extremely well organised and there weren't any shortages. Within a week they got bakeries and a laundry service up and running and we were provided with things like sanitary towels . . . Compared to what people were going through at home our life bordered on luxurious.'

The hospital was notified that casualties were coming in by a bugle call on which a long G note would be played. Audrey was responsible for the pre-op tent and resuscitation, which included all the drips – blood and saline.

'It was quite dramatic when the casualties began arriving. The ambulances came along the metalled roads and through the field where a big red cross made of canvas was pegged out on the ground, to show that we were a hospital. We continued taking in casualties until the surgeons couldn't cope any more. There was always someone being operated on and another man waiting.'

Audrey was startled, on seeing her first convoy, to note that the men often still had their rifles, or even grenades, and were very reluctant to part with them. 'It was as if they found it hard to realise that their situation had changed and they were no longer fighting for their lives.'

Resuscitation was something of a euphemism. This was where the men who were too ill to be operated on were placed.

'They had dreadful injuries. They were only boys – 19 or 20, younger than me. Some had had all their guts blown away, others had terrible chest wounds . . . I wonder if they knew they were dying. They used to talk to me about their parents. They wanted to see their mothers. There was one lad I particularly remember. He didn't want me to go off duty. I suppose he was afraid of dying. Most of them only lasted two days, then they were removed to the morgue tent and buried.'

Battle conditions demanded modifications to certain medical procedures. The nurses found themselves looking after a far higher number of amputees than would be found in civilian nursing. Under normal conditions the flap of skin would be stitched over the stump to give a more cosmetically appealing effect, but in Normandy the surgeons left the wounds open. 'They didn't look very nice but with battle injuries there is a high risk of gas gangrene. The wounds are often muddy and dirty and sometimes it's quite a time before the injured man receives medical aid. The surgeons gave preventing infection a higher priority than appearance.'

The girls soon adapted to field conditions – sometimes with felicitous results. Audrey learned to tie the bottles containing blood for transfusions to handy guy ropes. 'When the bottles, which were made of glass, were empty, we rinsed them out and threw the rinsing water on the ground outside the tent. A few days later there would be wonderful mushrooms growing there which the cooks would fry for us for breakfast.'

Dorothea Chisholm's first convoy turned out to be a group of Canadians who had been 'shot up', as they bitterly described it, by Americans in one of the notorious instances of friendly fire that happened in the fighting after D-Day.

Fresh from the starched-sheet world of civilian hospitals Dorothea was shocked at the rough and ready nature of field-hospital nursing – but deeply impressed, as were all the new recruits, by the efficiency of the army organisation when it came to the treatment of casualties.

There were no sheets on the beds. Just Army blankets and pillows. Sheets were kept for covering the patients up while they were undergoing surgery. We had the men straight from the casualty clearing stations. They were dirty and bloody and still in their uniforms. We didn't even undress them for surgery as it was important to keep them warm. We washed their hands and faces and sometimes we cleaned their teeth, which they hadn't been able to do for ages. Then we cut off the uniform where the wound was. If it was the arm we cut off the sleeve, if the leg the trouser leg.[2]

Every wounded man who came to the hospital had a label tied to a buttonhole in his battle jacket describing the treatment he had already received at the field dressing station and when he had received it. Those who had received the new wonder drug, penicillin, had yellow labels, those who had had sulphonamide, its predecessor in fighting infection, red. Men who had been given morphia for pain relief had it written on their foreheads in indelible pencil. 'It enabled us to know when another injection was due,' Dorothea explains. 'You can't give morphia too frequently and you wouldn't necessarily give it to someone who was going to have surgery. In those days we used to give penicillin in three-hourly injections, so it was important to keep those injections up.' This meticulously observed system, Dorothea believes, not only saved lives, but protected the medical staff.

'We'd have boys in who had trodden on landmines and had their genitals blown off . . . there were terrible stomach injuries . . . You felt so sad for these young men. All the tension . . . and what you had seen would build up and occasionally you would break down, but most of the time you coped by keeping busy.'

German resistance in the weeks following D-Day meant that Meta Kelly's hospital, the 75th, could not set up as the land earmarked for it was still in enemy hands, so she was diverted to another hospital, the 81st, which was already up and running.

'The fighting was so intense that there was no regular routine in the hospital and we were sent wherever we were needed. We used to see Matron in the morning and she would tell us where we going that day. Some nurses went to a nearby convent to assist the nuns who were nursing casualties, some helped out in 81st. For that period I always worked in different clearing stations under canvas.'[3] In the end the field designated for the 75th became available and on 7 July the unit moved. There was no let-up in the work, however.

> As soon as we were ready to admit casualties we were overwhelmed. Hundreds came in and within days all our beds were filled. You just rushed round from one stretcher to the other seeing if they needed another dose of penicillin. The wounded made very little noise and on the whole they were very brave and uncomplaining. What most of them wanted most, unless they were dying, was a cigarette, and although it may seem shocking to people today that a nurse helped a patient to smoke, we were glad to light one for them.

Despite the horrific physical injuries what upset Meta was the number of soldiers whose nerves had been shattered by the horrors of war.

> We had a lot of what were known in those days as 'battle fatigue' cases. They were very drowsy and behaved as if they couldn't be bothered to move and just lay there quietly. But when the gunfire started up, which was usually after dark, they sprang into life and started desperately digging with their bare hands at the tarpaulin that covered the ground. Like animals looking for shelter they were trying to get underground. It was a dreadful thing to see and I used to have a terrible time calming them down, which we did with a combination of sedatives and soothing talk. They were nearly always evacuated back home within 24 hours but it horrified me to think that in an earlier age they might well have been shot.

The nurses came across all the nationalities that were fighting on the Allied side. 'The British were grateful for anything you did for them,' Dorothea remembers, 'and the Canadians were also very nice lads. I looked after a very tall Canadian Indian with long black hair and a face that looked as if it had stepped straight out of a Western. He was very badly wounded and must have been in a lot of pain, but he never groaned or showed any expression on his face. By contrast a French soldier who had a septic finger made a lot of fuss.'[4]

Meta Kelly, like many other QAs, found the Americans' informality startling.

I was on night duty when an enormous American officer from Texas was admitted. He had a pretty bad head wound and was unconscious. He was too big for our beds and we had to extend the bed with boards to accommodate his legs. The second night he started coming round. I was the only sister on duty and I sat with him, talking to him as much as I could and using his name – the idea that people could respond to communication when they were unconscious was just starting to be discussed then. The third night I was on my way round the ward speaking to each patient, when I noticed the Texan sitting up with his pillows plumped up, looking quite bright. He must have recognised my voice because as soon as he saw me, with my diminutive frame, he exclaimed: 'Gee, Sister, is that you? Where I come from many a good-sized squirrel is bigger than you.'[5]

Many of the casualties were head injuries who were housed in a ward by themselves where they lay, silent and comatose, their heads shrouded in plaster of Paris 'helmets'. Brenda McBryde, who had sailed to France with the 7th BGH, worked for a time in one of these 'Heads'. Despite the fact that the men were unconscious, strange things happened in 'Heads'.

One day a burly Guards Sergeant Major was admitted.

He was brought in from the theatre in a very boisterous mood and it took the surgeon, an orderly, Janet and me to get him into bed and keep him there. Then he started singing. In a deep and penetrating voice he sang clearly and distinctly all the words of a song whose melody was familiar but whose lyrics most certainly were not, and would have been more at home in a rugby football changing room . . . The surgeon was just about to make a hasty retreat when an amazing transformation took place in the ward. One by one the unconscious men, responding to the barrack-room choruses, joined in, till the whole tent resounded. Still with eyes closed and lying totally immobile like rows of white-capped angels, our ward full of head injuries rollicked through every verse.[6]

After the fall of Caen, and later still when the Allies closed the Falaise gap and overran German positions, the hospitals began to receive more and more German wounded. These were a mixture of SS troops and members of the Hitler Youth, teenagers whose hostile and aggressive behaviour was more typical of the brainwashed fanatic than the soldier. The cost in life to the Germans of defending northern France had been horrific and by now Hitler was drafting whoever he could into his armies. In the six weeks after D-Day the German army had lost 97,000 men killed, wounded or missing. This included twenty-eight generals and 354 lieutenant generals. Among the wounded was Field Marshal Rommel who had left the front for the last time after his car was strafed by Allied aircraft on 17 July.

Dorothea Chisholm found nursing the Hitler Youth troops hard.

> Many of them came to us with limbs already amputated by their own doctors. We were told it was German medical policy, if a wound looked nasty, to simply take the limb off on the field. They were really young, 16 or 17. At one stage in Normandy we had them all down one side of a ward. You wanted to feel sorry for them, but they were so unpleasant it was hard. We had to empty their pockets and one lad handed me some small things made of metal. I was holding them in my hand when an RAMC officer came in and saw them. He took them off me straightaway. They were detonators. The German boy was laughing his head off.[7]

German Other Ranks were guarded by RAMC NCOs armed with rifles. But medical corps men were not the most bellicose and there were instances of German wounded escaping. Audrey Hayward may well have foiled a break-out. 'By now the wards had electric light, but only two bulbs and they were very dim. I was doing the rounds of the POWs ward on night duty when I saw the Sergeant who was supposed to be on guard. He had left his rifle at one end of the ward and was standing under one of the light bulbs deep in a book.'[8]

How the Germans were treated varied from hospital to hospital. Under the Geneva Convention they were entitled to the same treatment as Allied troops, which meant they should have equal access to penicillin, but, not surprisingly, the army often took the view that the ultramodern drug, which was still very expensive, should be saved for Allied casualties. German wounded arrived with their own supply of sulphonamide which they kept in their pockets. Meta Kelly's hospital was scrupulous in treating German and British wounded alike, according to medical necessity. 'But I heard from another QA that in their field hospital they did not give penicillin to the Germans.' Some of the nurses found it hard that Germans should be given the best, especially when they behaved so badly. In Audrey Hayward's hospital Germans in the resuscitation tent, who were not expected to survive, were given orange juice. As this was a luxury unobtainable to British civilians it caused a lot of resentment and the matter was raised with the CO. He, however, sanctioned the treatment, quoting the Geneva Convention.

Meta worked in the officers' ward, which included Germans. 'Patients were classed according to rank and not nationality. The only difference between the way Officers and Other Ranks were treated was that the Officers were served sherry in the evening.'

A major factor that helped prevent the QAs from identifying too personally with wounded troops was that after D-Day, with the German air force all but destroyed and the skies safe, it became army policy to fly most of the injured back to be nursed in military hospitals in Britain. This meant that most Allied casualties only stayed in a field hospital for a few days and that after a while the QAs were nursing more German than Allied patients.

In the first few weeks in France the nurses were too busy dealing with the deluge of casualties to mind much about their living conditions. Water rationing was irksome, but like their colleagues in North Africa they soon worked out a reasonably satisfactory system of strip washing. They all, however, loathed the primitive lavatories, which were a board with holes in fixed across a trench. A screen of tarpaulin shielded them from the men, but there were no indvidual partitions. In some hospitals Matron had her own personal privy.

Despite having been an enthusiastic Girl Guide Dorothea Chisholm found it a challenge:

> It was very muddy and it was a terrible palaver. We had trousers and leather boots and tin hats and gas capes on. One day the hessian blew down while some of us were in there and the men were queuing up for breakfast. They were very chivalrous and to a man all turned their back. The latrines took away any sense of hierarchy. You were quite likely to find yourself sitting next to Matron. I did try to get some privacy by getting up early. I put on

my tin hat, left the bell tent and crept towards the latrines. There was no one there. Bliss. Until suddenly a little chap from the pioneers appeared carrying a shovel and also wearing a tin hat. I didn't know whether to stay seated or try to get up, but he simply said, 'Good morning sister,' and continued on his way. I suppose he had come to throw earth into the trench and hadn't expected to find anyone there.[9]

The Americans were even more nonplussed by the enforced return to nature. Dorothea saw a perplexed-looking American nurse standing outside a ward carrying a full bedpan. 'She asked me what she should do with it. "Sling it in the hedge," I told her. She looked horrified.'

On occasions the uncomfortable conditions and the army equipment that didn't work proved a welcome source of humour.

Audrey Hayward came back to her tent one night to find her tent mate jubilant. 'We all detested the canvas baths that you were meant to be able to have a whole-body wash in. They invariably collapsed and the water ration meant you couldn't get your body covered anyway. On this occasion my friend shouted, "Look. I've got my back under water." She had achieved this by sticking both legs up in the air. What she didn't know was that she had forgotten to lace the tent up."[10]

Matron in a civilian hospital would be quick to crush any sign of undue femininity from her young staff, but in the field hospitals of Normandy, where the lives of thousands of young men hung by a thread, Matron's attitude underwent a sea change. It was a firmly held belief of General Montgomery, who commanded Allied land forces in Normandy, that the presence of British nurses comforted and cheered the wounded men; to maximise this effect they had to look like women. Accordingly, despite the practical difficulties of negotiating guy ropes, they were all required to wear their traditional white caps. Audrey Hayward was so concerned about catching lice from the German wounded, many of whom, in the Germans' retreat, had been left for days without personal care, that she appealed to Matron.

'I asked her if I could cover my hair with a sling to protect it, but she was adamant. The men's morale was more important than whether I got lice or not. I had to wear my veil.'

The Matron of Meta Kelly's hospital had equally strong ideas about appearance: 'She was a wonderful woman, absolutely dedicated to the patients, and although she sympathised with our feeling tired she was adamant that we should not look it. In the very early days she summoned us to her tent. Wondering what she was going to say we hurried in, to be told: "I'm tired of seeing you going round looking so tired all the time. These men have been in battle and they are wounded. They don't want to be looking at tired wan faces. Go to your tents and put some lipstick on." '[11]

Throughout that summer British, Canadian and American troops battled against a German force that may have been increasingly depleted, but was determined to go down fighting. Field Marshal von Kluge's force held the British Second Army in a bloody battle for Caen that lasted a month – the ancient town, by now a heap of ruins, finally fell on 9 July. In one incident to the west of the town a lone German Tiger tank destroyed a column of twenty-five Allied tanks and armoured vehicles. With Caen in Allied hands the British Second Army was ordered south towards the town of Falaise. The plan was to lure the German 15th Army away from Brittany, where it was defending strategic ports. This enabled the Americans to take Brittany in just one week and then, under the charismatic General Patton, to head east and north to encircle the Germans. That the plan succeeded so brilliantly was due in large measure to Hitler's despotic control. Instead of allowing his commander to retreat through what came to be known as the Falaise Gap, he ordered him west to the defence of Brittany, allowing it to close behind him. The gap was not closed until 17 August. Those Germans trapped inside the ring were pounded by a remorseless artillery barrage by the Americans. Just south of Falaise the Allies buried ten thousand German dead and took fifty thousand prisoners, many of them wounded. In the chaotic retreat the Germans abandoned their wounded in their field dressing stations.

As the line of battle moved up towards Belgium the pace of work became less hectic. Some of the girls moved up with the troops, while others were able to enjoy the occasional trip out into the surrounding countryside.

By September the rate of casualties had slowed down sufficiently for the QAs finally to get some off-time in the day and even the occasional day off. Paradoxically, although she had been immured in a world where injury and death were the norm, it was only when Audrey Hayward got away from the hospital that she realised the full cost of the D-Day landings.

> We decided to have a look at Caen. We walked through fields until we came to the crossroads where we had a good chance of getting a lift from a passing jeep. Two Americans were going to Caen and they gave us a lift. It was then that we saw for the first time the devastation. We drove through villages where all the windows had been blown out. We could see inside where tables still laid with food had been deserted and we saw cattle lying dead in the fields. Caen itself had been very badly bombed and one shell had gone right through the roof of the cathedral.[12]

One day a couple of RAF officers who were waiting for planes to be delivered invited them to a party.

> It was night time when they came to collect us. The driver pulled in to the side of the road and explained that, as there were no facilities for ladies at their mess, it might be advisable for us to spend a penny before we arrived. He told us not to go into the field because they'd all been mined, but just to pop round the corner of the hedge. That's when we saw hastily dug makeshift graves where soldiers had buried their comrades beside the road. The bayonet would be stuck in the earth with the dead soldier's tin hat and number tied onto it to identify him.

The autumn of 1944 in northern France was cold, wet and miserable. The QAs had abandoned their grey dresses and were nursing in boots and gaiters, treading on duckboards to try to keep out of the mud. It was so cold that the army allocated them a rum ration. But they could never stay warm in their tents at night. The cold would wake them and the only way to thaw stiff limbs was to light their paraffin-fired Beatrice stoves, and reheat the cold water for fresh hot-water bottles.

Many of the other hospitals had packed up and moved further up the line but Meta Kelly was one of the last ones to desert 'Harley Street'. By late autumn, sick of the mud and the cold, they had transferred to Nissen huts and were able to strike up friendships with the French.

'There are stories of how unfriendly and hostile the French were to the Allied troops but that was not my experience. We got to know the people in the local farm quite well. In the middle of this desperate battle they were continuing to farm. They told us stories of neighbours who had been killed and had their cattle blown up, but as far as they were concerned, they were glad to be liberated."[13]

Knowing how limited the girls' facilities were the farmer's wife used to do personal washing for them in return for soap and cigarettes. 'By this time you could get all sorts of things from the NAAFI – whisky, soap, even champagne. I imagine it was all looted from the Germans who had looted it from the French in the first place.'

And, bliss to these young women who, on army rations, were always hungry, occasionally the farmer's wife would invite them in for a meal in their house. Meta spoke a little French and her friend Dorothy was almost fluent. 'That was my first experience of French cooking and I was struck by the leisurely pace of their meals – course after course, instead of everything on the same plate British-style. And everything was washed down with champagne!'

In a bizarre irony that will probably never recur in the history of man, if you were a member (officer class) of the British Liberation Army in Normandy in the late summer of 1944 you could get hold of champagne more easily than water – which, as Meta recalls, was not always useful! 'We got our water from a tanker which came round and delivered daily. When your ration had been used up that was it. One night one of the sisters was going round the camp trying to beg a glass of water. One girl shouted back from her tent offering her champagne instead. "I can't use champagne," the first girl complained, "I'm trying to clean my teeth!"'

The railway which connected Bayeux and Caen ran near the site of the hospitals. If the train driver saw the girls walking he would usally slow down and offer them a lift. 'The public baths were our favourite destination. We had to bring our own towels and we invariably had to queue for a long time to get in. After the bleak ritual of the canvas washstand, being able to soak our whole body in warm water was bliss.'

Dorothea Chisholm's No. 6 moved to Rouen, whose many magnificent medieval buildings had been largely spared by the war. Here they were based in an old convent hospital, a welcome change from tents. By this time the QAs had more German than British wounded.

'They got the best treatment from our RAMC surgeons, but they never expressed any gratitude. In Rouen I looked after an SS officer. Several of the German officers were really quite elderly. At that stage of the war it was like that – Hitler was reduced to drafting the very young and the very old. This officer had been wounded in the face and our surgeon, who was only a general surgeon, had done a wonderful job. I told him he'd had the best possible treatment and he was very lucky.'[4]

They did not know it but this would be their last autumn in wartime. Quickening events would soon take them into Brussels and from there into Germany itself.

In addition to the introduction of penicillin, another area of treatment that progressed in leaps as a result of the war was blood transfusion. Nurses completing their training just before the outbreak of war recall it as an awesome procedure, performed in an atmosphere of bell, book and candle. It was devoutly believed that the blood had to be blood heat and so it was put through a warming device before being used. One Sister, thus programmed, was surprised, when she arrived at her tented hospital after the Normandy landings, to see bottles of blood secured to guy ropes, bobbing about in the fresh air – and the patient none the worse for it.

In the intervening years great advances had been made in the collection and storage of blood. Blood banks had existed in Britain since the late 1930s but problems arose when whole blood was transported long distances, particularly to tropical areas. Doctors found that plasma, a major component of blood, was highly effective in treating shock in battle casualties and much easier to transport. After the defeat at Dunkirk there was an urgent need for plasma and the first mass-scale civilian blood-donation campaign was launched on both sides of the Atlantic. In the six months between 15 August and 17 January 1941, 14,556 big-hearted New Yorkers gave 'Blood for Britain'. The plasma was extracted and diluted with equal amounts of sterile salt solution and sent to Britain in litre bottles, six to a carton. The containers had to be kept small because in those early days they were brought over by Clipper flying boats. Dried plasma, however, was easier to transport than liquid and less prone to deterioration. The invention of freeze-drying revolutionised the transportation of plasma. Britain's two freeze-drying plants, one in Cambridge, the other in Beckenham, a suburb to the south of London, could not produce enough plasma to treat the war casualties until the Army Blood Transfusion Service built its own plant. The ABTS, which was the first military transfusion service in the world, was set up in 1939 and processed more than thirty thousand donations in its first year. Between 1943 and 1945 Britain produced a quarter of a million 400 ml bottles of freeze-dried plasma. QAs working in Egypt and the baking western desert recall the plasma being stored in refrigerated container-style lorries which were kept cold by petrol-run generators.

Throughout the war the British Blood Transfusion Service ran a campaign persuading people that it was their patriotic duty to give blood for the boys overseas. The blood was collected in refrigerated vans and driven to centralised depots where it was processed and prepared for shipment. Later on, as refrigeration and conservation techniques became increasingly refined, it became possible to transport whole blood. The blood was then flown in insulated crates to large blood banks in the major theatres of war. From there it was dispatched forward to mobile transfusion stations which could operate in the battle zone.

By the time the second front had been opened in 1944 the Army Blood Transfusion Service was delivering blood on an almost daily basis to the field hospitals of Normandy. One QA remembers: 'It was a bit like dealing with the milkman. We had a special annexe on the end of our resuscitation tent. We'd leave our "empties" which were glass bottles, there. Next time we went there'd have been a new delivery of closed and sterilised glass bottles.'

19

The Liberation of Europe

After the stalemates of Caen and Falaise, the Allies pushed through France and into Belgium at lightning speed, crushing German resistance. By Christmas the enemy had been forced back to their own frontier.

Many QAs were posted home on leave prior to being sent to India to nurse the casualties of the Burma campaign. Others, including Dorothea Davies and Meta Kelly, packed up their hospital and went to Brussels in the traditional convoy of bone-shaking army lorries. They whiled away the hours with sing-songs of popular tunes such as 'It's a Long Way to Tipperary', 'Run, Rabbit, Run' and 'Show Me the Way to Go Home'.

After the cold and mud of Normandy, newly liberated Brussels was like the promised land. Dancing and socialising were back on the agenda, and this time the Officers' Mess was a luxury hotel not a tent. Despite the city's extensive bomb damage, the shops were full of luxury goods – and there was no rationing. Whereas the French had been ambivalent in their reception of the Allies the Belgians were whole-hearted in their welcome and opened their shops and homes to the liberators.

'It was such a relief to be housed in proper buildings,' Meta Kelly remembers. 'Our new billet had been an old coat-hanger factory on the outskirts of Brussels – so we had plenty of coat hangers. More importantly we also had running water. In fact we had very nice accommodation, just two to a room – I still shared with my friend Dorothy – with our same camp beds.'[1]

Meta's hospital set up once again as a six-hundred-bedded hospital. Casualties continued to arrive in convoys of ambulances – there was fierce fighting for many days in the Ostend area at that time as the Germans strenuously resisted Allied attempts to take the port, a highly strategic gateway for supplying troops based in the north. Now that the hospital was further down the line, however, the men had been cleaned up, and in many cases operated on before they reached the base hospital.

Courted by officers in ritzy surroundings the QAs began to feel like women again.

> The Officers' Mess was right in the centre of Brussels in what had been a very smart hotel. We used to dance to a wind-up gramophone and we were never short of drink at that time – champagne flowed like water, and in Normandy we had had ready access to cider and calvados. We were even able to swap our battledress trousers which had never fitted, for skirts. We got them from the NAAFI. By that time there were quite a lot of ATS women [Auxiliary Territorial Service] in Brussels doing clerical work and driving ambulances. We were free agents in Brussels with not even a curfew, which was a great novelty for us, as even in civilian hospitals there was a curfew.

Towards Christmas things grew tense again as Germany launched what was to be her last great show of strength – the daring and totally unexpected assault on Belgium through the forests of the Ardennes. The Battle of the Bulge, which lasted ten days and was enormously costly in lives to both sides, was fought almost entirely by the Americans. They had great difficulty holding the German advance, which came within five miles of the River Meuse before being forced into retreat once more. Meta and everyone else in Brussels that anxious Christmas heard the guns in the distance.

'We were really afraid that the Germans were going to break through. People would say to each other in the morning, "Noisy last night, wasn't it?"'

In the main, however, Brussels was a place to have fun. The girls had proper off-duty time and leave. Meta got a 72-hour pass and went to stay at the Officers' Club where the bedroom could have come from a film set. 'The shopping in Brussels was unbelievable. We saw things we hadn't seen since before the war back home – perfume, make-up, Paris-type fashions. My sister was married with two small daughters and I bought them lovely party dresses. I bought make-up, too. We met lots of lovely Belgian families who invited us to their houses for meals.'

Throughout her stay in Brussels Meta had been becoming more and more depressed by the war and the suffering it inflicted. 'There had been so much killing. I just wanted it to stop and for the boys to be able to go home for good.' When the long-awaited end came she was still in Brussels.

'The city went mad on VE-Day. Church bells rang and everyone came out of their houses. Strangers danced with each other in the streets and people invited us into their houses to celebrate. We went to the Officers' Club and danced and sang and drank more champagne. It was absolutely wonderful.'

Soon after VE-Day Meta learned that her hospital was going to move with a reduced staff to Norway, so the QAs were all posted to different areas. Some went to Germany, including her friend Dorothy, with whom she had shared a tent ever since embarking for France. She was sent to Bruges. This time there were no battle casualties, but the usual assortment of the local sick and people coming through for evacuation. It was in Bruges, however, that she came face to face with what for her proved the most harrowing evidence of man's inhumanity to man in the whole of the war.

I had had a day off and I came back to the ward which I had left half full of not particularly ill people. I will never forget the sight. The ward contained about 30 living skeletons, whose haunted sunken eyes stared out at me. Each man had a number tattooed on his arm. These men had been liberated from Belsen.

When I first heard about the camps I thought their cruelty and savagery had been exaggerated for propaganda purposes. But here was living proof that it was all true. Many of them must have been in their twenties but they looked like 60- and 70-year-olds. The bulk of them were Jewish, Austrians and Belgians. I spoke in French to those it was possible to speak to, but they were very weary. Most of them just wanted to rest.

They were very ill, both physically and mentally, particularly with digestive problems – worms and dysentery. The consultant in charge of them said they were to be fed frequently, but in very small quantities. We gave them milk and eggs mainly. They were only with us for about two days and it was obvious many of them would not make it.

The Allied advance into Germany was so fast that in one town a German hospital train was found parked in a siding, full of wounded men. It had been there for two or three days, as its destination was by then within Allied lines. The men had simply been abandoned, without water or food and many of them were already dead. Luckily for them a British MO looked after them.[2]

By the time they made it to Germany the nurses had seen pain and suffering on an unimaginable scale. But for a handful of them the worst was still to come.

After her years in North Africa Molly Budge had followed her unit to Italy and from there had travelled to France with the D-Day invasion force. Three weeks before the end of the war, on 15 April, the British went into the infamous Belsen concentration camp and liberated the sixty thousand inmates. Molly's last duty in Europe was to tend the women and children who had been imprisoned there. In addition to starvation conditions, typhus, typhoid fever and cholera were rife in the camp. The work was so demanding the QAs were given stimulant drugs to keep them going.

> About six of us QAs went in a convoy of ambulances and lorries. Part of the procession was a tank with a huge flame thrower. The huts which the wretched inmates had lived in were hopping with lice and disease – and the flamethrower was used to burn down the worst of them. What we saw there was the most horrible experience of my life and for a long time I could not talk about it. There were bodies lying on the ground everywhere, many already dead, others dying. Josef Kramer, the camp Commandant, and Irma Grese,* the notorious female guard, were there when we arrived and we saw the great whips they had used on these defenceless human beings.[3]

While the men dug huge trenches to bury the dead, the nurses got to work to save as many as they could of the living.

* Both were hanged as war criminals in December 1945.

The first thing was to get some of the huts habitable, which we did by scrubbing and fumigating them. The huts they had lived in were so infested with lice we had to use blow torches to the doors and walls to kill them. Then we sorted the inmates into men, women and children. There were 500 children in the camp and on the first day they were all assembled up and sent to Palestine. The mothers did not seem to mind. They knew they would not be able to look after their children and they seemed relieved to know that someone would care for them. The men were so small and bedraggled they didn't look like human beings and the women were so skeletal I wondered how they had been able to conceive and bear children. They were pathetically glad to see kind people and they kept coming up to us, grabbing our arms and kissing all up our arms, saying 'Schwester, schwester' (Sister) over and over again. It was harrowing and, because of the huge numbers involved, unremitting work.

The prisoners were put into big baths and had their hair shaved off to rid them of lice. Their emaciated bodies were covered in sores which had to be treated and although they were desperate for food, feeding them was tricky. Their digestive systems had been damaged by years of abuse and we used to give them a special type of bread which I imagine was easier to digest. But whatever you gave them they would only eat half of it – the rest they would tuck away under their pillow in case they never got any more.'

Molly remained at Belsen for about a week while the prisoners were transferred to hospitals and until the place of suffering and horror was finally empty. In recognition of the shocking nature of their experience, the entire unit was sent to Denmark for a week's rest and recuperation.

Freda Laycock was another QA who experienced the horrors of what the Nazis had done to their victims in the concentration camps. Freda, one of eight children, of a farming family from Hensall in Yorkshire, was with the 10th British Casualty Clearing Station when they liberated Stalag XB at Sandbostel, between Bremen and Hamburg, at the beginning of May 1945. Many of the German women drafted in by the British to help with the Herculean task of nursing the broken survivors back to health broke down, terrified that they would catch typhus, and were unable to continue working. Freda, however, never lost her self-control nor forgot her duty to her patients. She spent VE-Day, when most other young women on the Allied side were dancing and celebrating, tending the sick and dying. Her diary of the last two years of her war service contains entries for those first days in Sandbostel, when she must have been suffering extreme emotional and physical strain. They are, however, pragmatic and unemotional – as one would expect from a QA:

May 6th
Up early packed left Zevan at 2. Arrived POW camp Sanbostal [*sic*] at 4 p.m. Had tea and went round wards. 1700 patients. Had a conference with MOs later about ward work.
May 7th
Meeting with German sisters. On wards at 12 midday. 270 patients on my ward. Very, very busy. Not enough staff, food or equipment. Patients in an appalling condition, starved and dying. Heard late at night it was VE-Day the following day.
May 8th
VE-Day hectically busy.
May 9th
VE dinner but I wasn't there. Went back on ward. Had a glass of champagne later.
May 10th
Better day, patients not calling out so much. Pyjamas issued patients look more civilised.

Freda's guts so impressed Major Hugh McLaren, a fellow RAMC officer, that he paid her a special tribute in his official report. His unflinching honesty in describing his own reactions to the squalor and degradation makes Freda's calm courage, by contrast, appear even more admirable.

The worst part of the stalag, dubbed the Horror Camp, was where eight thousand political prisoners had been kept. A different medical unit, which had arrived at the camp a week earlier, had taken charge of these men. They had been moved from their filthy huts to what the liberators dubbed the Human Laundry, a giant marquee filled with rows of trestles supporting stretchers, to be washed and deloused before being delivered by ambulance to the hospital. Major McLaren admits that he was so distressed by conditions at the hospital itself that he never had the courage to visit the Horror Camp. 'It seems that into a mass of dead, dying, and befouled humanity the SS had occasionally dropped a cartload of turnips or potatoes. Those who had the strength scrambled for food. Out of this human pig sty the likely survivors were picked out.'

Major McLaren and Sister Laycock were allocated to C Block of the hospital where huts built for eighty patients were crammed with as many as 320. On the first day six of the 'skeletons' in the beds were found to be already dead, two had been dead long enough to have rigor mortis. The Major's words paint a picture of almost unmaginable horror.

> My first sensation was one of nausea. The latrines had been blocked for days without discouraging the patients from using them.
>
> Two wards were equally offensive. On my first visit I was near to being sick. Standing on the floor or hanging on to the bunks for support were the merest skeletons of men. They were naked, unshaven and dirty. They defecated onto the floor where they stood. They had sunk so low that no trace of embarrassment was occasioned by the presence of the British or German sisters. Some 80% of the patients were too weak to rise from their beds. Moreover, they were in double tiered bunks. It was easy to see why the hospital was in this befouled state. Each nurse had 60 patients and one bedpan. The patients averaged between 6 and 10 motions per day with famine diarrhoea i.e. at least 2000 stools in our hut alone.

Major McLaren and his fellow medical officers predicted that the QAs would break down under the strain – even making bets as to which one would crack first. But none did, a fact which clearly made him proud. 'They became whiter and whiter in the face. Dark patches were visible under their eyes but it was the German sisters who first went sick or lame (over 10% for two weeks).' The German nurses were terrified of catching typhus. Major McLaren had the perfect remedy to shame them. 'It was certain cure to lead them along to see Sister Miss Laycock, in the middle of the typhus cases, calmly doing her work.'*4

* A copy of Major McLaren's report was found among Freda Laycock's possessions after her death by her daughter Kathryn Ingham. It was addressed, affectionately, in the Major's hand to 'Miss Laycock Chief Officer of the famous C Block'.

While women like Freda Laycock and Molly Budge were dealing with the miry underside of the Third Reich other QAs were discovering the highly civilised lifestyle that had been enjoyed until so recently by its faithful servants and their families.

Dorothea Chisholm had followed her unit from Bayeux to Rouen and from there to Ghent. By Christmas she had crossed the German frontier and was based in Iserlohn on the edge of the mighty Ruhr complex. Eighteen months earlier the area had been the focus of the famous 'Dambusters' raid. Using cutting-edge science Barnes Wallis's 'bouncing bomb' had breached the dams which fuelled the nucleus of German's industrial power.

The hospital was a converted SS barracks and the QAs were billeted in elegant houses which had belonged to SS officers. Now, for the first time, they came face to face with German civilians.

The Americans had been billeted there before us and they had done terrible damage to the houses. They had hauled furniture out and burnt it on bonfires. These houses had been beautifully furnished, with oil paintings hanging on the walls. Each one had a wine cellar. The Americans had shot up the pictures with their rifles, smashed mirrors and opened all the wine bottles and poured out the wine. Everywhere was swimming in booze. The officers' wives were living not far from their old homes and they approached us to ask if they could retrieve some of their belongings, photograph albums, and personal things. We were under strict instructions not to fraternise with the enemy. Some of the sisters were very hard and would have nothing to say to them, but when I looked at the family photos strewn around the gardens, which was what they wanted most, I found it hard to hate them. I know their husbands were SS officers, but you couldn't help realising that they were human beings.[5]

Just up the hill from the QAs' billet was a hospital full of Russians suffering from typhoid. They had taken to shooting at random and the Matron of Dorothea's hospital was concerned for the women's safety. 'Apparently you go a bit crazy with typhoid. We were ordered, when walking up the hill to our houses, to remove our white caps so that we did not make an easy target.'

The wards were still full of wounded, but Dorothea's work in

Iserlohn consisted largely of giving injections of penicillin to speed the healing of wounds.

> We still had to be careful where we went as there was a danger of mines. When we went out the officers who accompanied us had to carry pistols. It was beautiful countryside, with wooded hills and lakes which reminded me of my home in North Wales. The officers had taken over an old German pub which had a proper bar as their Mess. We used to meet them there and go for drives. Once we went by lorry to see the damage done by the British raid on the Möhne dam. It was quite an impressive sight – this huge block of stone which had been swept down the valley. As the weather got warmer, we used to swim in a lake.

By now there were no fresh casualties and many of the nurses were being recalled to Britain. Meta Kelly and twelve other QAs flew home to England in a huge Anson aircraft. Built for transporting troops, the old workhorse had no seats and the girls sat on the floor.

Europe's troubles were over. But thousands of British troops were still fighting a deadly jungle war in Burma. Many QAs would find their next posting lay east.

VI

INDIA AND BURMA

20

A Tiger for the Nurses

The person entrusted with administering this vast force of QAs – nine thousand of whom were serving overseas – was a veteran army nurse who did her training at St Bartholomew's Hospital in London during the years of the First World War. A forceful, articulate woman with strong features and intelligent grey eyes, Katherine Jones came from the small market town of Beccles, in Suffolk, and attended the fee-paying Highfield School. She joined Queen Alexandra's Imperial Military Nursing Service in 1917 and in 1937, when she was serving in Palestine, she was mentioned in dispatches. In 1938 she was brought back to Britain and appointed Principal Matron at the War Office.

Many areas of British life may have been unprepared for war, but the QAIMNS, with its strong army organisational traditions, was not among them. From as early as 1936 trained nurses who wished to volunteer for active service knew, in the event of general mobilisation, which units they were to join, had been issued with travel warrants to those units from anywhere in the country, and were expected to carry these documents with them at all times.

By the outbreak of war Katherine Jones was able to mobilise more than a thousand QA nurses to cross to France with the British Expeditionary Force. The first half-dozen landed in Cherbourg on 10 September, just a week after the outbreak of war. Miss Jones, then Senior Principal Matron, landed the following day. In July 1940, after the chaotic retreat to Dunkirk in which she took part, she was promoted to Matron-in-Chief QAIMNS. She was 44.

The network Miss Jones relied on to mobilise the first thousand nurses was the QA Reserves and the Territorial Army Nursing Service or TANS – a part-time body, made up of civilian nurses, who

volunteered to remain on standby for mobilisation in the event of war –
a parallel to the way that male civilians could be members of the
Territorial Army. As war loomed Matrons of hospitals up and down
the country were briefed to encourage their newly qualified nurses to
join the TANS. 'You didn't know what you were signing,' said one
newly qualified staff nurse, who joined the TANS in 1938, 'but if Matron
asked you to do something you did it.' For the duration of the war, the
TANS was absorbed into the Queen Alexandra Imperial Military
Nursing Service.

From the outset Katherine Jones was a passionate and articulate
champion of her nurses. This was the first time army nurses were, as a
matter of policy, being deployed right up to the front line, and Miss
Jones missed no opportunity to inform the British public, through a
stream of newspaper and magazine articles and radio broadcasts, of their
stoicism, dedication to duty and courage. She was intensely proud of
the way thousands of young women had adapted to the privations and
ordeals of war.

> They have lived in luxury hotels, villas, Nissen huts, tents, house-
> boats, dugout sunken quarters . . .
> They have sailed and are sailing with the Army to every war area
> and share its fortunes. At present they are serving in seven major
> commands . . . and constant requests come from all overseas sta-
> tions for more and more Sisters to be drafted to them. Reserves are
> everywhere serving up to the age of sixty, many of them in severe
> and exhausting conditions. In Florence Nightingale's day it was
> specifically stated that the nurses were for the base hospitals in the
> war area. Today, however, they share the hasards [sic] of total
> warfare.[1]

As evidence of this, Miss Jones cites the fall of Singapore in February
1942. When she was writing, two years later, the fate of the ten QAs
who had been posted to Hong Kong and the sixty who had been nursing
in Singapore was still largely unknown. They were presumed either
drowned at sea or prisoners of the Japanese.

Miss Jones found the idea of shipwreck particularly horrible and it
is for QAs who survived this ordeal that she reserves her particular
admiration. In a magazine article she asks readers: 'I wonder if you read

about the torpedoing of QAs on their way to North Africa – 212 of them?* The very next day 207 started to nurse . . . They were fitted out in soldiers' clothes – it's all there was – underclothes, battledress fore-and-afts and boots. But they don't appear to have nursed any the worse for that, and, indeed, it has proved to us that this clothing was the most suitable for the dreadful rain and cold in that part of the world in December and January.'

Miss Jones was particularly impressed with the stiff-upper-lip atti-tude of the nurses as they waited in the lifeboats for rescue.

> The Principal Matron told me 'there was no sign of any panic'. And one Matron, who was up to her armpits in water in a water-logged lifeboat only remarked: 'Yes it was terrible, because we thought the boat might sink at any moment, but it didn't do me any harm at all – none at all.' They were black with oil in one boat, and just before they landed, so it is said, the Principal Matron produced a comb from her pocket and, handing it round, she said, 'Here, tidy up a bit, and try not to *look* like survivors.'

Courage was a quality much esteemed in warfare and Miss Jones was keen to point out that, in this new type of war, male troops no longer had a monopoly of it. Returning from a tour of field hospitals in North Africa Miss Jones wrote with evident satisfaction: 'Among the indi-vidual QAs who asked to see me all but one wanted to serve on a hospital ship, or in a casualty clearing station or a forward hospital, or even to volunteer as parachutists! I've got several names of Sisters who want to drop from the skies with the RAMC.'[2]

By 1942 the Corps had grown to several thousand and was adminis-tered by a clearly delineated and highly efficient chain of command that embraced all corners of the British Empire. The ruling council was by this time based in Cheltenham, and consisted of the Matron-in-Chief, three Principal Matrons and two Matrons. The overseas staff comprised two Chief Principal Matrons, based in Delhi and Cairo, with Principal Matrons in each war area. India had four, Ceylon one, Egypt two, Iraq and Persia one, West Africa one.

In a radio broadcast made during the war Miss Jones, who in 1942

* This refers to the *Strathallan* which sank off the coast of Algeria on 21 December 1942.

was appointed Dame of the British Empire, stressed that all QA nurses are commissioned officers. 'A Sister has the equivalent rank of 1st Lieutenant, a Sister with ten years service has the equivalent rank of Captain, Matron Major, Principal Matron Lt Colonel, Chief Principal Matron Colonel and Matron-in-Chief Brigadier. Sisters and Matrons are addressed by their rank on duty. All ranks above that of Matron are addressed by their names Miss . . . or Mrs . . .'

An army Sister's duties, she informed her listeners, were twofold: administering and supervising nursing in the wards and nursing the dangerously ill and seriously ill patients herself; training the male nursing personnel.

In the sixty years since the war we have grown more and more egalitarian in our social convictions, distrusting hierarchy and un-questioning respect for rank. To Dame Katherine Jones, whose entire professional life had been dedicated to the army, however, rank and privilege were hard-won spurs. She waged a determined war of her own to have army nurses accepted as fully commissioned officers, in parallel with their doctor colleagues in the Royal Army Medical Corps, who all held officer rank. Her belief was that this would improve the status of nursing in society as a whole.

She prophesied that if she survived at all in nursing history it would be as the 'militarising Matron-in-Chief'.

> Having lived all my life in this [rank-conscious] atmosphere I have learned to appreciate its symbolism. To me, officer rank with all its symbols, its privileges, its duties and its traditions, is a living reality. It means responsibility and hard earned privilege reflecting profes-sional and military achievement.
>
> Can you therefore be surprised that conferment of com-missioned rank on QAIMNS and the TANS was the most signifi-cant day in my working life? To me it was the recognition of the status which a State Registered Nurse should enjoy in relation to the auxiliary personnel. As qualified doctors have conformed to the military pattern, so now State Registered Nurses of QAIMNS and the TANS were to conform to the same pattern with the same justification that they perform the responsible duties of a profes-sional non-combatant officer.

Miss Jones believed devoutly in the power of nurses to cheer the morale of wounded men, and they did this best, she held, when wearing the familiar, feminine QA uniform of grey dresses, white veils and grey half-capes trimmed with red. As the war dragged on, however, this woman who was born in the last years of Queen Victoria's reign, when women in trousers would have been unthinkable, was forced to accept that battledress was more practical.*

> It is clearly impossible for a Service of over 10,000 . . . to continue to wear an outdoor uniform, which though beautiful in itself and rich in honourable tradition, could no longer be renewed overseas and incidentally was not suitable for conditions of active service in camps and deserts, jungles and shipwrecks, or even at home under stress of clothing rationing and cleaning difficulties.
>
> These circumstances, as well as others, danger of machine gun bullets and the ruining of camouflage, drove us into outdoor khaki uniform and even into khaki battle-dress, slacks and boots and anklets.

Perhaps to her surprise she found that she rather liked the modern model – and suspected that the founder of military nursing would also have approved. 'I think that Florence Nightingale . . . would rejoice in the significance of this unfeminine apparel, for it means that we are getting ever closer to the front line.'

An unbroken thread in Katherine Jones's professional life was her willingness to campaign for greater recognition among doctors of the contribution made by nurses to saving lives. Doctors, she felt, were too ready to take all the credit themselves.

An article published in the *Journal of the Royal Army Medical Corps* after the war reproaches doctors for their lack of appreciation. The article, which is anonymous, purports to be by a doctor, but the passionate style is quite un-doctorish and the content bears so much resemblance to feelings Miss Jones expressed elsewhere, that there is a distinct possibility the article was a piece of pro-nurse propaganda planted by the Matron-in-Chief to give doctors food for thought.

---

* Queen Mary, who was President of QAIMNS during the Second World War, was vehemently opposed to the idea of QAs wearing trousers.

Likewise an allusion to laundry problems in the field suggests a female mind: 'How they manage their laundry must remain one of the major mysteries of the war.'

It is all too seldom that in medical or surgical case reports we find the physician or the surgeon making any reference to the nursing aspect of the treatment or of the great part this plays in the progress of the patient. It was once suggested that the introduction of the sulpha drugs and penicillin has made much surgery unnecessary. Be that as it may, nothing yet introduced has rendered nursing unnecessary or in any way made calls on the skill and devotion of the Nursing Service any less insistent . . .

. . . In any case of serious illness or of surgical emergency nursing is of paramount importance and those of us who have been patients are left in no doubt whatever as to the great debt we owe to our nurse.

Indeed the Matron-in-chief is at her most eloquent when she is describing, with something akin to a mother's pride, the vastly increased medical competence the modern QA has acquired as a result of the challenges of the war: 'The modern "Lady of the Lamp" is, as often as not, a slim, alert, clear-eyed young woman with an electric torch in her battle-dress trousers. She is an expert on blood transfusion and knows all about penicillin and has technical qualifications not dreamed about in the days of the Crimea. But she has the same spirit of devoted service as had the "Lady of the Lamp" in the wards at Scutari.'[3]

And was this huge advance in professional competence recognised and rewarded by the authorities? Of course not. Army nurses' pay was a glaring example of injustice.

In an address to the Federation of Professional and Business Women Miss Jones angrily contrasted the situation of nurses in the UK with that of other countries, notably 'America and all the Dominions'.

Year by year their status and salaries improved until, when war broke out in 1939 all these countries gave to their Army nurses the status (and later the rank) and the pay of a non-combatant officer i.e. $300 a year.

But what happened in the UK? The employment of women in

the Army, and in civilian war work, brought the true financial position of nurses to the full light of day. Their rates of pay did not compare with those of other professional women or with other officers of the Women's Forces. Even after the recent increases, a junior Sister, apart from certain allowances, must still serve five years to reach the salary of an ATS subaltern![4]

When wearing her campaigning hat Miss Jones comes over as something of a dragon. Her personal correspondence, however, reveals a more complex character. The wealth of letters she found time to write from Cheltenham, many of them addressed to anxious Matrons in trouble spots, reveal a warm personality, whose ability to empathise with others' tribulations is tempered by the gritty defiance in the face of adversity that was the hallmark of the war generation. She was particularly assiduous in maintaining a correspondence with Maud Buckingham, Matron of the Military Hospital, Imtarfa, Malta, during the terrifying time when the island was under siege. In one of these letters, dated 16 July 1941, she is insistent that, whatever the Germans say, rationing is not getting the British civilian population down:

> Your story of oranges and lemons does make our mouths water, although the stories told by Germany that we are starving are completely untrue. We would like an orange and a lemon sometimes although, incredible as it may sound, we were even able to buy half-a-dozen or so lemons at a time last week in Cheltenham. One wonders how they were brought and where they came from. In all other respects we are very well fed and can obtain all necessities without any trouble at all and although there is a lot of talk etc. about the rationing of clothing, there is still really plenty of everything in the country and England very much has its chin up.

She commiserated with Miss Buckingham's request for more nurses to deal with the explosion in casualties resulting from the regular bombardment of the naval dockyard. 'We are sorry not to be able to send you any more help at present, but I understand that a number of good trained orderlies have been spared and will be a great help in the hospitals where there is only a very short establishment of QAs. Our thoughts have been with you very much lately as we hear of constant air raids.'

In March 1942, when the siege was at its height, Miss Buckingham sent Miss Jones a cable, telling her that, despite the pounding the island was taking, all the Sisters were safe. Miss Jones's reply, while urging, with characteristic vigour, all concerned to continue to do their duty, reveals an unexpected vulnerability, the result, perhaps, of the loneliness all leaders feel in war. 'Thank you very much for sending me the cable. Good news like that seems to take a lot of the responsibilty off my shoulders. I know that your whole staff will have worked well and will have done all they could to help the poor unfortunate men who were, and are, damaged in these raids. QAIMNS will do their very best all the time . . . and keep up the morale. Please tell them not to fail to take what sleep they can when off duty during the day so that they can all pull their weight.'

She did her best to keep those who did not have much access to radio and newspapers up to speed with the fate of other QAs in trouble spots. Where it came to the Sisters caught up in the fall of Hong Kong and Singapore she wrote with, as it turned out, fatally misplaced trustfulness: 'We have been told that the Japanese have agreed to treat all prisoners with due regard to their national customs, such as clothing and food. We have at present no definite news of any of them and it may be some time before we know exactly how many had to stay behind in Singapore and how many were evacuated. In all there are a total of 10 QAs in Hong Kong and 65 in Singapore . . .'

Miss Jones retired as Matron-in-Chief of the QAs in 1944, but warned her public that this would not be the end. From now on she would be campaigning, on behalf not just of army nurses, but of nurses everywhere.

> For the past few weeks I have been able to look at this question more as a nurse than as a soldier and as time goes on the problems of the nursing profession as a whole will loom larger and larger in my mind and it may be that the military aspects of them will become a little less absorbing . . . but this I know, I shall not fail to recognise at once in Civilian as in Military nursing any of the straws which show which way the wind is blowing on the fortunes of our

profession. I shall always be jealous for the dignity of the nursing profession. I shall always be pernickety about the symbols of its rank. I shall always be a tiger on its behalf and a devotee in support of all efforts for its improvement.[5]

21

Contrasts in the Raj

After the tented hospitals of Normandy, India was regarded as a glamorous posting. In effect the scores of QAs who sailed for Madras and Calcutta as the war in Europe entered its final phase found themselves playing a waiting game. They were there for two reasons: in preparation for the anticipated invasion of India by the Japanese, and to nurse casualties of the Burma campaign.

In (what were to prove) the twilight years of the Raj India was awash with British military hospitals, from Bombay to Calcutta and from Delhi down to Pondicherry in the south. Army nursing in India had traditionally consisted of caring for servicemen who had succumbed to the numerous tropical diseases such as malaria, dysentery and dengue fever. This left plenty of free time for tennis, dancing, the races – the pink-gin-at-sundown socialising for which British India was famous. And, highly appealing to girls brought up in modest homes, there were servants to fetch and carry for them. What the young QAs didn't know, as they boarded their luxurious ships for the leisurely journey, was that they were about to enter a world of extreme contrasts. For India was also a world of snakes, poisonous insects and dysentery; of a thousand incomprehensible tongues, horrifying poverty and a caste system which would make the class-ridden world of wartime Britain look as egalitarian as Soviet Russia. Worst of all was the climate, which dried up the complexions of English women, made their hair fall out, gave them agonising prickly heat and made them long for the monsoon like a dying man thirsts for water.

The British Empire was a world in which white superiority was a given. Indians, Africans, Gurkhas, Burmese, invariably described as 'native troops', were nursed separately from British servicemen, often in inferior accommodation. Off duty a similar colour bar obtained and the Sisters did not mix with the Indians as social equals. Britain in the 1940s was an almost exclusively white country and few of the girls who had just joined the QAs had seen a dark-skinned person before.

Away from the protection of the hospital compound, the nurses were advised always to remain in groups. In a society where native women were rarely seen in public, many of the nurses found the attention they attracted intimidating. Outside the hierarchical world of the army, Indian men had scant respect for the women's officer status. It was a jungle in more ways than one. The QAs were particularly afraid of train travel. The trains had barred windows to discourage knife-wielding marauders who travelled on the roof or clung to the sides from entering the carriage and robbing the occupants. According to some nurses who served in India there were instances of QAs being murdered.

Phil Dyer joined the service in 1944. She had been posted first to a unit in West Africa and had sailed to India with African troops. Landing in Bombay she made her way first to Calcutta and from there to Chittagong on the border with Burma, in what was then West Bengal, but is now Bangladesh. Her overland journey had taken three hot uncomfortable days, fortified by the familiar army diet of bread and butter, bully beef, tinned peaches and cream. But at least she had been expected.

Her posting from Chittagong to Comilla, some 50 miles to the north, on Christmas Eve 1945 was a different matter. No reservation had been made for her on the train so arrangements were made for her to travel in the courier carriage with the instruction that she was on no account to let anyone into her carriage.

'A large carriage all to myself. The seats were thick with dust. The light of the carriage would not work and to add to the horror, there was no means of locking the carriage door. The train was full of natives – Africans on one side of me and Indians to the other and as far as I could gaze there did not appear to be another British person on the train.' As time passed the battery of her torch failed and she was left to sit in the dark. 'At 1 a.m. we reached a station where the platform was filled with Christmas revellers. At my refusal to let anyone in, I've got to say my two brass pips were badly sneered at. We arrived at about 3 a.m. and I had to wend my way over a lot of natives sleeping on the platform . . .'[1]

One of the first things Europeans had to negotiate was India's teeming labyrinth of races and castes and the impact this had on every aspect of life. 'We were face to face with Moslems, Sikhs, Hindus, Parsees, Anglo-Indians and one vaguely heard of Kashmiris, Pakistanis and Tibetans each with their own particular language. From our eternally smiling Africans we became very accustomed to the sad-faced doleful-eyed Indians who never outwardly appeared to find life amusing and we also learned how their various distinctions affected their mode of living from the untouchables to the Maharajahs.'

Some of the women accepted the inflexibility of the caste system more readily than others. One QA, working in a base near Teheran with predominantly Indian personnel, clearly felt little sympathy. The hospital was overwhelmed with Polish ex-prisoners, many of them very ill, and the nurse evidently expected the all-hands-to-the-pump approach that she could command in a British context. She soon discovered her mistake.

> The sweepers would sweep, deal with latrines and bedpans, soiled linen and water; the bhesties would deal with clean water and linen only; the ward boys would deal with food and feeding utensils only; the sepoys would make beds but not touch any soiled linen of dysentery patients, neither would they touch a bedpan or help any patient with one no matter how ill the man might be. They could not be relied upon to wash the hands and face of any patient and had an intense dislike of dead bodies. The medical officers were fully employed doing the round of patients. The RAMC orderly and the sister were the only people available at any time for any job from pitching tents and removing the dead to giving intravenous injections and dressing wounds . . .[2]

Unlike in North Africa or the liberation of France, where mobile medical units followed the line, most QAs in India remained in base hospitals, receiving the wounded from Burma in airlifts. For a start in the Burma campaign there was no battle line as such to follow, nor did the terrain permit the establishment of large field hospitals. But, as the tide of the campaign turned in the Allies' favour some QAs did cross the border to work in mobile first-aid units.

The deadliest enemy of Europeans in Asia, however, was neither snakes nor panthers – nor even the Japanese. It was disease. At dusk mosquitoes descended in clouds to feast on tender European skin and malaria cut swathes through the ranks of troops and nurses. The problem became desperate when supplies of quinine, the traditional remedy, became a war casualty. Most of the world's supply came from the cinchona plantations in Java and when Malaya fell supplies ceased. Things were so bad that by December 1942 for every thousand American servicemen there were six hundred cases of malaria. British troops fared even worse. The following year Lieutenant General William Slim, Commander of the Fourteenth Army – the nemesis of the Japanese in Burma – reported: '. . . for every man evacuated with wounds we had one hundred and twenty evacuated sick. The annual malaria rate (alone) was eighty four per cent per annum of the total strength of the army and still higher among the forward troops . . . A simple calculation showed me that in a matter of months at this rate my army would have melted away. Indeed, it was doing so under my eyes.'[3]

Many of the girls suffered appallingly from the mosquitoes. This was particularly so in the early part of the war when uniform rules still decreed the nurses had to work bare-legged in dresses. Mary Davies had been posted to India in December 1943 to join 65th Combined Military Hospital at Asanol, West Bengal. Her health suffered from the start. 'There were no precautions you could take to protect you from mosquitoes. There were Flit-type things provided, but they did no good. Nothing worked. I developed legs that were practically septic. I complained to Matron and was allowed to wear trousers in the ward at night. In the end I got a mosquito net and hung it over my desk when I was on night duty.'[4]

Many girls took quite a while to acclimatise to life in India.

The climate, the mosquitoes, the unfamiliar and sometimes downright dangerous creatures, were very trying and all the Europeans fell ill at some time or other. I got malaria really badly and had to take six weeks off work. I got a cornucopia of laryngitis, tonsilitis and pharyngitis and later otitis media [infection of the middle ear]. And after that I got dengue fever which gives you a very high temperature and pains in your eyes. The intense dry heat and the way it made you sweat was purgatorial for English skins and most of us endured the discomfort of prickly heat. As the summer grew hotter and hotter it affected your temperament and you began to long for the rains. When they finally came I would rush outside and stand in the lovely warm rain, letting it soak away the horrible prickly heat and even taking shampoo and washing my hair in it.

The catastrophic effect of malaria on Allied troops after the Japanese blockade of quinine galvanised medical research and a substitute was evolved. Mepacrine had already been used by British troops and nurses in North Africa in a dose of two pills a day four times a week. They were warned that their skin would turn yellow. There were side effects. Some of the women and many men were admitted with sickness and diarrhoea but were told they must go on taking it. Officers were detailed to see that each man took his dose. One or two of the QAs became so ill they had to go to sickbay – the side effects being almost as bad as having malaria.

It emerged later that mepacrine had never been regarded as a preventive treatment, as a contemporary report makes clear. 'The use of . . . Atabrine [mepacrine's commercial name] for prophylaxis is not recommended as a routine procedure, as the available information indicates that these drugs do not prevent infection. However, they are of definite military value in that they do prevent the appearance of the clinical symptoms of malaria so long as they are taken.'[5] Not surprisingly the 'military value' argument carried the day.

As the war entered its final phase, however, the apparently invincible mosquito met its Waterloo, much to the delight of the nurses, in the shape of DDT. Phil Dyer, nursing the casualties of Japan's last stand, laid a good chunk of the victory in Burma at the feet of this miracle chemical. 'DDT had also helped to achieve the victory of the Four-teenth Army . . . This anti-malarial precaution was sprayed from planes over thickly infested mosquito areas so reducing the malarial percentage that may have occurred to this wonderful unmechanised army. How defenceless were these mosquitoes against the potent fluid, and as they were sprayed with DDT their existence was terminated and they fell to the ground in mass production.'[6]

Like many QAs, Mary Davies came to love India. In the early days there wasn't an over-heavy workload and that left plenty of time for socialising. This was, though they did not know it then, the twilight of the Raj, and Europeans lived the good life to the full. Here, as in all the other theatres of war, women were hugely outnumbered by the hundreds of men billeted in the area, and Mary and Eve, the friend she had palled up with on the ship, were in great demand. They began receiving invitations to dances and, with nothing but their uniforms, wondered what they would wear. 'But the great thing about India is that there is wonderful material to buy – and very clever tailors to make it up. We used to choose our material, draw the design of the dress on a piece of paper and give it to a tailor or *dhersi*. They would make it up in next to no time – and charge a very modest fee.'[7]

Accustomed to doing their own chores the girls happily took up the pampered habits that in their home country were reserved for aristocrats. 'In the Mess we each had our own bearer, which was like a lady's maid. They were incredibly thoughtful and performed little services for you that were far beyond the call of duty. For instance, if you were going out to a dance they would ask you which dress you were going to wear. When it came time to get dressed there would be your dress, freshly pressed and laid out on the bed, and on top of it a little spray of fresh flowers, specially selected to match the dress.'

Social life centred either round the old India hands – British civilian couples who frequented 'the club', and were usually older than the young nurses – or the army. 'The manager of the local steel works used to invite us over for a meal and a swim at the club where we saw what happened to the English Memsahibs when they stayed in India too long. Their complexions had acquired a yellow tinge and they looked ill. They were conscious of it and told us they envied our youthful home-grown rosy cheeks. Eve and I used to say to each other that we didn't want to end up looking like them. Club evenings consisted of hard drinking and endless games of Ma-Jong.'

Invitations from the army were more welcome. 'We knew the officers quite well and they used to invite us over for dances. They were quite a relief as it meant we could put on long dresses. This helped protect us from mosquitoes which always seemed to go for the legs. Sometimes it would be gramophone records, sometimes someone would play the piano. The Americans were not far away and they used to invite us over too. Our NAAFI did not supply things like chocolate and stockings and they tried to shower us with these sought-after luxuries.'

Mindful of their amorous reputation, Mary held her American suitors at arm's length. Her friend Eve, however, succumbed to the charms of one of them, even though he was married.

The peacetime hospitals in British India were grandiose imperial buildings of brick and stone but during the war many smaller Indian-style hospitals, made of thatched huts known as *bashas*, sprang up to care for troops going into Burma. Irene Anderson was posted to one of these in the jungle town of Lohardaga, 80 miles from Ranchi near the Assam border. At that time there were no casualties, but the usual tropical mix of malaria, dysentery and jaundice and the odd road accident. As was the norm in those days, races and ranks were nursed separately.

> We had a British other ranks medical ward, a British other ranks surgical ward and an officers' ward. The rest were for Indians, who were also nursed according to rank – the Indian officers, who were called halvidars, had their own ward. The wards and living accommodation were bashas. It was incredibly hot, an unremitting dry heat with horrible dust storms which blew up suddenly. The bashas were built so that you could open them out and prop up the roof at each end to increase ventilation, but when a dust storm blew up you had to be quick and batten down the sides of the basha. We used to have to pull our veils over our faces so that we could breathe without inhaling dust.[8]

The heat, which caused sweat to drip off the body, meant that the girls changed their dresses twice a day. At night, because of the mosquitoes, they were allowed to change into khaki drill slacks and long-sleeved tunics, taking care to tuck their slacks into their shoes. Dehydration was a danger and everyone had to drink eight pints of lightly salted water – sterilised and brought up in bottles from Ranchi – each day. A huge chest was daily filled with ice to cool the patients' bottled water.

Irene loved being waited on. Her own sepoy brought her tea in the morning, cleaned her room and made her bed, a majestic four-poster draped from floor to ceiling with a mosquito net. A dhobi washed and ironed all her clothes. She got on well with the Indians, despite the fact that communication was limited. 'When we did the rounds of the Indian wards we had an English-speaking *sepoy* with us to act as interpreter. As far as talking to the *dhobies* and *beasties* was concerned, we picked up a smattering of Urdu – "char" for tea, "darwaz" table, "gildy gao" hurry up and "cheney" . . . sugar.'

There was no running water in the nurses' living quarters. All the bedrooms opened on to another room which contained a bath and a lavatory which was just a seat over a bucket. When they wanted a bath the *beastie* filled it and emptied it for them, using rainwater which was permanently hot from the sun. He also emptied the lavatory.

But despite the luxury of being waited on, all the Sisters were aware that they were in a country where hidden dangers lurked. They grew used to shaking their shoes before putting them on for fear of hidden scorpions. One Sister found a giant centipede in her bed. Jackals and hyenas, attracted by the food, roamed the compound and snakes – cobras and the deadly krait – were regularly found in the Sister's quarters. They all dreaded night duty. As Irene remembers:

> You were just one Sister responsible for all the patients and regulations decreed that all electric lights be put out at midnight. As the lights went out you would be left with just one storm lantern to write up your report. The HQ was also the theatre and you stayed in there writing up your notes, having told the sepoy to come and call you if he wanted advice or someone was calling for you. One night I was in the theatre all by myself when I heard an awful commotion and banging on the closed door. With my heart beating nineteen to the dozen I crept over to the window to see if I could see what the problem was. It was a goat foraging for food.

Eventually the time came for the troops who had been training for so long to go into Burma. A big farewell party was held at the club in Ranchi and Irene bought a sparkly sari and had it turned into an evening dress by a local dressmaker.

The party was over. Those nurses who had yearned for a bit more action were about to see their wish fulfilled. And they were to be tested twice over: first, as they witnessed the suffering of thousands of returning prisoners of war, men broken in body and spirit; and second, as they found themselves expected to nurse the enemy responsible.

If the QAs thought India a savage land, the jungles of Burma were in a different league.

22

'Hard-working and patriotic women'

The British army had been driven out of Burma by the Japanese in May 1942 and the next two years had been pretty much of a stalemate. The huge country, much of it trackless jungle, with the few roads and rivers standing out as highly vulnerable targets, favoured the covert guerrilla type of fighting at which the Japanese excelled.

Fighting alone, often for months at a stretch, in humid conditions that European troops found debilitating, the unseen enemy crept noiselessly up on his quarry, infiltrating the line and picking off columns of Allied troops from the flanks with rifle shots which seemed to come from nowhere. The snipers tied themselves to trees so that if they were shot the sound of the fall would not betray their position. The Sherman tanks and cumbersome artillery on which the Allies had relied as they swept across France were useless here.

Throughout 1942 and 1943 the Japanese seemed unbeatable. And then a number of things happened that were to turn the tide and send victorious Allied troops storming down the length of Burma in a matter of months.

The first was the appointment of Lieutenant General William Slim as Commander of a new Fourteenth Army. Slim was a 54-year-old veteran of the First World War and today is widely viewed as one of the ablest commanders of the Second World War.

The second was the creation of the legendary Chindits. This super-fit force made up of British, Burmese, Hong Kong Chinese, Gurkhas and West African troops was the brainwave of the gifted and somewhat eccentric Brigadier General Orde Wingate. It excelled at penetrating far behind enemy lines, cutting off supply lines and harrying the Japanese from the rear. Wingate believed the war in South-East Asia could only be won by playing the Japanese at their own game – using lightly equipped units living in the jungle in small groups, supplied from the air and receiving orders via radio. Possessing a dry wit Wingate was supposedly the author of the quip: 'The impossible we do in a day. Miracles take a little longer.'

A third catalyst was the Japanese decision, in March 1944, to invade India.

They struck simultaneously at the British stronghold of Imphal and the more northerly town of Kohima. But the experience of the Chindits had shown that an army can be successfully supplied from the air and the besieged dug in. At Kohima, a small group of defenders fought on doggedly until they were relieved. At Imphal, where sixty thousand British and Indian troops were encircled, the bitter siege lasted three months, well into the monsoon season which was unusually heavy that year. Now the tables were turned: the Japanese began to run out of food and supplies as a result of the Chindits having cut their supply lines. On 22 June the siege was finally lifted. Superior Allied air power, the severity of the weather and the high incidence of disease among the debilitated Japanese troops were key factors in the victory. It had cost them dear. The Japanese recorded over 53,000 dead, sick or wounded – nearly sixty per cent of the 88,000 who had launched the attack. Allied casualties at Kohima and Imphal, by contrast, numbered 16,700.

The triumphant defence at Imphal signalled the fight-back to victory in Burma. By 20 March the central city of Mandalay had fallen and four days later the Burma Road was once again open to Allied traffic. General Slim's Fourteenth Army drove southwards in a two-pronged advance on either side of the mighty Irrawaddy river which flows out at the strategic port of Rangoon. On 1 May a battalion of Gurkhas was dropped by parachute near the mouth of the river and easily overcame a small pocket of Japanese resistance. Now the way was clear for Allied landing craft to sail up the river. When they arrived in Rangoon the Japanese had already abandoned the city. There were further sporadic skirmishes between May and August, but in essence the Burma campaign was over.

Mary Davies had been one of those who asked for transfers to be nearer the action. Based since 1943 in Asanol, an important rail junction 150 miles north-east of Calcutta, she saw her first war casualties nearly a year after she was posted to India, in January 1944, when a troop train arrived in the night from Burma bringing nine burns victims for treatment.

Her request was granted and she was transferred to Dacca, nearly 200 miles further east, not far from the Burmese border, to join 62nd Indian General Hospital. 'This was a proper building to which extra huts had been added. The Indians were nursed in the huts and the European Officers in wards in the main building. I like to think they got identical treatment but the officers' beds were more generously spaced than the Indians. Most of the patients had been transferred from field hospitals in Burma and were suffering from malnutrition.'[1]

As she arrived, convoys of wounded and ill ex-POWs were flooding into the hospital. By the end of December 1944 three wards, built for sixty, had seventy patients each. Throughout the early part of the following year casualties poured in. In a month the hospital population soared from 715 to 950. On 13 February 1944 a note in Mary's diary read: '. . . very bad casualties. No good standing there weeping. You've got to get on with it.' On 17 February she wrote: 'Convoys of very bad battle casualties arriving daily.' Mary particularly liked one of the wounded men. He was a Gurkha named Bhup Singh. He had lost his right arm and, being a member of a proud warrior culture, was deeply depressed by his mutilation.

She was amazed at the stoicism of the troops. A note in her diary for February 1944 notes wonderingly: 'But they're all so cheerful.'

In addition to the usual gunshot wounds, burns and fractures, many of the troops fighting in Burma suffered from gas gangrene caused by having lain undiscovered in the jungle for days before being found.

One QA fresh out from England had a brutal introduction to the particular sufferings of the victims of this lonely guerrilla warfare. Sarah McNeece arrived in Bombay and travelled by train to Calcutta before taking a paddle steamer up the Bramaputra river to join the 17th British General Hospital. It was a long, dusty and tiring journey and Sarah was looking forward to her bed, but there was an acute shortage of QAs and the Commanding Officer told her she was to go on night duty straight away.

They had a young officer who had just come in, having been terribly badly wounded in the battle of the Irrawaddy [mid 1944]. He was in a vehicle which had been attacked by snipers. The driver had been killed outright and he had been left for dead. He had been there days before anyone found him with both legs and one arm broken. He had been in theatre all day having his limbs set. And they didn't give him much of a chance. He had double pneumonia, gas gangrene and typhoid and was on five drips by the time I saw him. Nothing in his body was working. He had a raging temperature and my job was to tepid sponge him constantly to try and bring his temperate down.[2]

Sarah nursed her patient faithfully, night after night. When she ran out of tepid water she had to get more – one bucket of cold water, one of boiling, from the cook house. This involved crossing open ground in the dark, where hyenas and snakes lurked.

It even involved a degree of physical suffering on her part. 'I used to sit next to his bed talking to him while he was unconscious. His suffering was appalling and every now and then a convulsion would seize him and he would lash out and grab any part of me in an excruciatingly tight grip. I was black and blue with bruises. Once he even got hold of my hair and didn't let go till the pain subsided.'

After three weeks the officer regained consciousness. It fell to Sarah to persuade him to eat, an experience that brought her into further contact with India's intimidating fauna.

It was very frustrating. I don't think he wanted to live. I tried to tempt him, telling him he could have anything he wanted. In the end he said he'd have a spoonful of peach Melba! I flew up to the cook house and asked them to rustle up something that resembled peach Melba – the army always had tinned peaches – and rushed it back. He only ate enough to cover the back of my thumb. It was a real challenge to get him to eat solid food. I badgered and cajoled him and in the end he said he might eat some toast. Once again I tore up to the cook house and asked for half a piece of toast, quickly, before he changed his mind.

The toast was prepared and the cooks wanted to cover it, but Sarah dismissed them, keen to get back to her patient. 'Before I had taken more than a few steps an enormous vulture swooped and snatched the toast out of my hand. I went back and found all the cook house staff doubled up with laughter. "You'll be wanting it covered this time will you, Sister?" they said.'

The officer survived his terrible injuries, largely thanks to penicillin. Though it had been discovered (by British scientists) in 1940 it was not available to civilians in wartime and the nurses were deeply impressed by its miraculous healing effect. Gwladys Aiken first heard of it in Italy in 1943 when she heard a Canadian Medical Officer deliver a lecture to QAs working on a hospital train. She soon saw for herself how it radicalised recovery. 'In the hospital in Bari . . . One of my patients had been admitted with severe shrapnel wounds in his back. The wounds were horribly infected, reddish purple and filled with an ugly pus . . . This young man would surely have died without the administration of the wonder drug.'

At first the drug, which, because of its cost, had to be used with the utmost frugality, was administered by a procedure known as insulation. 'A carefully measured amount of penicillin was brought in by the orderly in a special case. From a small teaspoon I would blow the penicillin into the wound through a special mask which protected the wounds from my germs and allowed precise aim. As I was cleaning the wound, I remember seeing the lung moving inside the chest wall. It was the first time I had ever witnessed something like that, and it was quite dramatic.'

In those early days it substantially increased the Sisters' workload and involved considerable discomfort for the patients. Phil Dyer, nursing wounded troops in Chittagong in December 1944, noted:

It was really incredible to think that the particular fungi grown to produce Penicillin was doing such wonderful work for the Burmese campaign . . . As time went by . . . the various ranges of sulphonamides were being forgotten . . . In those days it had to be given three hourly day and night, which meant a constant flow of work preparing, sterilising, and giving the injections and no sooner had we completed one round of injections to the various patients when it was time to start the next.

Little did we realise that a few years after the war science would be wonderful enough to discover a penicillin solution that need only be given twice a day – Distaguine – and the joys of not having to continue the course for more than four or five days. How the patient must have suffered to endure the three hourly intra muscular injections.[3]

As the Burma campaign wore on and the number of hospitalised troops rose, the pressure on the nurses increased. Many, already seriously overworked, succumbed to malaria, amoebic dysentery and dengue fever and, as many women's war service expired, the corps was severely overstretched. Illness was a major problem for the troops, too. They contracted malaria and dysentery in such numbers that Lieutenant General Slim remarked that his army was disappearing before his eyes.

Constance Wane, Matron-in-Chief South-East Asia, praised the courage of the QAs in Burma, but warned in June 1945 that numbers were nowhere near enough for the task involved.

> Nursing officers are often asked to volunteer to go still further forward to Field Ambulances and Advanced Dressing Stations . . . These units are very close to the front line and in some cases have been cut off from all communication with our own forces except by air. The great trouble is that there are not enough of these hardworking and patriotic women to staff our military hospitals as we would like them to be staffed and the result is . . . overwork and strain and no off-duty time for rest and recreation during rush periods after heavy fighting has taken place. Drafts are continuously arriving from the UK as reinforcements but these do little more than replace the wastage due to sickness and the repatriation of time-expired nursing sisters.[4]

The high numbers of casualties had a positive spin-off for nurses. As medical officers were overwhelmed by the size of convoys, the nurses were allowed to stray into what had been strictly doctors-only territory. Throughout December 1944 and January 1945 Phil Dyer, stationed at the 74th Indian General Hospital at Comilla, was called on to perform tasks that she would have been forbidden to do at home. 'Our Medical Officer, being so busy receiving patients, could not always be present at the admissions. This was to our advantage as we became well acquainted with the stethoscope and commenced to do our own investigations for a diagnosis . . . Besides becoming adept at diagnosing we learned to do many treatments which we would not be allowed to do at home. What a great thrill I had at setting up my first blood transfusion and doing a lumbar puncture.'[5]

As 1945 wore on the numbers of wounded were boosted by hundreds of troops who had been Japanese prisoners of war. The discovery of the brutality of the Japanese towards prisoners sent shock waves round the Allied world, where it had been assumed that the Japanese would observe the terms of the Geneva Convention.

The victims included men who had been forced to build the infamous Burma railway, later immortalised in the film *Bridge on the River Kwai*. Deprived of protein for years on end, beaten and tortured if they collapsed on the job, unable to protect themselves against the many tropical diseases endemic in the fetid jungle conditions, 160,000 prisoners died in captivity. Among the most emotionally taxing work the QAs undertook was nursing the living skeletons who survived.

Audrey Hayward had been posted to India after following the British Liberation Army through Europe. Like Irene Anderson she was sent to Lohardaga, near the Assam border. Nurses sent to these areas in 1945 were there to tend casualties from what was expected to be a prolonged campaign with stiff resistance from the Japanese. But in the event Slim's tactic of creating his own jungle fighters to beat the Japanese at their own game proved so successful that the Burma campaign was unexpectedly swift. Those who came into the hospital were liberated prisoners of war.

They were in a terrible shape, suffering from severe malnutrition and deeply traumatised by what they had been through. Because of the lack of protein and roughage they suffered a lot of colitis and other bowel trouble. Many had to have colostomies. As the time drew closer for their going home the men became very disturbed. They didn't want to go home to wives and sweethearts with a bag and they appealed to the doctor to close up their bowel. The doctor was moved by their situation and agreed to close up one or two, but tragically, they died, which after surviving so much suffering, was almost unbearable for everyone. After that we didn't close any more.[6]

The returning prisoners were also mentally damaged. 'They had been so deprived of everything that whatever you gave them was hoarded. If you gave them a mackintosh to go out in, or put an extra blanket on their bed it would disappear. You'd find they'd stuffed it into their locker. It was a reflex.'

Tragically the freedom they had so longed for over three-and-a-half years was a state they couldn't handle. As Audrey recalled: 'Our Colonel said "These men have had an awful time. They must have freedom above all else." So they were allowed to go into Ranchi, which was the nearest big town, about 80 miles away, and do whatever they liked. But they couldn't cope. They got drunk, they got lost . . . they went missing . . . The Colonel felt so sorry for them and had meant well. But it was the wrong thing.'

Meta Kelly was also posted to India after her stay in Belgium. Already sick of war and longing for the end of all the killing, she was depressed by the fights that sometimes broke out between the ex-POWs.

After spending so many months, or in some cases years, combating one enemy you would have thought these men would have presented a united front, but apparently human nature doesn't work that way. I was accompanying the doctor on his rounds of the other ranks one morning and we found one patient had a black eye. When the doctor asked him what had happened he replied that he had walked into a door. Some way further on in the round we found another man – this time with a sprained wrist. This chap refused to say how he had come by his injury and I was a bit upset. After the doctor had gone one of the patients, a very nice chap, called me over and said, 'Sister, sometimes people have scores to settle.'

I think the doctor understood, but to me it seemed so sad after all they'd been through at the hands of the Japanese, that they were still fighting among themselves. I really felt for these men. They were tired and weary, and yet they never seemed to sleep well. Perhaps they had nightmares, or were still too afraid to relax properly. On top of that some of them had written home and found that things were no longer as they had been – and were worried about whether their wives and girlfriends were still waiting for them.[7]

The transformation of fit, optimistic and cheeky young men into bowed wraiths who looked decades older than their real age fanned a hatred for the Japanese among the nurses which tested their neutrality as healers to its limit. Phil Dyer describes the revulsion she felt at being called on to treat an enemy who had shown such cruelty to *its* prisoners.

I trembled with fear at the thought of having to attend them . . . That first night the RAMC orderly and I went down to the Japanese wing I would have given anything to run away . . . I looked down on 28 Japanese prisoners all looking like human scarecrows – small-boned, emaciated-bodied men, their eyes were the only live part about them and they were alive with hatred. I felt I could not do anything for them and . . . my eyes also filled with hatred, not towards them individually but to the whole human race they represented. Turning my back, I proceeded to leave the ward. Then as my footsteps led me nearer the exit I thought 'what if my brother, instead of being killed, had been taken prisoner, either by the Germans or the Japanese and a nurse had turned her back on him as he lay helpless in bed entirely at her mercy . . .' I retraced my steps and we proceeded to replenish blood transfusions and saline drips, attend to wounds and give nourishment. Their conditions were very poor and very few survived to be interrogated later. OK was the only word they understood.[8]

The dislike the nurses felt for the Japanese was matched by what bordered on hero worship for General Slim, the accomplished and personable British commander. On one occasion General Slim paid a visit to the hospital in Comilla where Phil Dyer was based. The attraction of the spirited young Sister to the hero of the hour is unmistakable.

On one particular evening we were playing table tennis when several army officers walked in. To my astonishment I saw one was General 'Bill' Slim, accompanied by the Matron. Introductions were made all round. To my surprise when it was my turn, General Slim asked me if I enjoyed table tennis. At my reply he asked me if

I would honour him with a game. I felt so very humble competing with the great man. After several knockabouts he made me feel very much at ease. I think it was the hardest game I have ever played, being determined that I would try and beat him. I did eventually – the first and last part of the Burma campaign that he was ever defeated.

Then suddenly it was over. On 6 August 1945 the Allies dropped the first of two atom bombs on Japan. On 2 September Japan surrendered unconditionally. Today's judgement of the act that finally defeated Japan dwells on the horrors of nuclear carnage – the bombs killed more than a hundred thousand outright, twenty thousand of them children, and many more in the ensuing decades. But at the time there were few mixed feelings. Only rejoicing that no more young soldiers would have to die, or be invalided back to a life of bleak dependency.

For the QAs there remained one more task, one some found the most harrowing of all – bringing the prisoners home.

23

Bringing Home the Prisoners

As the gruelling Indian summer of 1945 wore on and the war in the East showed no sign of ending, Irene Anderson began to long, not just for the cooling monsoon, but for something more exciting than tending endless cases of dysentery and malaria. When the Chief Matron India Command visited Lohardaga and asked for volunteers to work on a hospital ship she jumped at the chance. 'I had no idea what a hospital ship would be like. I just wanted to be closer to the action than I had been in Lohardaga.'

Irene embarked aboard the veteran vessel SS *Tairea* as part of an invasion force to recapture Malaya from the Japanese. She left the harbour in Bombay full of shipping ready for the anticipated battle and sailed escorted by the pride of the British fleet, the two magnificent battleships HMS *Nelson* and HMS *Rodney* and the French battleship *Richelieu*. They arrived at Penang, but had only been there a few days when they heard that the Allied troops who had landed had found no opposition as the Japanese had surrendered. The atom bombs had been dropped while they were underway.

Now the brief changed. There would be no battle casualties. Instead the Captain was ordered to sail to Hong Kong and bring the prisoners out of Stanley camp.

The *Tairea*, a large old-fasioned vessel with three tall grey funnels and vivid red crosses painted down both sides of her hull, was one of a fleet of hospital ships which performed heroic tasks throughout the war, taking wounded men off, and conveying them to base hospitals behind the lines. She had been built in Glasgow in 1924 as a passenger ship plying between British India and Japan. The ship already had an impressive war record by the time Sister Anderson joined her. She had used her lifeboats to recover wounded from the campaign at Kismayu, Somaliland, in 1940. In 1942 she served at Madagascar, Alexandria and Smyrna. In July 1943 she attended the landings at Sicily and later returned to Sicily to rescue survivors of her sister ship *Talamba*, which had been bombed by German planes. Over the next eight months the old ship would make eight return trips bringing thousands of POWs out of Hong Kong, Singapore, Burma and Malaya to be nursed back to health in India.

The *Tairea* was staffed by a team of doctors, a Matron and nine Sisters. In addition to the Royal Army Medical Corps, who were British, there were several members of the Indian Medical Corps on board. The ship had 506 beds divided into six wards on three decks. The beds were fixed to the side of the ship in two tiers and the Sisters had individual cabins. To their delight, now that the danger of malaria was no longer so present, the Sisters were expected once more to wear their flattering tropical uniform of white dresses, white veils and white canvas shoes.

Their first port of call on that trip was Hong Kong. The trip was recorded by cinema newsreels and images of the emaciated human cargo were broadcast to a horrified world. 'We sailed with all our lights blazing – we were the only ship in the convoy to be allowed lights as we believed the Japs wouldn't bomb a hospital ship. This was wishful thinking as the Japs had no respect for anything. As we entered Hong Kong harbour we had a destroyer in front of us and a minesweeper on either side as the seas were mined.'[1]

On the first trip, in addition to troops, they collected 506 civilian prisoners, many of them women and children.

> They were brought to the dock by ambulance and loaded onto the ship. I was not prepared for the sight of these poor emaciated people and it upset me dreadfully. I gazed in horror at their legs which seemed frighteningly deformed – the two little bones, the tibia and the fibula, hanging onto the huge patella with just a bit of skin holding them together. I was engulfed in a feeling of hatred for the Japanese. It was a scene of utter misery. There was no rejoicing. Most of them were very quiet and frightened – as if they didn't really know what was happening. There was an Irishwoman who

had not been interned as the Southern Irish were neutral during the war, but whose husband and children had been. Because they were British. She had just been reunited with the children she had not seen for three and a half years. It was very emotional.

Many of the former prisoners were too weak and ill to survive the journey and the nurses found these deaths, when freedom and loved ones were just a short journey away, almost unbearable. 'We had burials at sea on every trip. It seemed so sad to be losing people after they had been set free . . . but some of them were just skin and bone and it was inevitable. When someone was being buried the Captain stopped the ship, prayers were said and the body was lowered over the side.'

One case particularly upset Irene. 'She was a Czechoslovakian woman whom I willed to stay alive. Just before she died she said to me: "I know I'm dying, Sister, but don't mind, because I'm free."'

Many of the prisoners had developed tuberculosis, still more had dysentery and all were suffering from long-term malnutrition.

We kept the very ill in bed, giving them plenty of fluids and feeding them food which was pureed for them in the kitchen in tiny quantities. Feeding them was a very slow process as if you gave them too much they were sick. Many of them had hookworms. They were disgusting things which burrowed into the skin of the legs. The only way to get them out was to roll the tail round a small piece of wood, like a matchstick. You had to do it gradually or it would break and you would have left the head in. It took several days.

But worse even than the physical problems they suffered, from some of which they would never recover, was the mental damage prisoners had suffered. Indian prisoners, who were segregated from whites in special Asians-only camps, were treated worse than any other group. A high number were repeatedly tortured in an endeavour to force them to join the Japanese-sponsored Indian National Army, raised in Singapore under Chandra Bose to assist in their invasion of India. They were incredibly brave and endured untold pain. The Gurkhas resisted to a man.

There was a price to pay, however, and many of them were unhinged by the time they were rescued. Several Indians jumped overboard during the rescue trips. 'The Captain always turned the ship back to look for them but we never found them.'

The saddest thing for the nurses was the high number of their own young men who had become mentally disturbed as a result of the torture and ill-treatment.

> Often there were as many as two hundred of them. They were regarded as too dangerous for us to nurse and were looked after by orderlies. They could be very noisy and some were violent. You could hear them shouting and throwing their food about when they were being fed. The worst cases were straitjacketed, which after all they'd been through seemed dreadful. They spent most of the day in bed, but once a day the orderlies would bring them up onto well deck, beneath the main deck, so that they could get some sun. The crew put a big net over well deck to prevent them from throwing them-selves overboard. We were on a higher deck and we used to look down at these rows of straitjacketed young men lying on the deck and feel hatred for the Japanese and their brutality. I won-dered what would happen to them when they got home.

The liberation of the tens of thousands of prisoners marked the symbolic end of the war and the *Tairea* was given a conqueror's welcome as she sailed into Madras with her fragile human cargo. 'There were flags and bunting everywhere, all the ships in the harbour tooted their horns and a Gurkha pipe band played us a welcome on the dockside. I held some of the children up to see the band.'

On a Singapore trip Irene and some of the other Sisters went to Changi for a picnic and decided to take a look at the infamous jail. 'Even deserted it was a ferocious-looking place. We looked at the great guns which for so long had been aimed at the defenceless prisoners and we visited the cemetery. It was horrifying to think of the suffering of those victims, all so young, and to know that those graves had been dug by their fellow prisoners.'

Life on board the *Tairea* mirrored army routines on land. The Sisters worked morning and afternoon shifts, did night duty and had time off. Officers were nursed together, away from the men. Because, in addition to the medical staff a number of the crew were Indians, they had their own mess deck. 'We didn't have anything to do with them – they were nursed by orderlies and they had their own cooks. They had special needs – for example Sikhs had to be provided with special oil for their long hair. They even had their own Asian-style lavatories, which had a central drain instead of a pedestal.'

To provide a bit of recreation the nurses were given 24-hours shore leave whenever they arrived in port and before they took on patients. The Captain gave a dinner on each trip and the nurses were able to invite friends. 'We had got quite pally with the officers from another ship called the *Prince Albert*. If we were in port at the same time as them they would invite us to dinner on their ship and we would reciprocate.'

The war had ended on 14 August when the Japanese signed the unconditional surrender, but in some parts of what were then the Dutch East Indies (now Indonesia), isolated groups of Japanese guerrillas continued to attack Allied forces. When the *Tairea* sailed into Batavia, the capital city (now Jakarta), she ran into one of these pockets.

'The harbour was full of wrecked ships and we had to sit there for two weeks while the Army subdued the resistance. We had to stay on the ship for most of the time as it was felt the situation was too dangerous, but towards the end we made one trip to a market where I swapped an old shirt for a pineapple.'

During their war service QAs faced all kinds of dangers – air raids, shipwreck, imprisonment. Yet the only time Irene Anderson felt genuinely afraid was when a social outing the Sisters had planned went wrong. The *Tairea* carried a little boat that she had picked up from one of the ships sunk off Sicily. One day three of the nurses decided to go ashore for a picnic with some of the ship's officers. The launch's motor broke down as they were making for the shore and they began drifting out to sea.

The area was full of shipping and we hailed people to save us. One of the ships answered our call and came alongside. They let down a rope ladder for us to climb. It was the most frightening thing I have ever done in my life. The side of the ship towered about 50 feet above me and the ladder wobbled about all over the place making my legs swing out behind me. I was sure I was going to fall into the sea and was paralysed with vertigo. In the end they sent one of the officers we'd gone out with to go up ahead of me. He kept saying 'don't look down' and somehow I managed to get on to the ship.

Phil Dyer left her hospital on the Burmese border at about the same time. The ship on which she sailed was taking ex-POWs home to England. What shocked her was how disorientated the men seemed, as if they had become frozen in a time warp.

It was heartbreaking to see these men on their arrival at the ship. The years had not been kind to them due to the atrocious treatment bestowed upon them by the Japanese in their various camps. They had all suffered torture of mind and body . . . Mentally the new world they had been released into was strange to them, and everything was extremely bewildering. Many phrases they could not understand. The King's English had vastly changed in three and a half years. Perhaps they thought we had become mentally unbalanced as we spoke in terms of 'Bang on', 'Wizard Prang' and such things.

Physically they had nearly all suffered from one or many types of tropical diseases. Malaria, dysentery, typhoid, black water fever, jaundice, gastric ulcers and various others. Due to a deficiency of vitamins and iron in their meagre diet, their whole physique was in a very poor condition. Many had developed beriberi through lack of vitamin B.[2]

Sister Dyer was cheered by the speed with which many men seemed to recover during the trip. But she could see they were in turmoil as the prospect of home became a physical reality. She wanted to talk to them – but about what? The horrific nature of what they had been through turned conversation with 'normal' people into a minefield.

Psychologically, although they were all so grateful to be alive, they were frightened to pick up the lost threads of the life to which they were returning. It was difficult to really converse with these men while on board. We had so little in common with their past and each one of them avoided the subject of what he had endured. If we spoke of our trials and tribulations, they appeared so trivial in comparison with what they had gone through. If we spoke of our gay times, we felt they must be very embittered to think that some had managed to have a pleasant time out of the war.

Mary Davies left her hospital in Dacca in early November 1945 for a posting to Surabaya on the Indonesian island of Java. Her mission, too, was to nurse back to health newly liberated prisoners of the Japanese, this time mainly Dutch.

As Irene Anderson had found when the *Tairea* tried to sail into Batavia, Java was a dangerous place. Mary's ship docked at the end of November, more than two months after the Japanese surrender, but while she was there two British NCOs were killed by snipers. Surabaya had been the scene of fierce fighting and the place was in ruins, with no electric light or running water. Decomposing bodies of Dutch civilians floating in the sea bore witness to the ongoing danger posed by hidden Japanese snipers who refused to admit that the war was over. Water was so scarce they used seawater to wash the wards at the Field Ambulance to which Mary had been posted. The girls longed for a bath, but using their canvas washstands, had to make do with the small amount of water that was delivered daily. The patients were eighty Dutch women and children who had been imprisoned by the Japanese. 'The tortures these women had been subjected to were unspeakable. They had had cigarettes pushed up their nostrils, and several had been sexually tortured.'

All the time she was in Java Mary and the rest of the QAs – they were a team of twelve – were subject to a curfew which, in those days before gender equality, was 7.30 p.m. for women and 10.30 p.m. for men. The danger was from Japanese snipers. 'You couldn't go anywhere on your own. If any of us wanted to go to the bazaar we had to have an armed guard to go with us.'

A month later Mary moved and met up with all the staff from her old hospital in Dacca. Here, among the Dutch ex-prisoners and patients still recovering from battle injuries, were familiar faces from India. To one in particular she was able to bring a measure of comfort.

I met up again with my Gurkha friend Bhup Singh. He was still feeling very low, having lost his right arm and knowing he would not be able to use a kookri again. One of the senior officers in our unit had lost his right arm before the war in a skiing accident, yet he had adapted wonderfully – for example he was a brilliant dancer.

I thought it might be helpful if the Brigadier had a chat with him. He accepted willingly and taught him all sorts of things. I saw Bhup Singh again some time later and he was a different man.[3]

By the spring of 1946 the British were thinking of handing Java back to the Dutch and many of the QA Reservists were nearing the end of their war service. As Mary Davies prepared to set sail for Singapore it was Japanese prisoners who roped up their trunks. 'One couldn't help contrasting the way they looked with the men and women who had been *their* prisoners. They were not walking skeletons. They were well fed and humanely treated . . .'

Among the tens of thousands of prisoners being liberated were the QAs who had survived after the fall of Singapore and Hong Kong. Instead of nursing injured troops they had spent their war comforting people dying of starvation and treatable diseases.

At Stanley camp, where Daphne van Wart had been incarcerated since the rapes and massacres of Christmas Day 1942, when the Japanese overran Hong Kong island, the end took everyone by surprise. 'The Japs got very drunk in their house on the hill and never came to collect the roll call lists, so we were confined to barracks until the interpreter arrived . . . met the British administrator and told him: "We are no longer at war. We are friends now." And we were all given a roll of toilet paper (we called it the Victory roll) . . .

'We heard later that we only had about eight days to live as we were becoming a liability. We were going to be killed in groups of thirty.'

Not until Admiral Cecil Harcourt arrived from Singapore at the end of August with six hundred men to receive the surrender from Vice Admiral Fujita and Lieutenant General Tanaka did freedom become a reality for them. There were fifteen hundred Japanese on the island and Harcourt sailed the aircraft carrier HMS *Indomitable* into Hong Kong harbour, sweeping for mines as he went. Expecting resistance he stepped ashore with a revolver in each hand, but there was none.

Daphne van Wart eventually sailed home on a Liberty ship, the *Admiral Hughes*, from Manila. There were just twelve nurses and four thousand troops on the ship, many of them American. Daphne decided the Americans had had rather a soft war when, at a meal on board, an American officer refused to eat leg of chicken and demanded breast. 'I was so angry I leant across the table and seized his plate saying: "You should have been hungry like I was and you wouldn't be so fussy."'

The memory of the days when Britain had stood alone against tyranny were still fresh in people's minds and being British commanded universal respect. The QAs were moved by their reception when they called in at Honolulu: 'A steel band was playing American music. When the conductor learned that there were British on board he leant forward and said to the band: "Take off your hats and stand up, you buggers," and they played the national anthem.'

The Japanese surrendered on 14 August following the dropping of atom bombs on Hiroshima and Nagasaki on 6 and 9 August, yet it was not until twelve days later that Captain Siki told Margot Turner and her fellow prisoners on Sumatra that they were free. Margot herself was ill in the hospital when the news came, and her friends felt she would not have lasted much longer.[4]

The Japanese then produced a complete range of items that would have saved lives had they been forthcoming earlier – 'medicines, for lack of which our friends had died', as Margot bitterly observed. Bandages, quinine, vitamin tablets, powdered milk, butter, giant mosquito nets, all looted from Red Cross parcels, appeared in large numbers. Best of all, in Margot's view, was soap, a luxury that had disappeared from their lives for three long years. The Japanese finally allowed the men from the neighbouring civilian camp to come over and be reunited with their families, though according to Margot there were very few of the British men left alive. To the relief of the exhausted women they took over the hard manual work.

For all their joy at the war being over, however, the prisoners were still marooned deep in the jungle, apparently forgotten by the world; until one day when a South African parachuted into the camp and told them that their existence was known, but that it had been hard finding them. During the second week in September another plane flew over dropping fresh bread and medical supplies. Margot and her friend Netta Smith were flown out a few days later.

Margot was sufficiently recovered to note with contempt the change in the attitude of the Japanese. 'We went from the camp as we had come – in Japanese open trucks. We had the same Japanese truck drivers who had been so insolent to us when we had arrived; now they were offering us sweets . . . On the train journey to Lahat the Japs, who had treated us like cattle before, were coming round with curry, but we had brought our own rations and had the satisfaction of refusing theirs.'[5]

Margot flew to Singapore and was sent to the luxurious Raffles Hotel to recuperate. From there she sent a telegram to her mother, who had simply been told that she was missing. She sailed for Engand on 26 September on a ship containing roughly fifteen hundred men and ten women. The journey took nearly a month and it was late October before Margot was reunited with her mother. An old friend of Margot's went with her mother to meet her at Hove station.

'Margot was very thin and yellow-looking and had some of her front teeth missing. But she was mentally very cheerful.'[6] Her ordeal had left scars. One of her teeth, as we have seen, had been knocked out by a Japanese guard, another had been extracted in Singapore as she had developed an abscess just before she was liberated. She was also rather lame – the result of an injury incurred when a large log fell on her foot and probably broke a bone. For some time afterwards wearing shoes hurt her.

Right to the end the QAs were sharing the suffering at the sharp end of the war. Where there were soldiers – even in the hell of Japanese prison camps – the QAs were there.

24

Last Act

The war did not end at the same time for everyone. QAs who were young and had enlisted relatively late in the war were kept on after their older sisters, who had seen several years of active service, were demobbed. In the ugly aftermath of six years of fighting and devastation there was still plenty of work for nurses to do. Prisoners had to be nursed back to health and civilian populations cared for in countries that had been laid waste.

In the Far East, QAs took up the challenge of nursing back to health those newly released from the Japanese camps, many of them Javanese and Indian.

After the overthrow of Singapore the Japanese treatment of the Indians was particularly harsh. They were put to work on building and engineering projects such as the airfield at Changi where hundreds died as a result of hard labour, insufficient food and lack of drugs. Sadly many continued to die in the recovery camps, where many drugs were still in short supply.

A Captain in the Royal Artillery described the challenge facing nursing staff: 'When discovered by officers of this Department in the early days of liberation these unhappy people were in a pitiful condition. All were destitute. Some were starving. Many had beriberi and skin diseases were highly prevalent, particularly among the children. The people had no money except Japanese dollars and had sold all their possessions including their scanty clothing for food.'[1]

Four hundred were taken to a camp at Thompson Road, given mosquito nets to protect them from malaria, supplied with decent food rations and handed over to British nurses, one of whom was Lieutenant

Christie QAIMNS. Predictably the situation improved so dramatically that the Captain was able to report that in just two weeks 'no less than 100 children were cured of scabies'.

With evident satisfaction he notes: 'Miss Fernandez and Mrs Christie have supervised the making and distribution of clothes for all the children and most of the women. A regular system of bathing and washing the children has now been in force for two months. The hookworm which was prevalent at first has now practically disappeared. The camp is now a happy unit of well fed people . . .'

It is interesting to note what daily rations were considered to be necessary for these people in contrast to the harsh regime they had been enduring for the previous four years. It also reveals how much food was available on the island, which the Japanese witheld. According to the officer the allocations were:

> Men: 11 ozs rice
> 2½ ozs soya beans
> 7 ozs fresh fish
> 8 ozs fresh vegetables
> 1 oz coconut oil
> ⅔ ozs sugar. ⅔ ozs salt every day.
> Women and children draw the same ration with the exception of rice. Women draw 8 ozs of rice and children 6 ozs daily. The rice ration is the same as that in force for the rest of Singapore Island but the shortage of rice in the opinion of the Medical Authorities is amply compensated by the large protein content of the fish and the high vitamin content of the fresh vegetables.

The constant discovery of more destitute Indians on other parts of the island, as well as the return of many others from Siam, French Indo-China and what were then the Dutch East Indies made it necessary to open another camp at Hartley Road. These people too benefited from the efficiency and compassion of a QA nurse.

An article in the Tamil newspaper published in Singapore in December 1945 pays warm tribute to the Florence Nightingale-like effect of QA Cecilia Blair. The article confirms that most of the inmates in

Hartley Road camp were 'those who were taken to Sumatra for the construction of the railway'.

> 430 Tamil labourers are well looked after in Thomson Road Camp, after being brought by Japs from Kuantan and left stranded in a village 4 miles from Sembawang.
>
> Of the 430, there are 130 children. They were suffering from malaria, beriberi, scabbies [*sic*], tropical ulcers, T.B., V.D. and malnutrition and when found, they appeared like moving skeletons. Most of them are cured by the efficient nursing of and proper treatment of Mrs Blair, who belongs to the British Military Nursing Service. It is no wonder that all the inmates of the Camp are most grateful and affectionate to Mrs Blair because she became very attached to the children there. Major W. Rose brought us in his jeep to see those who were struggling for life, entrusted to this Sister. We will never forget the kind service rendered to us by this woman.

Towards the end of 1946 Irene Anderson was posted to Naples. Her task there was to nurse the army of occupation which comprised a wide variety of nationalities, including Poles, Rumanians and Chechens. Her time was taken up with general nursing, road-traffic accidents and treating injuries resulting from fights between the occupying Allied forces and the Italians, usually over food. Italy had been bled white by the months of fighting and its people were starving. Sadly, even with the war over there were still some deaths, one of which upset her greatly.

> They brought a young lad in one night. He'd come from a ship and he had a bad throat. They thought he had tonsilitis and had been giving him sulphur drugs. You have to drink plenty when you take these drugs and he hadn't been made to drink enough. In fact he had diphtheria. We did a tracheotomy but it was was too late and he died. He can only have been about 18. I cried over that boy's death. I thought of his mother. He had come through the war. It was so needless to die of such a treatable illness when the world was at peace.[2]

However Irene did save a life in Italy.

One night a big tall British soldier came in bleeding heavily from a facial injury. It was a jagged circular wound, made by the end of a broken bottle. He had been to his own unit for help but no one had been able to stop the bleeding. I got him on to a bed and made a ring-shaped dressing that followed the outline of the cut and applied as much pressure as I could. The next day, before they could operate, he had to have three pints of blood. If I hadn't stopped the bleeding he would have died.

Active service continued to come up with surprises of the sort not often encountered when nursing on the home front. 'Some of the men had got married during their active service and one chap had married a French Moroccan woman. She was admitted one day with a bad cough. She had a violent fit of coughing in front of me and coughed up an enormous worm, it must have been between two and three feet in length.'

Gradually, however, even the youngest of the QAs came to the end of their service.

Daphne van Wart eventually arrived in Southampton on 4 November 1945, five and a quarter years after leaving England. The Matron-in-Chief and staff were on the quayside to meet them. When Daphne shook hands with her, Matron said, with characteristic restraint: 'Your father *will* be pleased to see you.'

The atmosphere was like an extended carnival at the thronging ports, where thousands of euphoric returning troops were embarking for home and loved ones. Mary Davies finally left Indonesia in the spring of 1946, arriving in Singapore in April, where she and other QAs spent an enforced holiday swimming and sunbathing as there was no further transport immediately. When a ship was eventually made available it was so crowded that eight girls had to cram into one cabin. Mary disembarked at Hong Kong and was assigned to No. 28 Indian General Hospital, perched high on a peak with magnificent views over the harbour. There she helped prepare wounded patients for return to their homelands aboard hospital ships. One of their more tragic cases was a young soldier who had been attacked by a shark while swimming, losing one leg and suffering serious injuries to the other. At the end of October Mary filled in her release papers. She sailed home aboard the *Empress of Australia*.

'As we cast off people in the hospital up on the hill were waving sheets to us. We stopped in at Colombo for one hour to refuel and then were on our way home again. I arrived back in London on December 14th after three years active service. I went by troop train to Netley where I was demobbed.'

For many QAs the homecoming, dreamed about for so long, proved bitter-sweet. Though they were delighted that the killing had stopped, they found they missed the excitement and energy that accompanied the danger. Civvy street seemed dull as ditchwater. Phil Dyer had already observed among returning prisoners of war this sense of detachment from the world around them. Now it was her turn. Returning from India at Christmas she found that people she had once felt close to now seemed part of another life.

> My home life had completely altered. Friends had either been killed, got married or divorced. All and sundry appeared to me to be complete strangers and I felt extremely disjointed with everyone, finding that there were very few people with whom I appeared to have a lot in common . . . so 'I wandered lonely as a cloud' wishing quite often that I was still with my unit and friends who had become so much a part of my life, having endured the trials and tribulations of Army life . . . I was not alone in this strange transition. Innumerable service people . . . continued to do so for many years after the war.[3]

Dorothea Chisholm landed at a freezing Tilbury at Christmas 1945 having been transferred to Poona after the end of the war in Europe. Digging in her trunk to find gloves for numb fingers used to the balmy heat of the tropics, she found they had all been devoured by moths. She and her fellow QAs took a train to Southampton and from there went to the great military hospital at Netley to be demobbed.

> And then we were just turned loose. We did not know what to do. I went up to north Wales on three months leave and I was bored to death. There was a terrible feeling of flatness and anti-climax. I didn't want to go back into a hospital. I was grown up now and I didn't want to be bossed around by some Matron any more. Everything had just finished . . . all the company . . . all the

excitement . . . My poor parents were so pleased to see me but I wasn't happy to be home. My sisters all had babies but I didn't know whether I wanted that. I had got engaged in Germany but I had broken it off in India because I'd been having too good a time.[4]

Dorothea realised that this feeling of being an outsider was even worse for the men, many of whose close friends had lost their lives, but that didn't make it any easier. 'There had never been anything quite like it, no matter how dangerous and how horrible it had been. It had been the most intense experience of our life. The reason you felt so isolated was that no one who hadn't been there knew what it had been like.'

For now, however, the urgent question for most QAs was: what do we do with the rest of our lives? Some, including Phil Dyer and Molly Jennings, had married during the war, and were looking forward to their lives as wives and mothers. Others married soon after they returned home.

A small proportion decided to join the regular QAs, renamed after the war Queen Alexandra's Royal Army Nursing Corps. One of these was Daphne van Wart.

On her return to the UK Sister van Wart was sent to Anstie Grange, near Dorking, which was the training centre for new recruits to the QARANC. There, in a manner that would have delighted the recently retired 'militarising' Matron-in-Chief, she was taught to be a modern QA, marching, saluting and calling superiors 'Mam'.

When she decided to become a regular she was sent to the Cambridge Hospital, Aldershot, where an element of surreal humour surfaced about the army's medical preoccupations: 'When I had my medical there were no King's Regulations for checking QAs who had been POWs of the Japs. Instead I was asked if I had got flat feet or a hernia!'

Nurse van Wart marched in the London Victory Parade in May 1946 with Miss Dyson, the Hong Kong Matron who had shared her imprisonment at Stanley. No effort was spared to ensure that the QAs would come over as members of a military force. 'We were trained for a fortnight by a Sergeant Major of the Welsh Guards – a week in Wellington barracks and another week in Bushy Park under canvas. His parting words were "Woe betide any of you young ladies if I see you marching out of step down the Mall."'

In the light of everything Daphne had gone through as a POW it must have been galling to discover that the King (George VI) did not recognise the QAs. 'As we passed the saluting base I could lip-read the King saying to the Queen (who held the programme), "Who are these?" But Daphne took the charitable view that HRH was foxed by the unfamiliar military uniform. 'We were ahead of the ATS, also in khaki. In those days we were better known for our grey and scarlet uniform.'

Few returned to civilian nursing, fearing that the authoritarian yoke at which they had already chafed as trainees would prove unendurable now. Fresh back from India and believing that even the hidebound world of nursing had to have been shaken up by the war, Audrey Hayward was prepared to give it a go. She accepted a post as Sister in Midwifery at a hospital in Redhill in Surrey. Little had changed, including the fact that, irrespective of age and status, they still had to live in nurses' homes. The start was not auspicious.

> I was interviewed by the hospital management committee sitting round in an imposing semicircle with me in the centre. The first question I was asked was 'wouldn't I feel homesick?' I pointed out rather tartly that if they looked at my application they would see that I had recently returned from India. The other thing I found irksome was that nurses were not allowed to use the marble steps at the front of the hospital. They were reserved for the hospital management committee. We had to use a back staircase. I was grown up now and held a responsible job, yet in this world it was as if time had stood still. I soon left. I wanted to be my own boss so I trained as a Health Visitor.[5]

The experience of having been a QA instilled in many a taste for adventure which could never be satisfied by life as a golf-playing wife in the Home Counties. Meta Kelly met her future husband, an RAF officer, in Ranchi. After the war he joined the Colonial Service and was posted to Nigeria, where they remained until the 1960s, when he joined the British Council and was posted to Somalia. Mary Davies joined the Colonial Nursing Service and set off on her own for Kenya in 1949. With a European doctor and his wife she ran a forty-bed hospital for Africans in the Teita Hills in south-west Kenya. She married an executive of the East African Railways and Harbours and did not return to the UK until the 1960s. At the age of 49 she, like Audrey Hayward, trained as a Health Visitor.

Observers of QAs commented throughout the war on their grit – their steely determination to put their own feelings of fatigue or discomfort aside and 'get on with it'. Few embodied these qualities more vividly than Margot Turner.

In his account of her extraordinary life Sir John Smythe wrote: 'There is a lot of luck about dying, just as there is about living. If a person had a bad go of Banka Fever the chances were they wouldn't recover – however strong their physique and however high their morale.'[6] The survivor of two shipwrecks and three years in a brutal Japanese internment camp in which so many had died, Margot had been outstandingly lucky. One might have thought her many ordeals would condemn her, as they did so many other victims of Japanese brutality, to the unchallenging twilight life of a mental invalid. Not Margot. The speed of her recovery from those years among the disappeared impressed everyone who met her. Just over six weeks after returning to Engand she was back at work – as a QA Regular. In 1947 this remarkable woman was posted overseas again. After an outstanding career in the QARANC which saw her running military hospitals all over the world, and despite frequent bouts of pneumonia – the legacy of her years as a POW – in 1962 she was appointed Matron-in-Chief and Director of the Army Nursing Service.

Even now there is something that draws QAs to each other. Despite their dwindling numbers, almost every week old QAs meet in restaurants and tearooms the length and breadth of Britain. They would not have missed their wartime experiences for the world and are intensely proud to have been there. But they share more than memories. Women of character, they also share a philosophy.

Sixty years after those momentous events they still subscribe to the same life view as Dame Margot Turner. Asked to explain how she had kept going through the bitter days of her captivity, this woman, whom her friends described as modest and non-intellectual, replied: 'I don't think about myself very much. I think about what I have to do.'

It could stand as an epitaph for the whole corps.

Source Notes

Introduction

1 *The Tale of a Field Hospital*, Sir Frederick Treves, Cassell & Co., 1900
2 *Queen Alexandra's Royal Army Nursing Corps*, Juliet Piggott, Leo Cooper, 1990

Chapter 1: 'Not when they have work to do'

1 Sister Mary Mulrey, 101 BGH, quoted in *Unsung Heroines: Women who Won the War*, Vera Lynn, Isis, 1991
2 *Army Sisters in Battledress*, M. Butland, unpublished m/s, QARANC Collection, Box 8, Ref. 2, AMS Museum
3 *Nurses in Battledress*, Gwladys M. Rees Aikens, Nimbus, 1998
4 Piggott, op. cit.

Chapter 2: The Making of a QA

1 Interview with Molly Budge
2 This and the following excerpts from an interview with Audrey Hayward
3 *The Maturing Sun: an Army Nurse in India 1942–45*, Angela Bolton, Imperial War Museum, 1986
4 *A Nurse's War*, Brenda McBryde, Chatto and Windus, 1979
5 Ibid.
6 Aikens, op. cit.
7 This and the following excerpts from an interview with Dorothea Davies (née Chisholm)
8 Brenda McBryde, op. cit.
9 Ibid.
10 Ibid.
11 Ibid.
12 Aikens, op. cit.

Chapter 3: A Baptism of Fire

1 This and the following material from the Diaries of Miss H. A. Luker, IWM Documents, WW2 papers, Hospitals ref. Misc 373
2 This and the following excerpts Dame Katherine Jones, private papers, AMS Museum
3 This and the following excerpts from Mary Evans, post-war BBC radio broadcast, WW2 broadcasts env. 2, AMS Museum
4 Edwards (first name unknown), post-war BBC radio broadcast, WW2 broadcasts env. 2, AMS Museum
5 Miss C. L. Robinson, post-war BBC radio broadcast, WW2 broadcasts env. 2, AMS Museum
6 Dame Katherine Jones, op. cit.
7 Piggott, op. cit.
8 Phil Dyer, quoted in *When Life was Grey and Scarlet: a Recollection of Life as an Army Nursing Sister 1943–1946*, unpublished m/s, 1953. QARANC Collection, Box 8, AMS Museum

Chapter 4: 'Do English women never cry?'

1 Papers of Mrs D. Ingram (née van Wart), IWM (item 93/18/1)
2 Papers of Mrs Day Joyce, IWM
3 This and the following material from *Quiet Heroines*, Brenda McBryde, Chatto and Windus, 1985
4 Ibid.
5 Daphne Ingram, op. cit.
6 Ibid.
7 Hong Kong file, AMS Museum
8 This and following material, *Captive Christmas*, Alan Birch and Martin Cole, Heinemann, 1979
9 Miss Jones, letter dated 29.1.41 in error for 29.1.42
10 Sgt J. H. Anderson, Prosecution Exhibit PX-1593A, Tokyo War Crimes Trial records, FO648 Box 116, Department of Documents, IWM
11 A. F. Gordon, Prosecution Exhibit PX-1591, Tokyo War Crimes Trial records, FO648 Box 116, Department of Documents, IWM
12 Ibid.
13 Mrs Andrew Levinge, Prosecution Exhibit PX-1590, Tokyo War Crimes Trial records, FO648 Box 116, Department of Documents, IWM

14 Testimony of James Barnett as quoted in *The Tokyo War Crimes Trials*, ed. R. John Pritchard, Garland, New York, 1987
15 Sgt. J. H. Anderson, op. cit.

Chapter 5: Into Captivity

1 *Quiet Heroines*, Brenda McBryde, op. cit.
2 Ibid.
3 Daphne van Wart, op. cit.
4 Ibid.
5 Ibid.
6 *Quiet Heroines*, Brenda McBryde, op, cit.
7 Ibid.
8 This and the following extract from Miss Dyson, QAM 71/1975, AMS Museum
9 Daphne van Wart, op. cit.
10 Molly Gordon, QAM 71/1975. AMS Museum
11 Ibid.

Chapter 6: Friday the Thirteenth

1 This and the following material Dorothy Garvin, QARANC Collection, Singapore file, AMS Museum
2 Catherine Maudsley, QARANC Collection, Singapore file, AMS Museum
3 This and the following extract Evelyn Cowens, QARANC Collection, Singapore file, AMS Museum
4 Olive Spedding, QARANC Collection, Singapore file, AMS Museum
5 L. M. Hartley, QARANC Collection, Singapore file, AMS Museum
6 Evelyn Cowens, op. cit.

Chapter 7: Shipwrecked

1 Dorothy Garvin, op. cit.
2 L. M. Hartley, op. cit.
3 O. W. Gilmour, quoted in *Home Port Singapore: A History of Straits Steamship Company Ltd, 1890–1965*, K. G. Tregonning, Oxford University Press, 1967
4 L. M. Hartley, op. cit.
5 Dorothy Garvin, op. cit.
6 Singapore files, AMS Museum

7 This and following material Margot Turner, QARANC Collection, Singapore file, AMS Museum

8 Beatrice le Blanc Smith, QARANC Collection, Singapore file, AMS Museum

9 *The Will to Live*, Sir John Smythe, Cassell, 1970

10 Dorothy Garvin, op. cit.

Chapter 8: The Disappeared

1 Vivian Bullwinkel testimony as quoted in *The Tokyo War Crimes Trial*, ed. R. John Pritchard, Garland, New York, 1987

2 *The Will to Live*, Sir John Smythe, op. cit.

3 Ibid.

4 *Wilma – A Woman's War: the Exceptional Life of Wilma Oram Young*, Barbara Angell, New Holland (Australia), 2003

5 Sir John Smythe, op. cit.

6 Margot Turner, op. cit.

7 This and the following extract Margot Turner, op. cit.

8 Betty Jeffery, quoted in *The Will to Live*, op. cit.

9 Margot Turner, quoted in *The Will to Live*, op. cit.

10 This and the following material Margot Turner, quoted in *The Will to Live*, op. cit.

11 Netta Smith, ibid.

12 Margot Turner, ibid.

Chapter 9: Sailing the Seven Seas

1 Aikens, op. cit.

2 *The Royal London Hospital Nurses' League Review*, nos. ix and x, 1940–41

3 Miss I. F. Bussell, QA Reserve, AMS Museum

4 This and following material from an interview with Audrey Hayward

5 Miss I. F. Bussell, QA Reserve, AMS Museum

6 *The Royal London Hospital Nurses' League Review*, no. xiv, 1945

7 Ibid.

8 Phil Dyer, quoted in *When Life was Grey and Scarlet*, op. cit.

9 The *Royal London Hospital Nurses' League Review*, nos. ix and x, 1940–41

10 Ibid.

11 Phil Dyer, quoted in *When Life was Grey and Scarlet*, op. cit.

Chapter 10: The Cruel Sea

1 *Quiet Heroines*, Brenda McBryde, op. cit.
2 Joan Hunter-Bates (later Moore), quoted in *Quiet Heroines*, Brenda McBryde, op. cit.
3 *Quiet Heroines*, Brenda McBryde, op. cit.
4 William Bromage, BBC WW2 People's War (Internet)
5 This and following material, Eric Munday, quoted in *SS Ceramic: the Untold Story*, Clare Hardy, Central Publishing, 2006, and from author interviews
6 This and following material, 'Twelve Days in a Lifeboat 10–20 October 1942', J. H. Bates, *Grey and Scarlet*, Hodder & Stoughton, 1944
7 Donald Delves, BBC WW2 People's War (Internet)
8 The Sinking of the SS *Amsterdam* 1944, Patrick Manning, BBC WW2 People's War (Internet)
9 Recording 17665 Sound Archive, IWM

Chapter 11: Flowers in the Desert

1 *Quiet Heroines*, Brenda McBryde, op. cit.
2 This and following material, from an interview with Molly Budge (later Jennings)
3 Quoted in *Grey and Scarlet*, op. cit.
4 *Quiet Heroines*, Brenda McBryde, op. cit.
5 Interview with Molly Budge
6 *Quiet Heroines*, Brenda McBryde, op. cit.
7 Ibid.
8 Ibid.
9 Dame Katherine Jones, 'Bridgebuilding', probably unpublished radio broadcast
10 Quoted in *When Life was Grey and Scarlet*, op. cit.
11 Ibid.
12 Dame Katherine Jones, 'Bridgebuilding', op. cit.
13 Violet Bath, quoted in *Front-Line Nurse*, Eric Taylor, Hale, 1997
14 Ibid.

Chapter 12: Under Siege in Malta

1 This and the following material, from Maud Buckingham, private papers, 84/28/142, IWM
2 Dorothy Mackie private papers, 84/28/142, IWM

Chapter 13: Operation Torch

1 Interview with Mary English
2 Mamie Ward, 85/6/1, IWM
3 Ibid.
4 Aikens, op. cit
5 This and the following material from an interview with Mary English

Chapter 14: Life of Comradeship

1 *Sand in my Shoes: the Tale of a Red Cross Welfare Officer*, Sylvia Skimming, Oliver and Boyd, 1948
2 Ibid.
3 Ibid.
4 Ibid.

Chapter 15: Swept off their Feet

1 Interview with Mary English
2 Interview with Sarah McNeece (later Saville)
3 This and following material Betty Biggs (later Cole), *The Wanderings of a Wartime QA*, unpublished memoir, AMS Museum
4 Interview with Irene Anderson
5 Interview with Mary Davies
6 Betty Biggs, op. cit.
7 Interview with Audrey Hayward

Chapter 16: 'The QAs are here'

1 Sylvia Skimming, *Sand in my Shoes*, op. cit.
2 Interview with Mary English
3 This and following material, Gwladys Aikens, op. cit.
4 Gwladys Aikens, op. cit., and *Shipping* magazine, December 1993
5 Dame Katherine Jones, private papers, AMS Museum
6 Interview with Mary English
7 Dame Katherine Jones, private papers, AMS Museum
8 This and following material from an interview with Mary English
9 These paragraphs were written by Newbold Noyes Jnr, son of the owner of the *Washington Star*, and first appeared as a coda to *Nurses in Battledress* by Gwladys Aikens, op. cit.

Chapter 17: 'Come and see what we are part of'

1 This and following material from an interview with Dorothea Chisholm
2 This and following material from an interview with Audrey Hayward
3 This and following material from an interview with Meta Kelly

Chapter 18: Operating in the Orchards

1 This and following material from an interview with Audrey Hayward
2 This and following material from an interview with Dorothea Chisholm
3 This and following material from an interview with Meta Kelly
4 Interview with Dorothea Chisholm
5 Interview with Meta Kelly
6 *A Nurse's War*, Brenda McBryde, op. cit.
7 Interview with Dorothea Chisholm
8 Interview with Audrey Hayward
9 Interview with Dorothea Chisholm
10 Interview with Audrey Hayward
11 Interview with Meta Kelly
12 This and following material from an interview with Audrey Hayward
13 This and following material from an interview with Meta Kelly
14 Interview with Dorothea Chisholm

Chapter 19: The Liberation of Europe

1 This and following material from an interview with Meta Kelly
2 *Sand in my Shoes*, Sylvia Skimming, op. cit.
3 This and following material from an interview with Molly Budge
4 Major Hugh McLaren's report was originally Appendix 5 of *Sandbostel. A report by Lt Col F. S. Fiddes RAMC Commanding No. 10 (Br) Casualty Clearing Station RAMC*, written and printed in the field, August 1945. Other details about Freda Laycock, including extracts from her diary, are reproduced with permission from her daughter Kathryn Ingham, who has set up a website commemorating her mother's war service: www.fredalaycock.org.uk.
5 This and following material from an interview with Dorothea Chisholm

Chapter 20: A Tiger for the Nurses

1 This and the following material Dame Katherine Jones, private papers, AMS Museum, QARANC collection

2 Dame Katherine Jones, *British Journal of Nursing*, October 1943
3 Dame Katherine Jones, address to the Association of Hospital Matrons, 2 September 1944; env. 2, WW2 Broadcasts, AMS Museum
4 Dame Katherine Jones, private papers, AMS Museum
5 Ibid.

Chapter 21: Contrasts in the Raj

1 This and following material Phil Dyer, quoted in *When Life was Grey and Scarlet*, op. cit.
2 Anon., Public Records Office WO/222/189
3 'From Atabrine in World War II to Mefloquine in Somalia: The Role of Education in Preventive Medicine', Peter Weina, *Military Medicine*, September 1998
4 This and following material from an interview with Mary Davies
5 Circular letter no. 56, Office of the General Surgeon, 9 June 1941
6 Phil Dyer, AMS Museum
7 This and following material from an interview with Mary Davies
8 Interview with Irene Anderson (later Leighton)

Chapter 22: 'Hard-working and patriotic women'

1 Interview with Mary Davies
2 This and following material Sarah McNeece
3 Phil Dyer, quoted in *When Life was Grey and Scarlet*, op. cit.
4 Constance Wane, article for publication 19 June 1945, ADV HQ ALF-SEA, env. 2, WW2 broadcasts, AMS Museum
5 Phil Dyer, quoted in *When Life was Grey and Scarlet*, op. cit.
6 Interview with Audrey Hayward
7 Interview with Meta Kelly
8 This and following material Phil Dyer, quoted in *When Life was Grey and Scarlet*, op. cit.

Chapter 23: Bringing Home the Prisoners

1 This and following material from an interview with Irene Anderson
2 This and following material Phil Dyer, quoted in *When Life was Grey and Scarlet*, op. cit.
3 Interview with Mary Davies
4 Netta Smith, quoted in *The Will to Live*, Sir John Smythe, op. cit.

5 Margot Turner, QARANC Collection, Singapore file, AMS Museum
6 Nancy Sutton, quoted in *The Will to Live*, Sir John Smythe, op. cit.

Chapter 24: Last Act

1 Captain J. P. Blackledge, Cpt RA, 22 December 1945, 167 2563, IWM
2 This and following material, from an interview with Irene Anderson
3 Phil Dyer, AMS Museum
4 Interview with Dorothea Chisholm
5 Interview with Audrey Hayward
6 *The Will to Live*, Sir John Smythe, op. cit.

Select Bibliography

Grey and Scarlet: Letters from the war areas by army nurses on active service (Hodder and Stoughton, 1944)

Adie, Kate, *From Corsets to Camouflage: Women and War* (Hodder and Stoughton, 2003)

Angell, Barbara, *Wilma a Woman's war the exceptional life of Wilma Oram Young* (New Holland Publishers, Aust.)

Bolton, Angela, *The Maturing Sun: an army nurse in India 194245* (Imperial War Museum, 1986)

Gruber von Arni, Colonel Eric and Searle, Major Gary, *Sub Cruce Candida 19022002: A celebration of one hundred years of Army Nursing* (The Queen Alexandra's Royal Army Nursing Corps Association, 2002)

Hardy, Clare, *SS Ceramic: The Untold Story* (Central Publishing, 2006)

Matanle, Ivor, *World War II* (Colour Library Books, Godalming, Surrey, 1989)

McBryde, Brenda, *A Nurse's War* (Chatto and Windus, 1979)

McBryde, Brenda, *Quiet Heroines* (Chatto and Windus, 1985)

Piggott, Juliet, *Queen Alexandra's Royal Army Nursing Corps* (Leo Cooper, 1975 and 1990)

Rees Aikens, Gwladys M., *Nurses in Battledress* (Nimbus Publishing, Halifax, N.S., Canada, 1998)

Roland, Charles G., *Long Night's Journey into Day* (Wilfrid Laurier University Press, Canada, 2001)

Skimming, Sylvia, *Sand in my Shoes* (Oliver and Boyd, 1948)

Sloggett, Diane, *Angels of Burma* (The Pentland Press Ltd, Bishop Auckland Co., Durham, 2000)

Smythe, Sir John, *The Will to Live* (Cassell, 1970)

Smythe, Sir John, *In This Sign Conquer: The story of Army Chaplains* (A. R. Mowbray, 1968)

Taylor, Eric, *Front Line Nurse* (Robert Hale, 1997)

Taylor, Eric, *Combat Nurse* (Robert Hale, 1999)

Travers, Susan, *Tomorrow to be Brave* (Corgi, 2000)

Index

Abbeville, 30
Aden, 129
Adriatic Sea, 202
aeroplanes, 5
Africa, 4, 111, 122, 138–9, 162
casualties in, 165–6
women in, 148
see also East Africa; North
Africa; South Africa;
West Africa
Africans, 118, 248–50
Afrika Korps, 138
Aikens, Gwladys, 22, 111, 113,
163, 195, 261
air ambulances, 176
aircraft carriers, 112, 151, 153–4
Albrecht, Miss, 155
alcohol, 143, 166, 225
see also champagne
Alexandra, Queen, 3, 19
Alexandra Military Hospital,
53, 76–8
Alexandria, 137–8, 141, 147–8,
268
Algeria, xiii, 160, 176, 185
Algiers, 126, 160–2, 169,
175–7, 181
ambulance trains, 35–6, 72
American Field Service, 204
Americans, 65
and Battle of the Bulge,
229
in India, 251, 254
informality, 12, 203–5,
218–19
and Italian campaign, 194,
199, 203–5

and luxuries, 143, 222, 254,
275
in Normandy, 214, 216,
218–19, 222–3
nurses, 169–70
and Operation Torch, 160,
164, 167, 175
and Pacific war, 102
and romantic relationships,
185
wreck civilian
accommodation, 235
amputations, 216
Anderson (later Leighton),
Irene, 113, 185, 254–5, 263
on hospital ship, 267–73
return to Italy, 279–80
Andrews-Levinge, Miss, 54,
56, 58
Anglo-Indians, 250
Angmering, 211
Anson aircraft, 236
antibiotics, 22
see also penicillin
ants, 145
Anzio, 10, 130–1, 168, 177,
191–2, 197–8
Arabia, 119
Arabs, 161, 165, 171, 174–5
see also Bedouins
Ardennes, 229
army biscuits, 143, 174, 193,
201
Army Blood Transfusion
Service, 227
army life, 18, 20–1
Army Nursing Reserve, 3

army tailors, 11
army units
7th Armoured Division, 137,
139–41, 146
1st Army, 10, 160, 192–3
2nd Army, 214, 223
8th Army, 10, 138–9, 180,
183, 192
14th Army, 251–2, 257–8
35th Nigerian Regiment, 118
Arnhem, 13
Arromanches, 209, 211
Asanol, 251, 258
askari, 132
Assam, 254, 263
Athens, 181
Atlantic Ocean, 10, 43,
115–16, 163, 196
see also North Atlantic;
South Atlantic
atom bombs, xii, 266–7, 275
ATS (Auxiliary Territorial
Service), 186, 229, 245, 283
Australia, 105, 124
Australian Army Nursing
Service (AANS), 93
Australian Navy, 90
Australian Red Cross, 91
Australians, 12, 90, 128, 202
nurses, 93–5, 105
Austrians, 230
autoclaves, 155
Aviemore, 28
Azores, 124

Bache, Private, 62
Balkan Beam system, 23

Bangladesh, 249
Bangor, 24
Banka fever, 105, 284
Banka Island, 87–8, 91, 93, 104
Banka Straits, 96–7
Barce, 184
Bardia, 138
Bari, 181, 192, 198, 261
  mustard gas incident, 194–7
Barletta, 193, 197
Barnett, James, 57
Barnett, Mrs, 87
Barrack Hospital, 153–6
base hospitals, 172–3, 192, 215, 229, 240
bashas, 254
Batavia, 79, 271, 273
Bates, Sister J. H., 126–30
Bath, Violet, 149
battle fatigue syndrome, 141, 218
Battle of Britain, 43, 153
  injured pilots, 24
Battle of the Atlantic, 115
Battle of the Bulge, 229
Bayeux, 210–11, 214, 225, 235
BBC, 30, 33
Beatrice stoves, 25, 139–40, 224
Beccles, 239
Beckenham, 227
Bedouins, 144–5
Begg, Mrs E. M., 54–7
Beirut, 184
Belgians, 228, 230
Belgium, 9, 27–8, 223, 228–9, 264
Belsen, 11, 230–2
Benghazi, 138
beriberi, 67, 104, 106, 272, 277, 279
Bethune, 28–9
Biggs (later Cole), Betty, 183–4, 186
Bizerta, 130
Black, Lieutenant Colonel George, 54, 57
black water fever, 272
Blair, Cecilia, 278–9
Blitz, 22, 115

blood transfusions, 216, 226–7, 244, 263, 265
Blyton, Enid, 174
Boer War, 3–4
Bombay, 79, 90–1, 120, 248–9, 267
Bose, Chandra, 269
Boulogne, 30–2
Bowen Road Military Hospital, 45–8, 53, 59, 65, 67
Bramaputra river, 259
Brand, Sister, 83
bravery (courage), 13, 241
bread, fried, 59, 171, 174
Bremen, 232
Brest, 33
Bridge on the River Kwai, 263
British Blood Transfusion Service, 227
British Council, 283
British Empire, 15, 43, 54, 151, 241, 248
British Expeditionary Force, 9, 16, 27, 30, 36, 239
British Liberation Army (BLA), 225, 263
  currency, 210
British Red Cross Society, 2
Brittany, 33, 223
Bromage, William, 123
Bruges, 230
Brussels, 30, 226, 228–30
bubonic plague, 145
Buck, Virginia, 192–3, 198–9, 202
Buckingham, Maud, 152–9, 245–6
Budge (later Jennings), Molly, 16, 139–46, 149
  and liberation of Belsen, 231–2, 235
bugle calls, 215
Bullwinkel, Vivian, 93–6
Burma, 102, 132, 179, 185, 236, 249, 255–7, 263, 266
  care of casualties, 228, 248, 250, 254, 262–3, 266
  effectiveness of penicillin in, 261–2
  liberated prisoners, 268, 272
  and quinine blockade, 251–2

Burma Road, 258
Burma–Siam railway, 92, 263
Burmese, 248, 257
burns, 24–5, 197–8, 200–2
Bushy Park, 282–3
Buxton, Mrs A., 54–7

cabin fever, 118
Caen, 212, 214–15, 219, 223–5, 228
Cairo, 141, 145, 241
Calais, 31–2
Calcutta, 182, 186, 248–9, 259
Cambridge, 227
Cambridge Hospital, Aldershot, 282
Campbell College, 185
Canada, 4, 176
Canadians, 65, 214, 216, 218, 223
Cape of Good Hope, 111, 121
Cape Town, 42
'Captives' Hymn', 98
Carmarthen, 207
Casablanca, 160
casualties, among QAs, 5, 10, 80, 82
  at sea, 115, 121, 130–2, 162
casualty clearing stations, 14, 21, 152, 164, 172, 176, 241
  10th British Casualty Clearing Station, 232
  No. 12 Casualty Clearing Station, 28–30
  in Italian campaign, 192, 194, 197–8
  in Normandy, 215, 217
Catalina flying boats, 182
Catholics, 199, 202
Ceylon, 79, 89, 132, 241
Chamberlain, Neville, 28
champagne, 225, 229–30, 233
Changi, xii, 73, 270, 277
Chechens, 279
Cheltenham, 241, 245
chemists, dispensing, 183, 208
Cherbourg, 27, 33, 36, 239
children
  Japanese liking for, 65
  in Singapore, 277–9
China, 43

China Station, 43
Chindits, 102, 257–8
Chinese, 55, 65, 68, 91, 99, 257
  nurses, 52–4
Chisholm, Dorothea, 206–9,
  216–17, 220–2, 226
  in Germany, 235–6
  homecoming, 281–2
  training, 22–4
Chittagong, 249, 261
cholera, 102, 231
Christian, Princess, 3
Christian upbringing, 180
Christie, Lieutenant, 277–8
Churchill, Randolph, 166
Churchill, Winston, 28, 43,
  138
cigarettes, 143, 209, 218, 225
Clark, Paddy, 81
Clipper flying boats, 227
colitis, 263
Colombo, 281
Colonial Nursing Service,
  284
Comilla, 249, 263, 265
concentration camps, 11,
  230–2
Constantine, 161
contraception, 180, 185
convoys, 10, 111, 114, 116,
  121–4, 132, 151, 154
Cooper, Molly, 97–100, 106
Coventry, 158
Cowens, Evelyn, 74–5, 77–9,
  91
Crimean war, 1–2, 244
Currie (later Davies), Mary,
  47–51

Dacca, 186, 259, 273
Daily Telegraph, 2
Dakar, 122
Damascus, 184
Dambusters raid, 235
Davies, Dorothy, 225, 228,
  230
Davies, Mary, 186, 251, 253–4,
  258–9, 273–4
  homecoming and
  subsequent career, 280–1,
  283–4

Davis, 'Taffy', 123
D-Day landings, 10, 19, 102,
  131, 179, 206–14, 224, 231
DDT, 252
Deeble, Jane, 3
Delhi, 241, 248
dengue fever, 248, 251, 262
Denmark, 232
depth charges, 112, 132, 162
diarrhoea, 67, 234, 252
digging in, 197
diphtheria, 145, 279
  epidemic in Hong Kong,
  62–4
Dönitz, Admiral Karl, 196
Dover, 31–4
Dowling, Gwen, 90
Drummond, Irene, 93–4
Dryburgh, Margaret, 98, 101,
  106
DUKWs, 211
Dunkirk evacuation, 28,
  30–4, 36–7, 42, 226, 239
Dunlop, Mrs, 82
Durban, 124, 159
Dutch, 65, 85, 88, 90, 97–101,
  273–4
  doctors, 99–100
  nuns, 97, 105
Dutch East Indies, 87, 271,
  278
Dutch Military Hospital, 79
Dyer, Phil, 249, 252, 261–2,
  265, 272–3
  homecoming, 281–2
  sea journey to India, 118–20
dysentery, 61, 102, 104–6, 117,
  144, 230, 248, 254, 262, 267,
  272
Dyson, Miss, 65–7, 282

eardrums, burst, 201–2
earthquakes, 4
East Africa, 5
East African Railways and
  Harbours, 284
Eden, Anthony, 91
Edinburgh, 22, 67, 159,
  206–7
Edward VII, King, 3
Edwards, Sister, 34

eggs, 113, 144–5, 157, 171, 174,
  231
Egypt, 5, 137–9, 151, 160, 227
  Principal Matrons in, 241
  romantic episodes in, 181,
  183
Eighth Army News, 181
El Alamein, 138
El Tahag, 139
ELAS, 181
Elder Dempster line, 114
Emergency Military Nursing
  Service, 74
emergency rations, 209
English, Mary, 160, 162,
  164–5, 169, 176
  marriage, 180–1, 185
  and Italian campaign,
  192–4, 197–202
English Channel, 31, 34, 161,
  209, 212
ENSA, 118, 143, 146
Equator, 113
  'crossing the line'
  ceremony, 117
'Eternal Father Strong to
  Save', 133
Evans, Mary, 33–4, 148
Eve (Mary Davies's friend),
  253–4

Falaise, 215, 219, 223, 228
Far East, 89, 121
Farouk, King, 149
Federation of Professional
  and Business Women, 244
Female Auxiliary Nursing
  Yeomanry Service
  (FANYS), 132
Fernandez, Miss, 278
Fidoe, Elizabeth, 54, 56–8
field dressing stations, 21
field hospitals, 140, 145–6,
  206, 221–2, 241
First World War, 5, 9, 16,
  152, 196, 239, 257
flame throwers, 5, 192, 231
Flanders, 5, 192
Foggia, 181, 194, 197
Folkestone, 42
Fonteyn, Margot, 24

Force K, 151
France, 89
  Allied advance and
    liberation, 179, 228, 250,
    257
  and D-Day landings,
    209–11, 231
  German defence of, 220
  German invasion, 28, 31
  living conditions in, 221–2,
    224
  occupation currency, 210
  and outbreak of war, 16, 27,
    239
  Vichy, 137, 139, 160
  see also Normandy
Freetown, 122, 128
French Indochina, 278
French North Africa, 137, 160
French, 175, 211, 225, 228
  casualties, 192, 218
friendly fire, 214
frostbite, 5
Fujita, Vice Admiral, 274
Fulham, 181

Gallipoli, 5
Garvin, Dorothy, 71–3, 80–5,
  90–1
gas gangrene, 216, 259–60
Gaumont Cinema, 118
Geneva Convention, 46, 50,
  121, 220–1, 263
George VI, King, 283
George Cross, 159
German 15th Army, 223
Germans
  attack hospital ships, 121
  behaviour in occupied
    France, 211
  casualties, 9, 175, 219–23, 226
  civilians, 235
  and Italian campaign,
    191–2, 194, 199–203
  prisoners, 164, 167, 169,
    175–6, 220
  resistance to Allied
    advance, 228–9
Germany, 2, 282
  Allied advance into, 226,
    230–1

and phoney war, 27–8
rearmament, 16
reunions, 126
surrender of, 69, 107
Ghent, 235
Gibraltar, 2, 4, 162, 165
Girl Guides, 221
Glasgow, 22, 160, 267
Glen Dessary, 28
gliders, 211
Goodwood House, 208
Gordon, Amelia (Molly),
  54–8, 67–9
grapes, 194, 201
Graziani, Marshal
  Rodolpho, 137
Greece, 89, 167, 181, 194
Greenock, 111
Grese, Irma, 231
Grey and Scarlet (Jones), 158
guerrilla warfare, 257–9, 271
Gulf of Guinea, 128
Gurkhas, 141, 201, 248, 257–8,
  269–70

Hall, Miss, 35
Hamburg, 232
Hammersmith, 118
Hampshire Regiment, 130
Hanublin, Mrs, 156
Happy Valley racetrack
  rapes, 52–3
Harcourt, Admiral Cecil,
  274
'Harley Street', 214, 224
Hartley, Sister, 76, 81, 83, 91
Hartley Road camp, 278–9
Hayward, Audrey, 17–18, 21,
  114–16, 186
  in India, 263–4
  in Normandy, 210–11,
    214–16, 220–2, 224
  subsequent career, 283–4
'Heads', 219
health visitors, 283–4
heat exhaustion, 129, 144
Helmieh, 145
Helpmann, Robert, 24
Hensall, 232
Hindus, 201, 250
Hindustani, 119

Hitler, Adolf, 16, 28, 31, 176,
  214, 220, 223, 226
Hitler Youth, 220
Holland, 9, 13, 28
Holweg, Dr, 100
Hong Kong, 4, 41–3, 180,
  240, 280
  defences, 43–4
  drug shortages, 60–3, 69
  food shortages, 59–61, 63,
    67–8
  internment in, 58–70
  Japanese invasion, 9–10, 14,
    44–57, 246
  liberation of, 267–8, 274
  surrender of, 57–8, 71
Hong Kong Volunteer
  Defence Corps, 49, 51,
    53–5
Honolulu, 275
hookworms, 269, 278
Horlicks, 129
Horrocks, Lieutenant
  General Sir Brian, 13
hospital ships, 5, 10–11, 31–6,
  111, 241
  attacks on, 121, 130–1, 146–7
  and North African
    campaign, 146–8, 161,
    165–6, 173
  St David sinking, 130–1, 177
  Strathallen sinking, 161–4
  Tairea voyages, 267–70
hospital trains, 9, 31, 34, 177,
  231
  see also ambulance trains
hospitals
  2/10th Australian General
    Hospital, 93
  No. 6 British General
    Hospital (France), 207–8,
    226
  No. 6 British General
    Hospital (North Africa),
    149
  7th British General
    Hospital, 219
  17th British General
    Hospital, 259
  29th British General
    Hospital, 210

56th British General Hospital, 122
63rd British General Hospital, 145
67th British General Hospital, 160, 164–5, 176–7
75th British General Hospital, 21, 211, 217–18
81st British General Hospital, 217
93rd British General Hospital, 169–75
17th Combined General Hospital, 73–4, 76, 82
65th Combined Military Hospital, 251
No. 2 General Hospital, 139, 146
No. 4 General Hospital, 35
No. 11 General Hospital, 36
No. 28 Indian General Hospital, 280
62nd Indian General Hospital, 259
74th Indian General Hospital, 263
No. 1 Malayan General Hospital, 74, 80
post-war, 283
pre-war, 15, 20
Hove, 276
Hunter-Bates (later Moore), Joan, 123

Imphal, 258
Imtarfa Military Hospital, 152, 245
India, 4, 89, 118, 132, 228, 248–56, 263–4, 273
caste system, 248, 250
climate, 248, 267
disease in, 251–2
hospitals, 254
Japanese invasion, 248, 258, 269
Principal Matrons in, 241
romantic episodes in, 182, 185–6
return from, 281–3
sea journey to, 111

social life in, 253–5
train travel, 249
Indian General Hospital, 76
Indian Medical Corps, 268
Indian National Army, 269
Indian Nursing Service, 4
Indian Ocean, 10, 111, 132–3
Indians, 248–50, 255, 271
casualties, 59, 148
officers (halvidars), 254
prisoners, 269–70, 277
in Singapore, 278
troops, 139, 201–2
Indonesia, 79, 106, 271, 280
Indragiri River, 90
Ingham, Sister, 81
insulation, 261
International War Crimes Tribunal, 53, 92, 94
Iraq, 5, 241
Ireland, 2, 114, 139, 185
neutrality, 269
Irish College, Rome, 199
iron rations, 12
Irrawady, battle of the, 260
Iserlohn, 235
Ismailia, 139, 183
Israel, 183
Italian 10th Army, 137
Italian air force, 150, 153
Italians, 141, 192, 194, 203, 279
casualties, 9, 192
prisoners, 137–8, 164, 169, 172
and tents, 143
Italy, 10, 180, 231
campaign, 130, 177, 191–205
fights, 279
food shortages, 192, 194, 279
German surrender in, 203
introduction of penicillin in, 261
and North Africa campaign, 137–40
road accidents, 203, 279
romantic episodes in, 182–3, 185
surrender of, 191
'It's a Long Way to Tipperary', 228
Ivory Coast, 122

Jakarta, 79, 271
Jamaica, 4
Janneson, Sister, 156
Japanese
attack hospital ships, 121
attitude to sick, 68–9
attitude to women, 53, 58, 64, 88
and bowing, 59, 61, 65, 98
brutality, 91–2, 246, 263, 270, 272
and Burma campaign, 251, 257–8, 263–5
casualties, 9, 256, 258, 265
change in attitude, 275–6
dead officer incident, 14, 49–51
expansionism, 43
hatred of, 256, 265, 268, 270
and Indian National Army, 269
invasion of India, 248, 258, 269
liking for children, 65
nurses, 60
prisoners, 265, 274
and quinine blockade, 251–2
soldiers continue fighting, 271, 273
surrender, xii, 266–7, 271, 273, 275
withholding of supplies, 275, 278
jaundice, 181, 254, 272
Java, 93, 251, 273–4
Java Sea battle, 90
Javanese, 277
Jennings, Molly, 282
Jerusalem, 186
Jews, 68, 230
Johore Baru, 74, 76
Jones, Dame Katherine (Matron-in-Chief), 36, 239–47, 280, 282
correspondence with Matron Buckingham, 152, 156, 245–6
publishes Grey and Scarlet, 158
visits North Africa, 169–70, 241

Jones, Violet Maud Evelyn, 42, 53, 77, 80, 82
Journal of the Royal Army Medical Corps, 243
Junkers 88s, 153–4, 195

Kai Tak airport, 43–4
Kashmiris, 250
Kelly, Meta, 211–13, 217–18, 221, 223–5
  in Brussels, 228–30
  homecoming, 236
  in India, 264–5
  marriage, 283
Kempei Tai, 99
Kenya, 132, 284
Kerr, Dr, 97
Kerr, Julie, 163
Kesselring, Field Marshal, 191–2, 199
King's African Rifles, 132
Kismayu, 268
kit, purchase of, 25
Kohima, 258
kookris, 141, 201, 274
Kota Bharu, 76
Kowloon, 43–5, 52, 59–60, 62
Kramer, Josef, 231
Kuala Lumpur, 76
Kuantan, 76, 279

La Baule, 27–8, 35
Lagos, 118
Lahat, 276
Lambeth, 16
landmines, 5, 138, 140, 192, 214, 217
latrines, 96, 100, 102–3, 142, 221–2, 234
Laycock, Freda, 232–5
le Blanc Smith, Beatrice, 83, 86, 88–9
Le Havre, 36
Le Mans, 33
Liberty ships, 196, 274
Libya, 137–8, 140, 183–4
lice, 222–3, 231–2
lifeboats, 12–13, 81–3, 93, 121–2, 124–5, 127–31, 162–3
Little Cedars of Lebanon Hospital, 184

Liverpool, 41–2, 71, 114, 124, 160, 206
  Blitz, 22–4
Lloyd, Marjorie, 123
lockers, 17, 21, 165, 202
Loebok Linggau, 105–6
Lohardaga, 254, 263, 267
London Hospital, 3, 31
London Victory Parade, 282–3
London Blitz, 22
Longridge, Major, 29
Lowestoft, 19
Luftwaffe, 9, 22, 28, 31, 41, 150
Luker, Helen, 27–31
lumbar punctures, 263
Lydia (Dorothy Garvin's friend), 80–1
Lye Mun passage, 44

Mac, Sister, 203–5
McBryde (later Fuller), Brenda, 21, 24–5, 219
McGregor, Sister, 81
Mackie, Dorothy, 159
McLaren, Major Hugh, 233–4
McNeece (later Saville), Sarah, 182, 259–60
Maconochie's stew, 143, 165, 193
Madagascar, 268
Madras, 248, 270
Maginot Line, 28
malaria, 43, 268
  among prisoners, 104, 106, 272, 279
  in India, 248, 251–2, 254, 267
  and Burma campaign, 262
  and quinine blockade, 251–2
Malaya, 44, 71, 73–4, 85, 88, 251, 267–8
Malays, 85, 99
Malta, 2, 4, 201
  siege of, 13, 149–59, 245
Manchuria, 43
Mandalay, 258
Manila, 275
Marchant, Sister, 156
marriages, of QAs, 180–4

Mary, Queen, 243, 283
matrons, 13, 19–20, 180, 222–3, 240–1
  Matrons-in-Chief, 239–47, 284
  military rank of, 242
Maudsley, Catherine, 73, 78–9, 91
Mediterranean Sea, 149, 161, 165, 176
  U-boat threat, 5, 10, 111, 121–2, 173
mental damage, 11, 86, 129, 141, 218, 264, 269–70, 284
mepacrine, 252
Mersa Matruh, 137
Mesopotamia, 5
Messerschmitts, 151, 153
Meuse, river, 229
Middle Ages, 152
Middle East, 89, 111, 124, 126, 145
Middlesex Hospital, 126
Middlesex Regiment, 44
midwives, 179–80, 186
military hospitals, 2, 15, 17, 221, 262
Millbank Military Hospital, 16
missionaries, 97–8
mobile hospital units, 17, 25
mobilisation units, 17, 180, 206–7, 211
Möhne dam, 236
Mombasa, 132
monkey meat, 101
Mons, battle of, 5
Monte Cassino, 191, 194, 197–8, 200–1
Montgomery, General Bernard, 138, 183, 206, 210, 222
Montreuil, 30
Morgan, Brenda, 46–7
morphine, 200, 217
mosquitoes, 251–2, 254
Mulberry harbours, 10, 209–10
Munday, Eric, 124–6
Munich crisis, 27
Muntok, 87, 94–5, 97, 104–5

Murray, Helene Bell, 83, 90
Muslims, 201, 250
Mussolini, Benito, 137, 139
mustard gas, 196–7

NAAFI, 225, 229, 254
Nanking massacre, 43
Naples, 192–3, 198, 201, 279
  Americans in, 203–5
National Society for Aid to
  the Sick and Wounded in
  War, 2
Netley, 2–3, 28, 45, 281
New Forest, 210
New Territories, 43
New York, 226
Newhaven, 32
Nigeria, 283
Nightingale, Florence, 1–2,
  46, 163, 240, 243
Nijmegen, 14
Nissen huts, 142, 176, 207,
  225, 240
Normandy, 214–29, 248
  D-Day landings, 10, 19, 102,
  131, 179, 206–14, 224, 231
North Africa, 10, 113, 151,
  179–80, 206, 231, 250
  casualties and hospital
    ships, 126, 130
  climate, 160, 169–71
  desert campaign, 137–49
  desert life, 141–6
  end of campaign, 191–2, 231
  food, 143–5, 171, 174
  hospital organisation, 172–3
  Matron-in-Chief visits,
    169–70, 241
  Operation Torch, 122,
    160–8, 175
  nurses' routines, 139–40,
    170–1
  social life, 174–8
  use of mepacrine in, 252
  water rationing, 10, 140, 221
  see also desert life
North Atlantic, 114, 117, 122
North Point Camp, 58
Northern Ireland, 113, 160
Norway, 230
Norwegians, 65

nurses
  American, 169–70
  Australian, 93–5, 105
  campaigning for, 246–7
  civilian, 283
  and doctors, 243–4
  German, 232–4
  increase in responsibilities,
    262–3
  Japanese, 60
  training, 2, 15, 17, 19–20, 173,
    179
  uniforms, 3, 5
  work routine, 19–20
nurses' homes, 19, 283

O'Connor, Lieutenant-
  General Sir Richard, 137
Operation Torch, 122, 160–8,
  175
Oran, 161
Order of Dannebrog, 4
orderlies, 1, 4, 17, 206, 270
  in Hong Kong, 61–2
  in Malta, 154, 158
  in North Africa, 146, 148,
    165
Orvieto, 200
Ostend, 228
Oswald, Miss, 81
Oxford, 50

Pacific, war in, 102
Padang, 90–1
Pakistanis, 250
Palembang, 97–8, 104, 106
Palestine, 141, 183, 232, 239
Pamican, 128
parachute silk, 146, 182
Parsees, 250
Pas de Calais, 29
Passchendaele, battle of, 5
Patton, General, 223
peanuts, 67–8
Pearl Harbor, 44, 71
Peebles, 20–2, 24–6, 111, 206,
  208
Penang, 90
penicillin, 217–18, 226, 236,
  244, 261–2
  equal access to, 220–1

Peninsular Wars, 1
Percival, General, 76
Persia, 241
Perugia, 200–2
pets, 146
Philippeville, 161, 164, 166–9,
  176–7, 185, 192
Philippines, 102
phoney war, 27–8
Pioneer Corps, 212, 215
Pius XII, Pope, 199
plasma, 226–7
Poland, 27
Poles, 250, 279
poliomyelitis, 145
Pom Pong island, 83
Pondicherry, 248
Poona, 281
Portsmouth, 209, 211
postings, 175, 180, 183
pregnancies, 180, 184–7
Primus stoves, 155, 174, 193
prisoner of war camps,
  Japanese, 96–107, 276
  and air raids, 103–4
  brutality in, 99–100
  entertainments, 98, 101
  food shortages, 101–2
prisoners of war, 12, 46, 53,
  282–3
  German, 164, 167, 169,
    175–6, 220
  in Hong Kong, 58–70
  Indian, 269–70, 277
  Italian, 137–8, 164, 169, 172
  Japanese, 265, 274
  Japanese treatment of, 91–2,
    246, 263
  liberated, 11, 256, 259, 263–4,
    268–70, 272–3, 277, 281
  in Rome, 200
  weights of, 103
  women, 60, 68, 100, 102,
    104
prostitutes, 42

Queen Alexandra Imperial
  Military Nursing Corps
  (QAIMNS)
  badge and motto, 4
  foundation, 1–5

homecomings, 280–2
medals and decorations, 5, 145, 163
military ranks, 15, 22, 53, 67, 112–13, 182–3, 207, 242, 249
mobilisation preparations, 239–40
numbers, 5, 15
pay, 53, 244–5
recruitment, 15–17
Regulars and Reserves, 16, 239
Roll of Honour, 122
social status, 2–3, 15
Queen Alexandra's Royal Army Nursing Corps (QARANC), 282, 284
Queen Mary Hospital, 48, 53
quinine, 105, 251–2, 275

RAF, 224, 283
bands, 208
defence of Singapore, 43
nursing service, 16
and siege of Malta, 152–3
Ranchi, 254–5, 264, 283
Rangoon, 258
rapes, 10, 14, 52, 56–7
rationing, in Britain, 19, 41
Rayment, Sister Ray, 105
Red Cross, 66, 69, 169–70, 174, 192
Red Cross armbands, 48, 53–4, 94
Red Cross parcels, 68–9, 104, 275
Red Sea, 111, 117, 119, 139
Redhill, 283
refugees, 29, 31–2, 43, 90–1
regimental aid posts, 21
resuscitation, 215–16, 221
rice, 59–61, 65, 67, 98, 102, 278
Richmond, Duke of, 208
Rimini, 181, 202
Roberts, Anne, 145
Robinson, Miss C. L., 35–6
Romanians, 279
Rome, 130, 191–2, 197–200
Rommel, General Erwin, 10, 138, 148, 160, 191, 214, 220

Roosevelt, President Franklin D., 197
Rose, Major W., 279
Rouen, 226, 235
Royal Army Medical Corps (RAMC), 37, 91, 128, 207, 268
admiration for QAs, xii
equivalence with QAs, 242
and German prisoners, 220, 226
in Hong Kong, 49, 53, 58, 60
in Italy, 197–8
and Normandy landings, 131
parachutists, 241
and siege of Malta, 157
Royal Army Service Corps, 198
Royal Artillery, 181
Royal Engineers, 124, 157
Royal Navy, 87–8, 90, 116, 130, 203
and convoys, 111–12
defence of Singapore, 43, 71
nursing service, 16
and siege of Malta, 152
Royal Red Cross, 159, 163
Royal Scots, 42, 44
Royal Tank Corps, 148
Ruhr valley, 235
rum ration, 47
'Run Rabbit Run', 228
Russell, Winifred, 82
Russia, 5, 248
Russians, 235

St Albert's Convent, 46–8, 50, 52, 59–60
St Bartholomew's Hospital, 239
St John's Ambulance Brigade, 52, 55
St Nazaire, 33–6
St Paul, 158
St Stephen's College, 46, 53–4, 58, 65, 67
St Theresa's Hospital, 60–2, 64–5

St Thomas's Hospital, 2, 27
Saito, Major Shunkiti, 60, 62, 64–5
Salerno, 130
Salonika, 5
salt, 68, 278
San Merino, 202
Sandbostel, 232–5
sandstorms, 142–3
sanitary towels, 68, 209, 215
SAS, 166–7
scabies, 278–9
scorpions, 142, 255
Scotland, 15, 27, 67, 111
Scutari, 1, 244
Sea Gladiator aircraft, 153
seasickness, 114, 116–17, 162, 212
self-discipline, 23–4, 212
Sembawang, 279
sexual relations, 179–87
Shackleton, Colonel, 45
Shaftesbury, 17–18, 114
Sham Shui Po camp, 59, 62, 64
Shanghai, 46, 65
Shau Kei Wan medical store, 45–6
shell shock, 5, 35, 141, 159, 197
ships
Amsterdam, 131
Abosso, 114–16
Admiral Hughes, 275
Ark Royal, 151
Arundel Castle, 160, 162
Barham, 151
Bismarck, 30, 116
Cameronia, 139
Ceramic, xii, 124–6, 128
Dorsetshire, 116
Dunnottar Castle, 120
Empire Star, 78–9, 84, 91
Empress of Australia, 41–2, 280
George V, 30
Hood, xii, 116–17
Illustrious, 154
Indomitable, 274
Invicta, 211
John Harvey, 196–7

Khedive Ismael, 132
Kuala, 80–4, 86, 88, 90–1, 93
Leinster, 130
Nelson, 267
Newfoundland, 130
Oronsay, 126
Paladin, 132–3
Petard, 132–3
Prince Albert, 271
Prince of Wales, 44, 76
Pumper, 197
Queen Olga, 148
Repulse, 44, 76
Richelieu, 267
Rodney, 267
St Andrew, 32, 130
St David, 130–1, 177
Somersetshire, 33, 147–8
Stentor, 122–3
Strathallan, xiii, 113, 126,
    161–4, 195, 241
Tairea, 113, 267–71, 273
Talamba, 268
Tanjong Penang, 85–6, 89
Tien Kwang, 80, 83
Vyner Brooke, 93–5, 105
Woodruffe, 123
shock, treatment of, 226
Shorncliffe Military
    Hospital, 42
'Show Me the Way to Go
    Home', 228
Siam, 278
Sicily, 4, 10, 167, 176, 181, 191,
    268, 271
Sidi Barrani, 137
Sierra Leone, 122, 128
Sikhs, 201, 250, 271
Siki, Captain, 101–4, 275
Simmons, Mrs, 54–8
Singapore, 13, 41, 43, 65, 97,
    159, 276, 280
    casualties, 75–6
    children in, 277–9
    daily rations in, 278
    defences, 71
    evacuation of, 76–80, 91
    fall of, 76, 88–90, 102, 122,
        240, 246, 277
    and Indian National Army,
        269

Japanese invasion, 9, 42, 44,
    71–6
    liberation of, 268, 270, 274
'Singapore ditches', 78
Singh, Bhup, 259, 273–4
Skimming, Sylvia, 169–78,
    192–3, 203
skin grafting, 24–5
Slim, Lieutenant-General
    William, 251, 257–8, 262–3,
    265–6
smallpox, 17, 145, 166
Smith, Mrs W. J. L., 54–7
Smith, Netta, 276
Smyrna, 268
Smythe, Sir John, 284
snakes, 248, 251, 255, 260
snipers, Japanese, 273
Somalia, 283
Somaliland, 268
South Africa, 3–4, 121
South Africans, 152, 275
South Atlantic, 113, 122
Southampton, 34, 36, 131, 139,
    208, 280–1
Southampton Water, 2
Spedding, Olive, 75, 77, 83,
    90
Spitfire pilots, 166–8
Spitfires, 151, 153
SS, 220, 226, 234–5
Stalag XB, 232–5
Stanley Internment Camp,
    58, 64–9, 282
    diet in, 65, 67–8
    liberation of, 267, 274
    medical care in, 68–9
State Registered Nurses,
    242
Sterling, Colonel, 167
stethoscopes, 263
Stewardson, Olive, 163
Stoker, Captain, 58
straitjackets, 11, 270
submarines, Japanese, 121,
    132–3
Suez Canal, 111, 119, 139
sulphonamide, 217, 220, 244,
    261
Sumatra, 85, 90, 97, 105, 275,
    279

Surabaya, 273
Syria, 139

Tanaka, Lieutenant-
    General, 274
tanks, 5, 138, 197, 202, 212,
    223, 257
Táranto, 192–3
Taylor (pilot), 153
tea (chai, char), 67, 145, 193,
    209, 255
Tecleburg, Dr, 100
Teheran, 250
Teita Hills, 284
Tenko, 98, 107
tennis, 15, 43, 248
    deck tennis, 118
    table tennis, 266
tents, British, 142–3, 170
Territorial Army Nursing
    Service (TANS), 16, 54, 73,
    239–40, 242
Texas, 219
Thailand, 71
Thompson, Margaret, 82
Thompson Road camp,
    277–9
Thomson, Kathleen, 46–7,
    59–64
Tibetans, 250
Tilbury, 281
Times, The, 1–2
Tobruk, 33, 138, 147–8
Tokyo War Crimes Trial, 55,
    93
topees, 117
torpedoes, 5, 34, 112, 122–6,
    131, 133, 148, 161–3
torture, 269, 273
tracheotomies, 63, 145, 279
Treves, Sir Frederick, 3–4
Trinitapoli, 193
Tripoli, 138–9
troopships, 111–21
    boat drill, 115
    camaraderie on, 120
    daily routine, 118
    entertainments on, 118–19
    food on board, 113–14
    numbers on board, 112–13
    U-boat precautions, 117

tuberculosis, 269, 279
Tunis, 138, 160, 164, 175
Turner, Margot, 83, 85–8, 91,
    93, 95–106
    liberation, 275–6
    subsequent career, 284–5
Tweed, River, 206
typhoid, 17, 102, 145, 231, 235,
    260, 272
typhus, 17, 231, 233–4

Ubin, 73
U-boats, 10, 41, 111, 115–17,
    122–6, 128, 151, 173, 196
    attacks on hospital ships, 5,
    121
    and Strathallan sinking,
    161–2
    U-515, xii, 123, 125–6
underwear, 12
uniforms, QAs', 5, 13, 16, 140,
    229, 283
    adoption of battledress, 207,
    224, 243
    and army tailors, 11–12
    and mosquitoes, 251
    old-fashioned, 18–19
    tropical, 41, 45, 268
    unsuitability in North
    Africa, 160–1, 166
    see also veils
United States of America,
    138, 176, 244

Urdu, 118
US 5th Army, 191
US Navy, 203

VADs (Voluntary Aid
    Detachment), 75, 83, 86,
    158
    experiences in Hong Kong,
    46–8, 53, 55–7, 63, 68
Valetta, 151
van Wart (later Ingram),
    Daphne, 41–7, 51, 59–60,
    65, 67–9
    homecoming and
    subsequent career, 280,
    282–3
    liberation, 274–5
Vatican, 199–200
VE-Day, 230, 233
veils, 11, 18, 45, 140, 142,
    222–3, 243, 254, 268
venereal disease, 1, 4, 43, 179,
    279
Venice, 192
Victoria, Queen, 163, 243
virginity, 180
vitamins, 68, 272, 275, 278
von Kluge, Field Marshal
    Günther, 214, 223
vultures, 51, 261

WAAF (Women's Auxiliary
    Air Force), 186

Wales, 15, 207, 236, 281
Wallis, Barnes, 235
Wanchai Naval Hospital,
    59
Wane, Constance, 262
War Office, 89, 91, 160,
    195–6, 239
Warrrack, Helen, 158
water rationing, 10, 45, 140,
    221–2, 225
Watts Carter, Molly, 97
Wellington, Duke of, 1
Welsh Guards, 282
West, Miss, 74–5, 77, 80, 82
West Africa, 17, 114–15, 122,
    126, 241, 249
West Africans, 257
West Bengal, 249, 251
Western Desert Force,
    137
Whitby, 21
Whitney, Captain P. N., 54,
    57
Wingate, Brigadier-General
    Orde, 102, 257–8
WVS (Women's Voluntary
    Service), 182

X-rays, 18
X-rayfilms, 155

Yamashita, General
    Tomoyuki, 71